Al Todd

The Conservation Diaries
of
Gifford Pinchot

D1211089

Pinchot during his tenure as Chief of the Forest Service, circa 1910. Grey Towers Collection.

The Conservation Diaries
of
Gifford Pinchot

—➤—◆—◀—

Edited by Harold K. Steen

Forest History Society
Pinchot Institute for Conservation

Copyright © 2001 by the Forest History Society

The Forest History Society
701 Vickers Avenue
Durham, North Carolina 27701
919 682-9319
www.lib.duke.edu/forest

All rights reserved, including the right to reproduce this book or portions thereof in any form or by any means, electronic or mechanical, including photocopying, recording, or by any information storage and retrieval system, without permission in writing from the publisher.

First edition

The Forest History Society is a nonprofit, educational institution dedicated to the advancement of historical understanding of human interaction with the forest environment. The Society was established in 1946.

The Pinchot Institute for Conservation is a nonprofit natural resource policy, research, and education organization dedicated to leadership in conservation thought, policy, and action. The Pinchot Institute was established in 1963.

Appreciation is extended to the USDA Forest Service History program and the USDA Forest Service Office of Communications for their support of this project.

Library of Congress Cataloging-in-Publication Data
Pinchot, Gifford, 1865-1946.
   The conservation diaries of Gifford Pinchot / edited by Harold K.
Steen.— 1st ed.
      p. cm.
   ISBN 0-89030-059-3 (cloth) — ISBN 0-89030-060-7 (pbk.)
   1. Pinchot, Gifford, 1865-1946—Diaries. 2. Conservationists—United
States—Diaries. 3. Conservation of natural resources—United
States—History. I. Steen, Harold K. II. Title.
   S926.P56 A3 2001
   333.7'2'092—dc21

                          2001003183

Printed in U.S.A.

CONTENTS

FOREWORD

For the past decade I have been living with Gifford Pinchot. After all, I now work, and practically live, in the shadow of his magnificent family home, Grey Towers. The French château with its stone towers and commanding view of the Upper Delaware Valley can put you in a trance. Legend has it that the house is haunted by James W. Pinchot, Gifford's father. Gifford's personal belongings are all around me. In every room, I see an image of his face, or something that reminds me of his life and work. The person who lived here must have been somebody, I mean *somebody*.

Those of us who have spent a career in forestry and conservation can't help but know about Gifford Pinchot. But the Pinchot I knew before, and the one you most likely know, is the creation of our culture. He is an icon, an abbreviated version of the man who actually existed in the flesh and blood. We have recreated Gifford to serve our own needs. The Gifford Pinchot of the second century of conservation is very modern in his thinking, politically correct, and ecologically versed. Every one of his statements is biblical. His populist values and beliefs are the core beliefs of our institutions.

The Pinchot I now know, as you may have guessed, is really different from the Pinchot of myth and legend. In some cases, he is bigger, stronger, more potent and capable than his myth. His interests and accomplishments are far wider than forestry and conservation—human rights, world peace, and the control of nuclear energy. But he is also more human, more vulnerable, more self-effacing and unsure than you would have expected. For me, he is more passionate and psychologically complex than I ever imagined.

Early in my tenure as Director of Grey Towers, I discovered a copy of the 1945 *Range Management Handbook* from Region 5 (California Region of the Forest Service). On the cover "Gifford Pinchot" is embossed in gold leaf. This was the government equivalent of the leather-bound gold-leaf edition—something special. More than thirty-five years after he was fired by William Howard Taft for insubordination, Gifford Pinchot was still receiving embossed copies of operating guidelines from the Forest Service rank and file. What kind of person was this? What did he do to make such a lasting and powerful connection with the public employees of this unique agency?

The Gifford Pinchot of myth and legend speaks to us in *Breaking New Ground*, his autobiography published posthumously in 1947. The Pinchot of myth has no doubts. Everything is certain. The truth is clear; he knows it and tells it straight: "The earth, I repeat, belongs of right to all its people, and not to a minority, insignificant in numbers but tremendous in wealth and power. I object to the law of the jungle." In a way, it is the gospel according to Gifford and was intended to be scripture. But who really was this prophet of conservation?

After ten years, I am still learning. What is most surprising is that not only do I still respect him (I stand in awe of what he accomplished), but also I am beginning to like him. He is far more human and sensitive a man than a first reading of his autobiography would lead one to assume. Not to kill the suspense, but I have not found anything that is unseemly or distasteful about the man. He seems to have led a highly moral life. Different, yes; weird and kinky, no.

There is more good news. *Breaking New Ground* ends in 1910, when Taft fired him. His diaries continue nearly to his death in 1946. His life after being fired as "forester" is as compelling and interesting as the one before. His diaries reveal that he never really left the agency; he did not have an official role, but he was always there. Called on frequently to lecture on the subject of conservation, he carried the beliefs and values of the agency as if they were engraved in stone tablets. He was the watchdog of what was right, good, and true. The agency leadership must have secretly hated him—except when they needed him to bail them out, as happened on occasion.

The diaries of Gifford Pinchot provide fresh insight into the man himself and how he thought, felt, and perceived the world. We are fortunate to have them. He was streaky in his recording information, however. There are significant gaps. Years are missing. Whether he did not record his thoughts or the writings were lost or misplaced, we may never know. What he did leave adds so much to our understanding of him that these diaries can be viewed as a companion to his autobiography.

They help dispel some unfounded (my biases are showing) characterizations of the man. He was not obsessed with the utilitarian uses of nature. Here is his diary entry for April 19, 1891: "...spent afternoon & till nearly 9 P.M. at edge of Cañon. Began to get some faint idea of its beauty and grandeur...It is so deep it masks the width & the width masks the depth, and a man can only wonder. At sunset it is magnificently beautiful & by moonlight magnificently terrible. But the great power of it lies in its serenity. It is absolutely peaceful."

Then there is the assertion that he was self-confident to the point of personality disorder. Read what he writes on June 15, 1891: "The satisfaction in getting to Grey Towers each time is something wonderful. But I never seem to get any work done here." Or July 3, 1891: "Worked in A.M. in a half hearted way. Made myself generally tired all day long. Am footless, useless, selfish, dumb & generally of no use to anybody." Three weeks later: "Am a footless ass…"

But most of all, we learn how incredibly connected Pinchot was. Hardly a day or evening goes by without multiple meetings, dinners, teas, or visits with the president, Supreme Court justices, senators and representatives, and a lineup of who's who in American political thinking.

At Grey Towers, we regularly conduct training for Forest Service employees. One of my goals is to make people feel "at home" and to introduce them, often for the second time, to what I call "Gifford Pinchot, Family Man." What was he was like at home, with his wife, with his family? What did he do? We know that he was "dry"; how did he unwind? I do not hesitate to say that understanding the complete Gifford Pinchot, warts and all, has a powerful impact on people. They seem to relate to him more and find him so much more appealing once they know the "whole" person.

Gifford Pinchot led his life ahead of the curve. He left us an extraordinary legacy, and we owe a debt of gratitude to Harold "Pete" Steen for his scholarship, his understanding of the history of forestry and conservation in America (which gave him the eye to know what mattered and what didn't), and mostly, his incredible endurance. Editing Pinchot's diaries was no easy task.

If you loved the mythical Gifford Pinchot, I hope you will forgive him for being human. If you felt estranged from this larger-than-life person, I hope you will welcome him into your home. The conservation diaries of Gifford Pinchot are well worth the read.

EDGAR B. BRANNON, JR.
Director
Grey Towers National Historic Landmark
Milford, Pennsylvania

INTRODUCTION

Trained in French and German forestry methods, Gifford Pinchot (1865–1946) was among the first to bring this new branch of knowledge to North America. By 1898 he headed the U.S. Division of Forestry, an agency that within a decade would evolve and expand into the U.S. Forest Service and become the centerpiece of the Conservation Movement. Pinchot left the agency in 1910 but remained active in conservation affairs through much of his long life. What follows is an extraction of conservation-related entries drawn from the much broader context that Pinchot's diverse career represents.

The diaries fill eight of the more than three thousand five-inch-deep standard archival containers in the Pinchot collection at the Library of Congress. Related to the diaries are his forestry journals and various notebooks, which require another thirty containers, and files related to his writings, which occupy another one hundred. Too, there are materials produced by close associates. These additional materials have been examined here only to search for information specifically related to the diaries. The principal published references are Pinchot's autobiography *Breaking New Ground* (1946), and *Gifford Pinchot: Forester-Politician* (1960), by M. Nelson McGeary.

Pinchot's diaries give insights into a wide range of topics and individuals. However, there are significant gaps of months and even years. The largest gap is from 1916 to 1936, although notes and appointment books exist for some of those years. Pinchot filled gaps for the latter portion of 1889 and all of 1890 and 1937 when he dictated the contents of the then-existing diaries as part of his preparation for writing his autobiography.

The generally complete materials from 1889 to 1915 and from 1936 to 1946 contain a trove of information on the nation's, and his, changing views about natural resources. In this book, those two periods of his life have been organized into Parts I and II. Selected examples of nonconservation entries have been assembled into two chapters, one for his earlier life and one for his final decade; these help us learn more about

Pinchot himself. An index of people named in the diaries who could be identified is appended.

For most years, the diaries were commercially prepared six-by-nine-inch books with one page available for each day. Seldom did Pinchot have so much to record that he would continue at the top of the next page. Fortunately, in those cases he was always careful to mark which information belonged to which date. At the end of each book were pages for memoranda, which he used on occasion.

For readability, Pinchot's frequent and innovative forms of abbreviation and his careful but still varied punctuation have not been duplicated in this edition; most alterations have been silent. Pinchot was a good speller, and he clearly made an effort to learn the correct spelling of people's names. Even more impressive during this age of word processors, he never crossed out what he had written; he wrote a finished product at first draft. There are, however, a few examples of tortured syntax, when a sentence did not evolve comfortably and he salvaged as best he could.

Pinchot wrote with a variety of nibs, and unfortunately the broad nibs make for difficult reading, as the letters tend to run together. A few pages are faded or show water damage, but overall, his classic nineteenth-century penmanship carries the day, and the entries are mostly very legible. The editor used a microfilm copy of the diaries and checked all questionable entries against the originals in the Library of Congress. Any word that was illegible or questionable in the original as well has been placed in brackets as, for example, [illeg.] or [replies?]. We can see in the dictated versions that when Pinchot ran up against a word or phrase that was illegible even to him, he skipped over it. In the very few places where Pinchot himself used square brackets, parentheses have been substituted to distinguish between his own and the editor's interpolations.

His style changed with the times. When he was exceptionally busy, as during the early years of the Forest Service, for example, the entries are rather terse. At other times, he wrote full descriptions of his activities and especially the things he saw, such as scenery.

There is both direct and indirect evidence that Pinchot did not always make a daily record; instead, he kept notes and from time to time wrote up back entries. Thus, the diaries often do not reflect his daily thinking but are a summary of the preceding days and weeks. There is also internal evidence that he was writing for history, and we can see him identifying people he obviously knew well to help the future reader.

In the diaries we find much on Pinchot's professional and political associates: George Ahern, Dietrich Brandis, Joseph Cannon, Bernhard Fernow, Henry Gannett, James Garfield, Henry Graves, Arnold Hague, Harold Ickes, Robert Underwood Johnson,

Diary page for April 5, 1897, reporting on status of Forest Service Organic Act as it surmounted congressional hurdles. At bottom, "not a clear day" is Pinchot's notation about Laura Houghteling; on this day, he was not able to "see" her. "Recession," referring to the public domain, is Pinchot's penciled note made sometime in the late 1930s as he reviewed his diary as preparation for writing his autobiography. Pinchot Collection, Library of Congress.

WJ McGee, Charles Mohr, John Muir, Frederick Newell, Overton Price, Theodore and Franklin Roosevelt, Charles Sargent, Carl Schenck, Harry Slattery, Herbert "Dol" Smith, George Vanderbilt, George Woodruff, and Raphael Zon are among those included. And of course, there is Secretary of the Interior Richard A. Ballinger, who became a near obsession for Pinchot following their 1910 battle.

Pinchot also addressed topics and issues. We can read about his forestry education, Biltmore Forest, Yale Forest School, creation of the national forests, evolution of the Forest Service, concern about water power, National Conservation Association, grazing and lumbering, transfer of the national forests to the Department of Agriculture, campaigns to keep the Forest Service in Agriculture, state versus federal jurisdiction over conservation, Pinchot's trips to the American West and abroad, World Conference on Conservation as Basis of Permanent Peace, and Progressive politics.

During his last decade, Pinchot spent a great deal of time on *Breaking New Ground,* and it is fascinating to watch him recreate his early years that we have already seen in the diaries. We can also see his various marks and notes in the diaries, as he reread them years later and selected what to him were the important events.

The full diaries from which conservation-related material has been extracted include much mention of health—Pinchot's and others'. He lived a robust life full of exercise, such as tennis, golf, medicine ball, woodchopping, horseback riding, and occasional chin-ups, and he enjoyed sportsman's pursuits, as we see from his many references to shooting and especially fishing. But he also recorded a great many visits to a range of physicians and dentists, as he suffered routinely from digestive disorders and tooth problems (he frequently chided himself for eating too much candy). He also noticed the health of visitors and especially that of his parents. As his general health declined during his later years, he jotted down his daily doses of medicine and related treatments.

No discussion of the Pinchot diaries would be complete without mention of Laura Houghteling, his fiancée, who died in 1894. Almost every entry for the next two decades contains a reference to Laura, ranging in length from a few words to a full paragraph. Nearly all of the Laura entries are written at the bottom of each page, with his daily activities recorded at the top. Perhaps the best explanation is the theory that Pinchot was a practitioner of spiritualism, and there is ample evidence to support this view. But since Laura had little enough to do with conservation, included here are only the few specific references from the top of the page where he recorded his activities, as he coped with his loss, so that we can learn more about Pinchot the man.

Pinchot was born to wealth in Simsbury, Connecticut; his maternal grandparents (the Enos) maintained a home there and one in New York City as well. His paternal grandparents lived in Milford, Pennsylvania. Gifford grew up in his parents' home in New York City and at their summer estate, Grey Towers, in Milford. After 1900 he also had a home in Washington, D.C., at 1615 Rhode Island Avenue. We frequently see the four addresses, especially Grey Towers or Milford, New York, and Washington.

The diaries of Gifford Pinchot provide both the substance and the flavor of conservation; there are real people making things happen despite seemingly endless obstacles. What did happen—what was accomplished—was extraordinary for the time. After all, federal involvement in natural resources ran counter to the trajectory of national history through the nineteenth century. Creation of the national forests reversed the trend, and although federal involvement during Pinchot's time seems modest by modern standards, it marks a huge shift in defining the proper role of government in conserving natural resources for future use.

Deep thanks are due Edgar Brannon and Rebecca Philpot at Grey Towers; Steven Anderson, Cheryl Oakes, Michelle Justice, Lorraine Swain, and Carol Severance (on assignment from Grey Towers) at the Forest History Society; Forest Service historian Jerry Williams; Al Sample of the Pinchot Institute for Conservation; and Peter and Nancy Pinchot for their interest and support along the way. Maksim Malik and Stanley Spain helped as often as needed to bring the computer nearly to heel. Sally Atwater's deft editorial hand smoothed an unusually complex manuscript; and Mary Beth Malmsheimer's design produced an attractive and readable book. Staff at the Manuscripts Division, Library of Congress, cheerfully processed many requests for material, and some knew enough about Pinchot to ask questions and in other ways demonstrate interest in the project. The U.S. Forest Service, via Grey Towers and the Washington, D.C., office, and the Forest History Society provided financial support.

Part I
1889 –1915

GIFFORD PINCHOT FROM YOUTH TO MATURITY

"Am trying to start fresh & do my work as I ought"

Gifford Pinchot was a likable man. As are most of us, he was complex and at times inconsistent. The reader will feel proud of him when reading diary entries that reflect altruism and embarrassed by those few that show pettiness. But mainly the reader will be impressed by the range of Pinchot's experiences and coincidences.

The diary entries that follow begin with Pinchot as a young man just graduated from Yale University and thinking very seriously about making forestry his life's work. They end a quarter century later with him in middle age, with no real job, and exploring his options. This chapter is about Pinchot as a person, his interests, his values—whatever is important to him. Pinchot as conservationist is treated in other chapters.

The reader will be startled to see that a man who accomplished so much was at the same time very, very hard on himself for his personal failings. At first, the "am no good" entries seem like a joke; surely Pinchot was not serious. But he was, and the reader will be saddened by the man's torment, as he again and again fell short of perfection.

Pinchot was a religious man. He attended church regularly—although he also worked many Sundays as well—and if you were visiting him on a Sunday, you probably went along. He studied the Bible and sometimes delivered a sermon as guest preacher when he traveled. He was open-minded and tolerant of other faiths. Religion was as likely a topic of late-night discussions with family and guests as were politics, literature, and conservation. Toward the end of this chapter we see Pinchot working with long-time friend Charlie Gill as they coauthor a book on the country church, which was published in 1913.

In the 1890s scientists were vigorously debating Darwin's theories, with much concern expressed over whether one could be a good scientist *and* a good Christian. Darwin himself had struggled over this issue for two decades before he, a devout Christian, could accept what his data revealed to him. The young and devout Pinchot, seeing himself entering a life of science, was troubled, too, and he spent two evenings reading

Natural Law in the Spiritual World, by Henry Drummond. Religion and science were not in conflict, Drummond wrote, and Pinchot noted in his diary, "Needed just such a book."

The spiritualism of Drummond's title was not precisely the spiritualism that Pinchot practiced daily for twenty years following the 1894 death of his fiancée, Laura Houghteling. Pinchot believed in the hereafter, and he also believed it possible to communicate with Laura. Thus it was that a few days before her death, he wrote to his father that they had "talked it fully over, and are not afraid because we know it can be nothing more than a temporary separation." Shortly, he began reporting on his conversations with Laura; they read books to each other, they "saw our house," they remained in love. During some "sittings," he could "hear" her voice. This continued love affair was no secret; Pinchot discussed it with his family and friends, and he remained close to "Mother" Houghteling and Laura's brothers. The spiritualism entries included here are but a very small fraction of those contained in the full diaries.

There had been at least two other women in Pinchot's young life, "M.H.F.," or Maria Furman, and "Trix," whose full name is unknown. Trix came on strong, even learning about trees, and Gifford obviously cared for her. Suddenly we read about M.H.F., who abruptly announced her engagement to someone else. From then on, we read only of Laura.

He was close to his family, especially to his mother Mary ("Mamee") and his younger brother Amos, and the relationships are obvious in the diary. Gifford inherited Grey Towers, the family estate in Milford, Pennsylvania, and Amos built a more modest home next door. The brothers remained very close, as family and as neighbors; each named his son Gifford. Amos died in 1944 and Gifford in 1946.

Pinchot's relationship with his father, as reflected in their letters, is more difficult to pin down. Gifford would write, "Dear Papa" or "Dear Father," signing "Your loving son Gifford." The response would be "Dear Gifford," but the distant man would end with, "Your Father, J.W. Pinchot." Even when Laura's death was imminent and James wired Gifford, "We are greatly distressed. Love and sympathy from all here," he still signed the telegram, "J.W. Pinchot."

Fishing was Pinchot's passion, and he would have fished every day, if he could. Some days at Grey Towers he would go out twice, trying different tackle. For saltwater ventures, he liked Bar Harbor, Maine; Block Island, Rhode Island; and anywhere off Florida. He also liked hunting and just plain shooting rifles and pistols. Game laws were looser then, and while hunting with Amos he shot and wounded a deer using only a pistol. True to the sportsman's code, they spent the next two days tracking the animal to end its suffering; they were not able to find it.

Yale University was important to Pinchot. He regularly attended reunions for his class of 1889, he assisted in fund raising for a variety of campus needs, and of course the Pinchot family endowed the Yale School of Forestry in 1900. Athletic himself, Pinchot followed Yale sports, especially football, and we see the scores posted regularly in the diaries. When in New Haven, he would sit in the stands and root (loudly, one would suppose) for Yale; a defeat of arch-rival Harvard or Princeton would be especially sweet.

Pinchot read voraciously and broadly. In fact, a favorite topic of self-admonition was his reading too late at night. The readings, reported here only in part, are impressive, and from time to time he offers us a brief critique. It seems strange that he felt it necessary toward the end of his life, as he was working on his autobiography, to write that although he had read a lot, he had learned little—part of the complexity of the man.

Pinchot was very concerned about his health, not all that surprising during a time when the leading causes of death were influenza and pneumonia. He led a life that would have exhausted most people, as it often did him, plus he long suffered from problems of the eye, skin, and digestive system. In January 1911 he enrolled in the John Harvey Kellogg sanitarium in Battle Creek, Michigan. The notion of preventive medicine—staying well rather than getting cured—was innovative, and the high-mindedness of Kellogg's program, which centered on obedience to natural law as a moral duty, obviously appealed to Pinchot. Kellogg's ban on alcohol and tobacco would not have been a problem, but Pinchot had a sweet tooth and probably thought twice about the restriction on chocolate. Even after Will Kellogg developed the still-popular cornflake and the Kellogg Food Company had become the family income generator, John Harvey continued to run the sanitarium and authored a series of books on diet and natural remedies.

In 1925, when he was 60, Pinchot had a thorough physical examination, and the physician's four-page report is included among his papers at the Library of Congress. The record shows his height to be 6 feet 1½ inches; weight, 175½ pounds; pulse, 60; blood pressure, 122/80. His overall health is "very good" but he is 10 to 12 pounds underweight for a man of his structure. The doctor noted that in earlier years, Pinchot's weight had averaged 150 pounds, and here and there diary notations confirm this lower number. The data support what photographs show: for most of his life Pinchot was a very slender man.

While chief forester, Pinchot had worked effectively as a political practitioner, moving the agency and its conservation mission to remarkable heights. After he was removed from office in January 1910, he found himself very active in the Progressive politics of Theodore Roosevelt and Wisconsin Senator Robert LaFollette. We can see his being attracted to the idea of running for elective office, that of U.S. senator from Pennsylvania. Although he failed to become a senator, he would serve two terms as Pennsylvania governor, on the heels of a brief stint as state forester.

Pinchot's spiritual relationship with Laura ends when he meets "Miss Bryce" in 1913. Cornelia Bryce becomes "Leila" in the diaries, and they marry on August 15, 1914; ten days later Mamee dies. In an early example of his working companionship with his wife, they go to Europe to help with relief work in a war that won't reach America for several years. That sort of ambitious public service will reappear during World War II.

No doubt Leila encouraged Gifford's support for the right of women to vote, but the diary shows that other women in his family, such as his Aunt Nettie, were also involved. He became active in the effort, even being elected vice-president of the Men's Association for Women's Suffrage, an interesting twist on the more conventional women's auxiliaries for things that men did. His belief was strong; as editor of *American Conservation* he included an article on "What Women Have Achieved," as well as a piece on the need to "save" the Indian. All this fit well with "progressive" republicanism, and we shall see more of it later on.

1890

5/28 London To Oxford with Nettie and others. Lunched with Guy Nickalls, single-scull champion, and saw bumping race. Mother under treatment of Doctor Quinn.

6/1 London Have been perfectly useless all this week and am disgusted with myself.

6/8 Paris Drive in Bois with Mother and Nettie, stopping to see deCoubertine's athletic games. Football would have disgraced a primary school, but still it is a beginning.

7/7 Paris Studied in morning. Afternoon with Hod [Walker]. Mme. DeBury gave me letter to Charles Richet.

7/8 Paris Presented letter. Richet, head of spiritualism in France. Long and most interesting talk.

12/5 At sea Seasick. Read Dumas's "La Marquise de Brinvillers."

12/16 New York Docked at 10:00 A.M. Father on dock.

12/21 New York …Eno there. Breakfast with Mr. and Mrs. Pryor and Dick Welling. Grandpa and Aunt Mary to dinner.

12/25 New York Christmas. Hubert Wells' wedding. He had our presents at lunch.

12/27 Train to Washington with Mother. She goes to see Blaine and Harrison about Uncle Jack.

1891

1/7 New York …Grandpa still soured on forestry.

1/11 New York …Mrs. Custer & Will to tea. Very pleasant time. No talks about forestry, which was a relief, for people seem to think I have distinguished myself. Which is nonsense.

1/18 Memphis Reached Memphis 2:40 P.M. Hole in the ground at first sight. Pavements awful…red mud, shanties & niggers the foremost features.

1/25 Paragould, Tennessee To church in

A.M. at the "Christian Church." They go wholly by the bible, so they say.

2/1 New Orleans Up about 6:30. Very much interested in the sugar plantations, with their stately masters' houses in groves of live oaks hung with Tillandsia and their straight rows of quarters. Also in the levees & the steamers moving along higher than we were. Like the canals in Holland.

2/6 Mobile Woke up with severe case of trots…

2/8 Mobile Church not open. Read Atkinson's account of the Alladin Cooker & Powell's trip through the Grand Canyon of the Colorado…

2/17 Cullman …Terrible feellessness & blues. Read & bummed around. Paid Dr. Halbfleish, owner of City Hotel, at rate of only $1.25 a day, in consideration of being a student. Smooth of him.

2/26 Milford Delightful day with Father about the place. Saw the dogs & the horses, all in good time, & got books & pamphlets I needed. It was delightful to be there again. The new pond & wall are fine, and I hate the idea of being away from the place next summer.

3/10 New York …Grandpa came in in A.M. with paper w. account of president's refusal to pardon Uncle Jack. Grandpa had set his heart at having it done, & it hit him hard. Was very very sorry for him & for Mamee.

3/12 New York …Must keep this diary daily. Have now (Mar. 24) written up all that is in red ink.

6/1 Winnipeg to Minneapolis …Bought Natural Law in Spiritual World and began to read it on train.

6/2 Minneapolis Reached Minneapolis about 6 A.M.…Read Natural Law…& was greatly impressed by it. Needed just such a book.

6/12 Simsbury, Connecticut …[While fishing, Grandfather Amos R. Eno] told me about early life & showed where he first kept

Yale University graduation photo, 1889. Grey Towers Collection.

store. His example is a marvellous one in energy, concentration and ability of judgment.

6/15 Milford …The satisfaction in getting to Grey Towers each time is something wonderful. But I never seem to get any work done here.

6/16 Milford Spent a good deal of the day in looking about the place with Father. It is very greatly improved since I saw it before going to Europe. Wall around the garden finished, new bridge over Sawkill commenced. Whole place with a better kempt air.

6/29 Milford Pseudo-work in A.M. Shooting & then tennis with Eno. Was nearly killed off by the same. Am in very bad condition physically.

7/2 Milford Semi useless work again in A.M. After dinner Mis. Dodge showed us a lot of bending & contortion things that Speck, Eno & I mostly could not do, and was really wonderful at them. Then we three ran down to Bremmans & shot a good deal with a Frank Wesson pistol. B. made 5 bulls out of 5 shots at 12½ yards 5 in. bull. Speck 4 out of 5. G.P. 3 out of 5. Toots had gone up to fish. I got 5 bulls out of ten shots as my best record.

7/3 Milford Worked in A.M. in a sort of half hearted way. Made myself generally tired all day long. Am footless, useless, selfish, dumb & generally of no use to anybody.

7/6 Milford …Have had a dandy time with them all of late, except that I have been so down on myself for not being able to talk or act like anything but an ass that it has spoiled some of the fun.

7/8 Milford Rotten as usual. This uselessness probably result of so much gadding about & so many late hours after that very severe western trip. Anyway am disgusted with myself most thoroughly.

7/26 Milford To Episcopal church. Heard most awful sermon fr. Mr. Lassiter. Fooled away the afternoon till we went driving.

7/27 Milford …Am a footless ass. Malaria or none, I have no business to act this way.

7/28 Milford Wasting time as usual. Shooting again in P.M. Also ride with Mamee. Loaded 100 pistol shells & shot them off.

8/9 Bar Harbor To Congregational Church with Mamee. To lunch with Trix, then for a walk with her. She knows a lot about the trees.

8/12 Bar Harbor Talked with Trix, as usual.

8/13 Bar Harbor …Trix on the piazza as usual.

8/29 Simsbury …Read "The Silence of Dean Maitland." Strong, useful, but somehow incomplete.

8/30 Simsbury …Heard fine sermon from Mr. Stowe on Will. "I am, I ought, I can, I will" are the foundation of growth & civilization …Am trying to start fresh & do my work as I ought from now on.

9/1 Milford …Fooled in afternoon chiefly with the books in the library arranging them by general subjects.

9/6 Milford …A useless day, of which I am greatly ashamed.

9/11 Milford Came down through the gorge above the falls with Mamee. A beautiful, beautiful time. She climbed splendidly. Once almost dropped her in the water as we came across just below the big pool where we had to wade the deepest. One of the pleasantest mornings I ever spent. Straight chumship.

10/1 Milford Went off into the woods with Trix after species of trees. Along the brook. Pleasant walk…T & I sat & talked on the porch both before & after supper.

10/2 Milford At work in the morning. Wasted a good deal of time. P.M. Trix and I drove to Port Jervis to meet Nettie, Eno & Johnstone. Trix is smoother than she was at Bar Harbor, decidedly, but somehow is not attractive…Am getting to feel the waste of this summer severely. Was awfully footless, malaria allowed for.

10/12 New York …Went home & ate grapes & cursed & cursed & cursed & read L'Homme.

11/16 Biltmore …My sacred mind still torn up at intervals. But letter I wrote wholly fine from anything but frank chumsship.

11/17 Biltmore …Met Miss Houghteling after lunch.

11/23 New York …Afternoon with Trix at Museum Natural History…Trix very much interested in forestry.

11/28 New York Work on book till 12. Then to see Trix & talk over her suggestions and corrections of mss. of book…Trix's corrections in many cases very sensible. She took lots of trouble about it.

12/2 New York Drove to Phila w. Trix & Mrs. Freddy…Private car down & back, w. free grub etc., big spread after lunch, which last was very impressive, and gen. a very generous set up on part of the camps. Saw a great deal of Trix, in fact saw nobody else. She & Brennan & Billy Rainsford had been jumping on me for being too narrow, and she told me about it very nicely. They are right, as I told her. Proctor came in in evening & told about his trip this summer. Gave me head of Rocky Mt. goat, unmounted! Way up!

12/3 New York Stiles says people at Bar Harbor were talking about an engagement between Trix & me. Cuss!

12/5 New York …Got big tortoise shell specs w. large round glasses. Very comfortable.

12/6 New York Heard Dr. Parkhurst on the value of suffering in forming character. Call at Grandpa's noon. Wrote diary, then to Communion Service with Father.

12/13 New York …Long talk with Father after church about Grandpa, money matters, Uncle Jack, etc. Things I cannot be too glad to know about.

12/15 New York At work on old letters & notes all day till 3:30, & again later in afternoon. Saw Trix & held an exam, so called, on Schlich I. Found she had really studied it.

12/21 New York Morning went out after presents…

12/24 New York …Eve dressed Xmas tree w.. Eno & Nettie. Mighty pleasant.

12/25 New York Lit the tree about 12:30. Mamee was delighted. Our presents very nice indeed.

12/31 New York …Thought not at all about end of old year, & made no resolutions for the New. That I have no end to be thankful for goes without saying. That I must make this next a better year than last.

1892

1/13 Spuyten Duuyvel, New York My chum buddy & I have been writing each other lots of notes since I got back trying to hit on a time when I could see her. Have been getting anxious so to do…Met Professor Douglas & went to his place…Awful dull time. And then to think that I was to have spent this evening with my chum if this engagement had not prevented! Wow! Mad clear through to think of it.

1/14 New York Got home about ten o'clock. Work. Then note from M.H.F. to come to lunch. Went to see her at 12, but did not stay to lunch. Found there was much more feeling than I have expected in myself. Was afraid to speak of personalities. Spoke of her reading more etc.…Mamee & Father must have noticed I was more or less broken up.

1/15 New York …Am getting a good deal worried about my chum buddy. Care more than I have for some time. Fear chum buddy does too. Puzzled what to do.

1/21 New York …Met M.H.F. there. Had been getting eager to see her…Asked me to come to see her…Said I would try…Very good time indeed with Kitty…Walked home with Kitty. She helps me to search with my chum buddy every time I see her.

1/23 New York After lunch before going to Dr. Lord's Mamee told me she thought M.H.F. was engaged to Bond Emerson. It hit me very hard, much harder than I had the least idea of before. Went off without saying anything.

1/24 New York Heard Dr. Parkhurst, but the event was note from M.H.F. before I was up, announcing engagement to Bond Emerson. Very nice note indeed. Made appointment to see me this afternoon. Feeling decidedly broken up, but thankful at bottom it all ended so. Pretty serious time.

1/25 New York …to Feneer's Club. Surprised

to find M.H.F. there. Good time with her. Feeling much better. Like Bond very much. Very thankful for this ending of my only chum buddy.

2/4 Biltmore …No news from home & none from M.H.F. Had expected her photo now.

2/7 Biltmore …to call on Miss Houghteling. Pleasant time.

6/2 Frankfurt …Got throat tablets. Feeling very cheesy…drank endless water…measles! O cuss, cuss, cuss.

6/3 Frankfurt …Then the nurse came, an old man, noiseless, tireless in attention, but not as clean in his person as in other things. Great relief to have him, anyway. He slept in the room.

6/5 Frankfurt …Got up in the afternoon and had a bath!!! O joy, oh rapture! Begin to feel like a white man again.

6/6 Frankfurt Better still…Old Depplebache read some, talked a good deal later on his favorite topic of mistreatment of privates in the army. Paid the old duck for four days, & then discovered (after he had gone) that I have counted half a day too much.

6/7 Frankfurt …Letters from Mamee & Laura Houghteling.

6/8 Frankfurt …Am getting simply disgracefully lazy. This must & will stop.

6/9 Frankfurt…drew check of Mamee's for 500 fr. Then settled at hotel 124.70 incl tips. Hence cost of measles = 10 days time nearly & about 180 marks. Prob in all about 200 marks or $50.

6/11 Leipzig …John Griggs waiting & we had a most beautiful talk. Went out & got some beer, being in Germany, and finished talking about one o'clock.

7/24 At sea Church in A.M. "The Bishop" officiated & made the most flabby remarks I ever heard from a clergyman.

8/3 Bar Harbor Croquet after breakfast. George [Vanderbilt] & Miss Webb against Adele & me. Wiped the ground with them.

8/6 Simsbury–Milford Long talk with

Grandfather & Aunt Nettie. Delightful time …Then went to Falls & saw them in the moonlight, & enjoyed it all immensely.

9/11 Biltmore Went to Sunday school…After lunch rode over & called on Laura Houghteling & then back here for supper.

9/28 New Haven Worked at letters a good part of the day on the train. Also read "A Window in Thums," which is delightful.

10/26 Biltmore …Afternoon late got some practice jumping on moving horse & picking objects from ground at a canter.

1894

1/15 New York …Stopping at Putman's to send Laura Thackeray's Ballads, Old Town folks & Spinster's Leaflets. Found Grandpa worse, after very bad delirious night…Dr. Loomis came in eve just before dinner & spoke encouragingly for Laura.

1/20 New York Not very good news from Washington. Expected to go down, but stayed, owing to expression of judgment from Mrs. Houghteling in letter to Mrs. Caufield. Wired for news & stayed.

1/21 New York Up very late. News from Grandpa not very good. About 12 rec'd telegram from Washington that progress for the week was slight.

1/22 New York Letter this morning not good. Exceeding anxious…Then good news after lunch…Things look brighter tonight than for a long time. Grandpa also much better.

1/28 Washington Laura had a bad night, as was expected from the medicine. But the symptoms were better…Sent Laura flowers …Laura held her own today.

2/1 New York A good report from Laura, although nothing definite. Grandpa fully rational.

2/15 New York One week today [Laura died]. In the office at regular work. Aunt Nell came to lunch & gave me a beautiful silver photo holder with L's initials on the back. It was most kind of her. Called on Mrs. Caufield who gave me a lot of beautiful letters written to her and others about L.

3/2 New York Part of the morning at the jewelers & trying to get a box for letters.

3/8 New York Regular work and old personal letters. Today the cover for The Blue Box was finished, and also reproductions of L's pictures. Some good, some not.

4/8 New York Up very late, & to hear Dr. Parkhurst, with Father. A good sermon on the nature of real success.

4/12 Biltmore …To Strawberry Hill [the Houghtelings' summer home] for supper. Spent the night.

4/15 Biltmore To church, where I sat with Mrs. Houghteling. Then to Strawberry Hill for dinner.

5/5 Biltmore …like a fool or worse I ate candy. Read The Story of My Heart by Jefferies.

5/17 Washington …I seem given over to eating. Have had to swear off candy till July 4.

5/20 Washington To church with Mamee …Wasted most of day reading A Gentleman of France, wh. is a good story.

5/27 Simsbury …Backgammon w. Grandpa after lunch. Found him not very consecutive …Read to Grandpa.

6/6 New York Graves and Nash came in the morning after I had been to Howard's about my Lady's silver box to hold her Blue Rose.

6/21 Milford …I keep falling behind the advances I have to make. My soul doesn't grow.

8/3 Simsbury Long talks with Grandpa in which he finally offered me $2500 a year to work for him—kind of work he refused to state. Also spoke at length about necessity for fitting myself for coming responsibilities. I said I would think it over.

8/4 New York …Saw about our letter box at Tiffany's this morning. It had to be returned for the finish was not right.

8/14 Milford …Afternoon read Mamee & Cousin Gussie my Lady's sonnet on Death and the Sculptor.

8/18 Milford Another useless self-indulgent day. I must get away, & shall on Monday.

8/26 Strawberry Hill To church with Mother [Houghteling].

9/9 Milford To church with Mamee & Amos …Later Amos told me he intended to join the Episcopal Church.

9/21 Milford Shooting, a ride with Mamee, & little ways of wasting time.

9/23 Milford Church, and a long talk in the afternoon with Mamee about my dear Lady. Talk with Father this evening about Amos at college. I think he has done well.

9/30 Strawberry Hill Read The Originality of Christ, my Lady's copy.

11/21 Strawberry Hill Packed in the morning and talked with Mother. Took train North.

11/24 New York Long talk with Father about forestry, especially at Milford.

1895

2/18 Simsbury Talk with Grandpa about his will, of which he showed me a copy dated Jan. 7, '95, and other business from about 9:30 till nearly six. Found him altogether wild and inconsistent in his talk, & unable to think consecutively.

6/25 New Haven Breakfast and then to Alumni hall for my speech which did not come off. Class meeting small.

6/26 New Haven Breakfast with Ted, & then worked at my speech. Father sat at the Pres.' right at the dinner. I was not much good, but said a word for forestry.

7/5 New York Long talk in the morning

with Mrs. Weir and Dr. Harwood about the nature of man, and God in man & nature.

7/7 New York …read about 50 pages of Social Evolution. I was very much struck by it.

7/26 Milford Shot a blue heron, 100 yards…from a boat, a wood duck flying 50 yards (rising from water & already 10–25 feet high), and a partridge sitting 35 yards. No misses.

8/11 Milford To church. Rainy day. Read Social Evolution.

11/17 New York …a ride in the Park on bicycle, and a talk with Dr. Parkhurst. I told him why I wanted to transfer my membership to an Episcopal church, and he said he thought I was right.

12/25 New York Christmas Day. We (Mamee, Father, Amos, & I) had our presents in the morning, and then I went to take the little Canfields some books. After lunch to see Uncle Henry (all four of us) & found him better. Then bicycle ride with Amos. Little Henry and Uncle Mo to dinner.

1897

2/25 New York Letters, etc. A nearly wasted day. Feeling perfectly useless.

2/28 New York To Saugatuck with Henry Eno to play golf.

3/30 Lakewood Walk in the woods with Smock & Harry & later at 12 took a carriage here studying the forest and shooting (.38–44) on the way. Loafed & rested here, & to bed early.

4/23 New York Book *[Primer of Forestry]* nearly all day. Made a fool of myself by reading…till nearly two A.M.

4/24 New York Book nearly all day. To the University Club (just elected) and Century. Acted very wrongly by reading again till nearly 1:30.

11/20 Washington …Sat up & read till 2 A.M. like a fool & worse.

11/21 Washington Church etc. Ride in P.M. A largely wasted day.

1898

1/2 New York Communion Sunday. To church with Mamee. Called on Mrs. Canfield. Wasted the evening.

1/4 New York Amos came back this morning. Uncle John seriously ill. Very busy all day with various small things…Took late train for Washington. Exceedingly tired.

2/1 New York …Office mainly. Dinner and good talk with the Rector. Registered as an anti-Platt Republican.

2/9 Philadelphia …Sat up reading Mark Twain's Follow the Equator.

2/13 New York Bible class with Amos.

2/21 New York [grandfather dies]…The rest of the day spent in writing and getting to the papers a correct account of his life.

3/17 New York Various errands. Geographical Society in A.M. P.M. Dr. Lord & down town. Eve Rector to dinner, & with him to hear Arthur Humbert tell about his African trip, with lantern slides. Very good show.

3/19 Milford Took 8:55 train with Father, & after lunch (Erissman's) went on the Hill and measured place for a dam above the Gorge. Evening worked it out. Showed about 43 M in standard logs for the round timber.

3/37 Asheville Church with Mother and Mrs. Canfield. P.M. spoke at Biltmore in the church.

4/1 Asheville Helped Mother pack for moving to Strawberry Hill in P.M. Dr. Battee found a spot in my left lung under the shoulder blade.

4/11 New York …Dinner at the Stimson's. The President's message about Cuba.

4/16 New York Letters etc.…Bicycle ride w. Harry Graves in P.M. Cliff Barnes to dinner.

4/21 Washington …War begun. Very hard to stay home.

4/29 New York Took 3:40 train for N.Y. with Mamee. Found that Amos had been drawn to go with the volunteer troop of Squadron A. Tried to see him drill, but failed. Then to annual meeting of Yale Club. Proposal endorsed to give rapid fire 4" gun to the Yale.

5/1 New York With Amos to see horses for his use in the troop. Did not find one. Evening help him pack his kit…Amos leaves for Hempstead with the troop in the morning.

5/2 New York Amos left at 6 this morning, and took the 34th St. Ferry with the troop about eleven.

5/4 New York Dewey Day. No news.

5/5 New York Send gauntlets etc. to Amos.

5/6 New York …looking up horse for Amos.

5/14 New York …To Garden City at 3:20. Found Amos well. Chance of their going to Chickamaunga.

5/15 Garden City To camp. Found Amos well & brought him back to lunch.

5/19 New York Amos came up to day. The troop is to start probably on Monday for Chickamaunga.

6/2 Washington Errands & trying to find horse for Amos.

6/6 Washington Errands. House & horse found, I think…Mamee & Father went home at four, & to see Amos at camp.

6/7 Washington …Saw about house, for which I offered 1800. Saw about horse for Amos…Out to camp. Very pleasant there.

6/9 Washington Amos came in from camp. Good time with him.

7/3 Washington Communion Sunday. Out to camp in P.M., & spent night with Amos.

7/4 Washington News of Sampson's splendid victory at seven this morning getting better and better as the day went on.

7/23 Washington …As I came away at lunch time saw bulletin that Amos's troop was ordered to Porto [sic] Rico. Lunch with Father, Ahern & Harry, & with them to Camp Alger to see Amos. His troop did start about midnight.

7/27 Old Point Comfort, Virginia Amos left about 9, & I followed to Newport News about 11. Found the men with their stuff packed & stayed with them till they started for the ship. Intensely hot. Saw Amos take his horse aboard the Massachusetts & then said good bye to him.

8/8 Strawberry Hill Mr. Houghteling met Laura tonight.

8/27 Ponce, Puerto Rico Left Relief with harbor master, & went straight on to Ponce. Found Amos at Miss Chanler hospital, doing splendidly after a very close shave. Could speak only very slowly, but out of danger.

9/9 Washington …Saw Secretary Wilson at his house. He was extremely nice. Told me confidentially there would be an investigation, & by the most competent men the president could find. All right about my absence. I told him some cases of brutality of volunteer officers.

9/28 Grey Towers Letters. Also errands. Harry came tonight. Mead left last night …Amos sat up on the top of the piazza in the sun. Doing finely.

10/6 Grey Towers Talk with Mr. Bigelow about the wisdom of collecting government publications. He advocates it. Letters. Golf in P.M. Talk in evening with Mr. B. about writing down accounts of daily occurrences. He said I should write my connection with forest work. Amos's horse came this morning. He enjoyed immensely having him about.

10/20 New York …Talk w. Father & Amos about buying part of Nehasene Park. No decision.

12/28 New York All day with Father counting securities & cutting off coupons.

1899

2/21 Washington Inspected houses & lots.

2/22 New York 9:50 train. Discussed house question.

2/28 Washington Bought the lot [probably 1615 Rhode Island Avenue]. $39,500. Paid $1,000 to hold it.

3/7 New York A rule for the coming year. No candy except at meals & on trains. No story book after ten thirty P.M.

3/28 Tampa–Waycross, Georgia When I got up there was a pelican sitting on the roof within 20 feet of my window.

4/24 Washington Arranged about sending things from office to house & Wash. Talk with Dr. Dillingham. He sticks to Banff for Mamee. A good place I think. Took 3:20 train. Read Louis Beck's South Sea Island stories.

5/12 Hartford Settled plans finally. Received $25,961.63 from division of rent from estate.

6/3 New York Receipted for, received, & deposited in U.S. Trust Co. check for $325,000—from the estate. Also heard we are to get money Grandma Eno gave us with interest.

6/10 Milford Cromwell paid over $8,263.32 each (I believe) as settlement for money given to Nettie, Amos, and me of Grandma Eno.

7/7 Washington …Wire from Father conditionally agreeing to the contract proposed for house & so signed it with Langley about six.

8/6 Menlo Park, California …Spoke in church in eve., about the unity of our life here & hereafter.

10/13 New Haven Various matters. Amos & I registered. Stopped at Saugatauk to see Will about his gift of a fence for Yale, & then to New Haven. Saw here Frank Houghteling, Lew Welch, Dr. Foster, Brewer, Baldy & others. Lew says there is a chance for a St. Gardens statue of Nathan Hale.

11/28 New York Various business. Rec'd interest

(my share from resid. estate) $10,——. Choosing electric fixtures with Father. Lunched with him.

1900

1/26 Washington Pretty well tired out. Did little all day. Dinner at Hague's with Admiral Dewey…

1/27 Washington Over the new house with Father, who is immensely pleased with it.

1902

6/9 Boston With Hodgson to sitting with Mrs. Piper. Admirable sitting. Cornelia [Eno]'s daughter threatened with dyphtheria. Loafed and capital sitting rest of day. Dined with Hodgson at the Tavern Club.

6/10 Boston Cornelia's daughter out of danger of having dyphtheria. Another remarkable sitting, including [Laura's] voice at the end. Loafed as yesterday. Went to Capronii's & bought a lot of Berge casts.

6/11 Boston Another sitting this morning, after telephoning Cornelia, [news that] all goes well, & reading her what I got yesterday. A wonderful sitting again, with the voice for a few moments at the end…Took 5 P.M. train, having forgotten to telephone Cornelia again. Read & copied sittings on train, & sent parts to Cornelia & to Mamee.

6/14 Washington …Old Jim has paralysis. I want to send him to Milford. It is hard to see the old horse breaking up.

6/15 Washington …Wrote James [Houghteling?] about the Piper sittings.

6/27 Grey Towers …Loafing. Fishing in evening with Father, Toumey, & Stuyvesant. Old Jimmy is recovering from his journey from Washington, and when let out today seemed in capital spirits.

Rules for 1903 [memorandum at end of 1902 diary]. No reading but my lady's books after I start for bed.

1903

3/8 Washington …To the Church of the Ascension. Quiet day. Did little. Evening to White House to take president guns [from the Philippines]…I have been getting too little sleep & reading too much trash of late.

6/7 Washington Arrived 7:30 A.M. Found all well. Garfield at the house. To church with him. Mail. Two letters from Amos.

6/18 Washington …Meeting of National Trust for Places of Natural Beauty & Historic Interest. Tether ball with Garfield.

7/23 New York to Grey Towers Breakfast with Uncle Mo, after going to Winchester store for ammunition. Errands. Took 10:25 train to Port Jervis, & found all well. Mamee especially so. A great pleasure to get to Grey Towers.

7/25 Grey Towers …Sighted rifle & packed in P.M., saw comet after dinner.

10/19 Washington …Arrive Wash. 5:10 P.M. Mamee well. Others away. Telegram that Nettie arrived safely. To Cosmos Club after supper. Willis Moore for a candidate of the Board Directors National Geographic Society offered me the presidency to succeed Graham Bell. After consulting with Newell decided to refuse, there being men who ought to have it, and I have too little time.

10/23 Washington …P.M. meeting Board of Directors of National Geographic Society. Moore reported I have been offered nomination for president & declined; also Greeley, but he was unan[imously] elected nevertheless, & that was just right.

1904

1/1 Washington

1. Read no play books while personal letters remain unanswered.
2. Read no play books after starting to go to bed.
3. Don't hurry.
4. Take good care of digestion.

1/4 Woodstock, Vermont Saw the quarry at Proctor…Woodstock, arriving at …Billings' house at 7:25 & getting to the lecture hall at 8. It must have been not less than 30 below zero at 8 P.M. I made a very poor talk, and had a pleasant time with the Billings afterward. Sleepy early, after a delightful day in the open air.

1/5 Burlington Started about 8:30 for a drive of 1½ hours about the Billings' farm. Lowest temperature of the night minus 44 degrees. Pretty chilly. Then took the train for White River Junction & talked with Miss Mary & Fritz Billings till about one. At Burlington about 6:30, & made a better talk in the evening. Senator Proctor introduced me in a most flattering way. After meeting another [attempt] to organize a Vermont Forestry Association. At night room so hot I had to break the double window.

1/24 On train to Chicago Took 6:55 train east. Read Sampson on Milton's sonnets, The Master Rogue, and that delightful book The Captain's Toll Gate. Stockton knew my Lady. Long talk with Taylor about religion. A fine, restful day.

6/1 Washington On train while reading a short life of Emerson, I suddenly had the thought that I must catch up quickly, for the end of probation is not far off. Surely it came from my Dearest. I am very happy tonight.

9/22 Grey Towers to New York Left at 6:30 with Joe Hunt, and after doing a lot of errands in N.Y. took 3:25 to Wash. Read part of Professor Weir's Human Destiny in the Light of Revelation. Found all well at 1615, & signed a lot of mail. Very tired.

10/18 Washington Routine. Amos came down in the evening, and we had a long talk about his future work. He inclines away from South America—toward law & politics. I am dreadfully sorry he will not be in Washington right along.

10/23 Grey Towers Talk about the office, & decision of the family to keep it in N.Y. I preferred Washington, but was overruled.

11/30 Camp +27 A perfect hunting day. Jim too lame to go out, so I hunted with Amos. After following trail nearly 4 hours, shot & hit a superb buck with the Luger, but it is not strong enough after all. Took up trail again after boiling tea & following 2 hours more. Occasional drops of blood. Camp again 6:30.

12/1 Camp +7 In. or two of light snow in the night. Amos & I took that deer's trail again & following him till 2:30, straight away from camp.

12/3 Camp —8 Loafed & read. Did a lot of very bad shooting with various revolvers. Read The Cloister & the Hearth & lay around.

12/4 Camp Finished The Cloister & the Hearth. A great book marvellously filled with human nature & truth. Walk with Jim before dinner, & together cut down a 33 inch birch before supper. Also read Thompson Seton's story of Monarch, which is good, but stale.

1905

4/30 Washington Long drive & good talk with Father. Read The Princess Passes, a capital book.

5/18 New York …To bed about 2 A.M. very tired. Read Dumas' Pauline. A beautiful story.

7/4 Washington Telegram that Father has nothing but a cold. Loafing & work. P.M. with Garfield & Murray to see athletic sports & a capital ball game. Evening loafed & worked.

7/5 Washington To office & disposed of mail, after seeing Dol Smith who was sick at the Cosmos. He came in late last night. Then to Church of the Covenant to the services for Mr. Hay. They were very simple & in excellent taste. Hamlin preached well.

9/23 Chicago–Winnettia Brotherhood convention. Supper at St. James's parish house

where the services were most interesting, in commemoration of the founding of the Brotherhood. We saw the room where it began. James made a capital talk.

9/24 Winnettia …This morning I saw Margaret Newhall, Frank's fiancée, who is obviously a very nice girl indeed, with poise & character. In the afternoon made my talk to the convention on public spirit. They seemed to like it. Supper with Lonnie Stagg & Cliff Barnes, and after a long talk with Cliff about the Religious Education Association.

9/25 Winnettia …Went to a banquet of the Church Club, at which the President introduced Rev. Mr. Guery as a famous negro educator. A good time.

9/26 Chicago Long talk with…Cliff Barnes about the work of the Religious Education Association. I believe it should come to N.Y. Then took the train east, with Willie Houghteling, just entering Yale. Had a good talk with him.

10/22 Milford To church in the morning. The Keans came up to lunch, and Joe Hunt arrived at lunch time. So we had a very good time. Later Joe walked down to the Forest Hall with Amos & me, and left at six. Amos & I had good talk about business matters & his law work. We both slept in the old room.

10/26 Milford Off with Father after breakfast to Buick Pond…Took our lunch & ate it at Watson's. Jim Heller drove us, & ate inhumanly. After lunch I went out & in an hour & a half flushed eight partridges (ruffed grouse), fired at four, & killed two, greatly to my delight & Father's. Saw two more on the way back. Got back at six after a most enjoyable & satisfactory day. A quiet evening. Great fun with young Gifford [Amos's son] when brought him the birds. I have been having fine times with him.

10/27 Grey Towers I spent this day on the river in Amos' cause. Went down to the mouth of the Raymondekill, pushed up in it, & cooked a chicken etc. Then poled back. A first rate time.

10/29 Grey Towers Instead of going to church, Amos, Pete [Hart] & I took a long walk up the Sawkill & around by the camp. A good trip. Harry Graves came for lunch, & had a long talk with him about all kinds of Yale Forest School matters. In the evening railroad rate discussion with Amos & Pete. I have had a real good time with Amos, who is much better this week in health.

10/31 Washington I was examined by Dr. West, who said I needed to go slow, or I might get nervous prostration.

11/8 Washington Came back with Huntington, who showed me his building for the Hispanic Society. Very fine, We had long talk about South America, & I urged him to act.

11/28 Cincinnati On train: at work & reading Macaulay's essay on Milton, all of which I like but the conclusion, which seems over-drawn.

1906

11/4 Washington Loafed & read & wrote letters. A solid hour of medicine ball with George Woodruff.

11/6 New York Second breakfast with Father, who looked very well. Voted for Hughes & the Judiciary nominator's Judges.

11/9 Washington Getting automobile pretty much all day. Finally bought Studebaker 30-35 HP, after trying it and showing it to Mamee.

11/24 Washington Regular business. Inspected quarters. Medicine ball with Garfield. Taft, Durand, Rosen & others to dinner. A very nice dinner altogether.

1907

11/14 New York Much of this day with Father. P.M. conference at lunch with Seth Low, N.L. Britton, Johnson of Orange Judd, about American Institute, & the chance to get it to take up Agricultural organization.

1911

1/2 Battle Creek Reception at lunch time. Met the whole staff. Good looking people. Lost my bath to go to a fool reception.

1/3 Battle Creek Business men of Battle Creek at dinner, 45 of them, and afterward I made a talk on conservation to a fine audience in the gym, about 1,000 I should think.

1/4 Battle Creek This afternoon we four (Horace Plunkett, S.S. McClure, & Irving Fisher, & I) saw Dr. Kellogg operate—Shortened round ligaments for one woman, and removed uterus and ovaries for another. Most deeply interesting…Kellogg is a very big man.

1/6 Madison Got on wrong train by some mistake I don't understand, & went to Milwaukee, & so didn't reach Madison till 7:45. Van Hise met me at train & went quickly to the meeting of students & town people. I was in time, for they had to move from the hall first chosen to the gym. Had about three thousand. Fine meeting. Gov. McGovern came also. Pleasant talk & supper after the meeting at Van Hise's where I stayed.

1/7 Madison Went over the campus with Van Hise, and then…the Forest Products Lab-oratory. Much impressed. Meeting of Forest Service people there. Hall made a fine talk & I followed.

1/8 Chicago Spent the morning on my talk for the evening. P.M. Lawrence & I had a walk. Very cold, & very high wind. We went to Lincoln Park. Quiet supper with Cliff Barnes at University Club, and then a fine meeting. About three thousand. Cliff says best & most enthusiastic meeting they have had. Joseph Fels came up after meeting. Long talk with him after at his hotel. A very powerful, egotistic, crude, & persistent man, who may do immense good if rightly advised.

1/10 Battle Creek Routine. Got tired on test & down to 154 stripped. Lecture by Dugmier in evening & good talk with him & Dr. Kellogg about food of African tribes afterward. Horace & I had a fine walk this morning, & good talk about the political future.

1/19 Philadelphia P.M. Horace & I went to Philadelphia & spoke to crowded meeting American Academy Political & Social Science. Irving Fisher also spoke. Fine big meeting. Topic conservation.

1/21 Washington …Evening meeting at LaFollette's house to organize National Progressive Republican League…I was on Nominating Committee & was elected to Executive Committee. A good meeting…Very busy. Lost a pound.

1/24 New Haven Good talk with Amos at breakfast. He was at Progressive Socialists dinner last night.

1/30 Jersey City Took Congressional Line & went straight to banquet. Nearly a thousand men there…T.R.'s name was most cordially received. It was a great meeting. Back the same night.

2/14 Washington Big dinner of Boy Scouts of America. They did stunts for us while we ate, & it was very interesting. I made a pretty poor sort of speech.

2/23 Washington Amos came down from N.Y. and we went to the meeting of the Nat. Prog. Rep. League at the Willard.

3/14 Ponta Delgada, São Miguel, Azores …Wonderful yellow sunset across island as we steamed away, brilliant long fleecy clouds near sun, & rising full moon.

3/15 S.S. Celtic Read Ferrero on Puritanism (a comparison of U.S. & Roman civilization) and did some work…Medicine ball.

3/20 S.S. Celtic Reading Seven Great Statesmen, Bismar[c]k…Mrs. Marcoe said she had something to say to me, and tonight urged me

whatever else I may do, never to go into the usual brand of politics & so forfeit the respect of the young people, which she says I have now universally. As I said to her, it is a heavy responsibility.

3/26 Rome …Talking about politics, Nettie asked me why I didn't turn Democrat & run for president.

3/28 Rome [David] Ruben again, and lunched with him. A very remarkable man, a Jew, whose main idea is to introduce the Jewish equity in the world, and take revenge for the persecution of the Jews by service [to] the human race.

5/7 S.S. Rotterdam Glassy smooth and no groundswell even. Foggy. Read The Brass-bounder all the morning. A fine story…This is beyond all comparison the most comfortable boat I ever was on.

5/13 At sea We had a capital crossing… Reading Promise of Am. Life. Played baseball a lot on enclosed deck.

5/14 New York Smooth at sea, but cold. The coast most beautiful as we came in. A most beautiful sunset like sequins or little flames on the water…I certainly was glad to get back.

5/16 Washington Amos & I took breakfast with A.J. Beveridge. Long & very good talk indeed. All about the political situation & what I should do. Short talk with T.R.

5/23 Oyster Bay to New York Came in with T.R. in auto, he driving. Archie along. Then Jim & I to Outlook with T.R., where he showed us forthcoming article on LaFollette.

5/25 Washington …talk with Bob LaFollette. He wants me to manage his campaign. Of course I can't. Has no one in mind. Told him of my talk with T.R. Made an ass of myself by reading late—Sam Blythe's The Great Bailey Myth.

6/2 Grey Towers …I went to see T.R. Told him of proposed speech against Taft. He said it was logical thing for me to do, and made no objection.

6/7 Grey Towers About the place at work pretty much all day…Evening went to High School Commencement in Forest Hall. Five girls graduated…Altogether delightful evening.

8/20 New York …Took afternoon train to N.Y. & went in. I don't think I ever hated to leave any place (of late years) as much as I did Grey Towers this time.

11/11 Washington …Dr. [WJ] McGee at dinner. Looking better but not yet altogether recovered from operation. Good talk. He is one of the bravest men I know.

11/15 Washington …Lunch with Roberston. Fine talk. Spoke afterward (hearing) before his Committee on Indust. Education & Technical Instruction as forest education and organized conservation (how we got public attention) & country life. Walk with Bill Kent. Supper with McGee at Cosmos Club, & talk. He is strong for Commission on National Efficiency… Reading Peter Ibbetson.

11/25 Washington …Called on Mabel Stevenson & Wayne McLeigh, who seemed to think I might be nominated for vice president if Bok won. I told him that was not my business.

12/25 Washington Christmas day. Tree in the morning…to see the Walcotts. Dr. McGee for dinner.

1912

1/5 Washington …Talk with Congressman Nelson. Explained Ohio vote and urged community of interest of all Progressives. He agreed with me.

1/15 Washington …Lunch with Dol & Price. Work on speech for 22d. Ride with Harry …Singing lesson. Evening letters, etc. Very cold. Fine ride.

1/22 New York [with T.R. and LaFollette] … Evening great meeting Carnegie Hall. At

8, line 4–6 wide extending more or less around whole building. Hall completely full. I spoke on waste & efficiency.

3/16 Philadelphia Spoke at Rural Life Conference in City Hall, Phila., mainly on the country church…Evening at banquet for Boy Scout movement.

4/8 Pittsburgh Met Senator Powell, & arranged for most of trip. Met various people. At noon lunch at Hungry Club, where I spoke on conservation & T.R. & esp. that he is in the fight purely for principle.

4/9 Pittsburgh Breakfast with T.R. & Alex. Moore. T.R. in fine fettle, and very well. Good talk with him about situation. As he says he has his fighting clothes on.

4/13 Milford Voted this day at John McCarthy's house in Milford Township for T.R. delegates at primary election. Voted Republican Ticket only.

4/16 Exeter–Boston Up at 6:30. Spoke to the boys at chapel for 30 min. about taking an interest in the nation, & how ability is second to vision and persistence. They seemed to like it.

6/22 Chicago Birth of the New Party this day.

7/27 Washington …saw Dr. McGee. Was pretty shocked at his condition. Long talk with him. His end is near, he believes, but is perfectly serene & content. A most wonderful and admirable man. Saw his doctor, who thinks condition hopeless, but may continue several months. WJ thinks 3 weeks. His will be a very great loss.

8/1 Chicago …Good news from home in letter from Mamee. Amos delegate from his district to the convention.

8/18 Washington All day on article on conservation & the cost of living for Progressive Campaign book, article for Boy Scouts magazine, & speech for Vermont etc. Saw McGee several times. Good talk after supper…Billy K. took me for a ride in his electric in P.M.

8/19 Brattleboro, Vermont …Made a reasonably decent speech, for me. Charley Gill came here to see me about the country church book.

8/28 Washington All day on Charley Gill's book. WJ in semi-coma all day. Knew me this morning and again this evening. Made some arrangements for last services at my house. Letter from Lawrence Houghteling raising serious questions as to what Medill is doing in Chicago.

8/30 Washington WJ stronger than yesterday. Knew me both morning and evening. In between & at night I did not wake him. Dentist for 2 hours…Charley's book all day. Making good progress. It will be a strong document, I am now sure.

8/31 Washington Working on Charley's book. WJ spoke to me today "I am glad to see you."

9/30 Omaha Up to this morning 27 speeches in this campaign.

10/3 Aberdeen, South Dakota… 36 + 2 = 38 [speeches]

10/14 Auburn, Indiana 52 + 2 = 54…At station heard rumors that T.R. had been shot at Milwaukee, but did not believe it.

10/16 Springfield, Massachusetts …Long conference with Charley Gill on county church book. Conference with Glenn & McFarland. Told them we wanted book published as part of a definite plan to carry this work forward & would insist. Agreed to let matters stand till we can submit finished mss.

1913

1/13 Providence …motor to Newport, where under auspices of Prog. League, I spoke on Conservation. About 550. Pretty fair talk, but not A1. They seemed pleased.

1/15 Columbus …Spoke on country church. First few chapters Gill's & G.P.'s book…Spoke again after dinner on conservation. Same audience [Columbus Club].

1/24 Washington …Miss Tarbell to dinner. She believes Standard Oil decision will really produce in end true competition. Also that we must be sure fundamentally.

1/26 Washington Horace Plunkett came. Wants me to quit active connection with politics and take up reconstruction of agriculture in U.S. Thinking hard about it. Barrett (Farmers U.) at lunch. Made unexpectedly poor impression— yielding to pressure and not leading his men …Quiet dinner at home. F.H. Newell came in after. Also strong I should take up agricultural work. He had seen Horace.

1/27 Washington …At dinner Coville, Newell, Holmes, Reger, Whitney Darton, Gannett, to consult about the McGee Memorial Meeting. Fixed date of April 17. Agree on publishing memorial volume, including letters. Made only tentative agreement on names of speakers. Very tired. Stomach bad. Have been eating too much trash.

2/3 New York …Dinner at Lawrence Godkins with Pritchett & McCarthy & Horace. Talk about agricultural cooperative…They all (Pritchett, McCarthy & Horace) want me to head an agricultural…society in U.S. I said I would consider it.

2/4 New York Met Horace & McCarthy with Amos at Pritchett's office. McCarthy repeated what he had told me (about Perkins) to Amos. Pritchett said he thought he could get half a million for agriculture society.

2/6 Washington …Dinner at the Beveridges. After discussion with Beveridge on trust question, in which he said Sherman law should be repealed. Also that he had letter writing to do with cutting out Sherman law plank from our platform. Said T.R. had prepared a statement on this plank which he showed him & Shafer, & that it did not at all agree with my account. Beveridge said his objection to the plank was that it did not contain provision for imprisonment.

2/23 Washington …I am dreadfully sick of speaking. Through for a time…No more engagements.

2/26 Washington …Very tired. Nap this P.M. Dinner at Russian Embassy with Mamee. Took in Mrs. Bayard. Delicious flounder au gratin— best fish I ever ate.

3/3 Washington Mail & catching up in A.M. Saw pageant at South steps of Treasury Department from Aunt Nettie's box & then suffrage parade from room in Grant Hotel. A wicked outrage the way it was handled by the police.

3/4 Washington Inauguration Day. With Amos up to Capitol to see the crowd. Then to see the parade from Grand Hotel. Missed Wilson, because we were late. Got tired of parade after a while.

3/6 Washington …Dentist in P.M. Quiet evening. Polly came in & told of hearing before Senate Committee on maltreatment of suffrage parade Monday. Am reading Quo Vadis again. Much impressed.

3/15 Washington …Evening dinner & reception. Peters & others. Miss Bryce came & Mrs. Brooks.

3/16 Washington All day with Charlie Gill on Country Church. Walk to zoo in P.M. He has rewritten chapter on Remedies, & it's the best work he has done.

3/19 Washington …Called on Miss Bryce & Mrs. Brooks.

3/20 Washington …Pretty weary tonight. Weighed 159 3/4, best for years.

3/22 New York Breakfast with Charley Gill at Century…He said Sage Foundation can't continue [his] Country Life work, so we decided

to offer the book to Federal Council of Churches.

3/27 Chicago About 2 hours late. At lunch time found Uncle Henry Wallace and Charley McCarthy at LaSalle Hotel. We spent afternoon & most of evening getting Plunkett's agricultural coop. plan going. We called it Agricultural Organizing Committee, adopted McCarthy construction with a few changes, & chose the nine members & then Uncle Henry went off at 10. We saw him to the train & talked late.

4/4 New York …Dinner at the Norman Whitehouse's. Florence, Miss Bryce, Mrs. Older, etc.

4/5 New York Met Charley Gill at MacMillans. Brett said they were not only willing but anxious to publish our book. Marsh then offered 10% on first 1,500, & 15% after. I asked for 15% on all copies sold.

4/8 Washington …Evening big dinner at Henry Whites to meet Bryan. Sat between Mrs. Peters & Miss Bryce.

4/10 New York Met Charley Gill at 9:30 at University Club & went to organizing meeting of Social Seminary Commission of Federal Council of Churches. After some debate Charley & I got our book recommended for acceptance by the Commission to the Council without McFarland getting any control over it, & had a special committee appointed to continue the work, in accordance with our proposition.

4/21 New York …Took 4:30 w. Charley to Oyster Bay. Good talk. T.R. read the first part of our book, was much struck by it, & said in reply to my request, that he would review it for the Outlook. Asked for a précis.

5/1 Chicago Met Uncle Henry Wallace, C.S. Barrett, McCarthy at La Salle Hotel. We went up to Barrett's room, revised & adopted const. of Agricultural Organizing Committee of

America, elected McCarthy as secretary, & directors, Godkin as Treasurer, Uncle Henry vice president & G.P. as president. Instructed me to apply in name of committee to Carnegie Foundation for funds, etc.…Read Stevenson's In the Forest.

5/4 Washington All day long on the page proofs of The Country Church, except walk with Beveridge in A.M., during which he said he never expected to run for office again, & urged me very strongly to run for Senate in Pa.

5/6 Washington …finished Country Church proof in a great rush—the last of it reached me at 12:30, and finally got away with a pretty clear desk at 3:05.

5/23 Washington to New York Finishing up mail, etc. packed up, took Congressional Line. On the platform as I walked up was Gen'l Wood. I crossed the platform & spoke to him, and as I turned away the man who was with him put out his hand & I shook hands before I recognized who he was. Then I saw it was Root. He was smiling in an embarrassed way. He had on a curly brimmed Panama hat, which may be why I did not recognize him. When I did I dropped his hand & walked away, and on the train debated whether I would go & tell him I had shaken hands by mistake. Decided against it…This day got insulting telegram from Horner of Ridpath threatening to enforce contract.

5/24 New York …Pritchett told me over phone he had failed to get money from Carnegie for Agricultural Organizing Committee. I wired McCarthy & Wallace.

5/31 New York Saw Pritchett who told me he felt sure we could get the money for A.O.C. next fall if Houston would write another letter emphasizing the need for our work.

6/2 Washington …Almost at once on my arrival Uncle Henry Wallace turned up. He had seen Galloway & Houston, and the mis-

understanding…(fearing duplication from work of A.O.S. & Department) was already by him removed. He was in great form, & we had a good talk.

6/6 New York …Saw T.R. & he agreed I should see…about Pa. senatorship, which he said very strongly he would be delighted for me to have.

6/10 Milford …Evening Mamee & I went over the main dates in the history for the family from 1865 to 1881. That was a good thing to do. I wrote them down.

6/22 Grey Towers Did not go to church …Miss Bryce came. Evening we listened to Gordon Brill read Amos' fine letter to "Mr. Chairman," being any N.Y. county chairman. It is very well done.

6/23 Grey Towers …Fishing with Miss Bryce near home. She wore a kind of blouse and rubber boots. Brook, too low for her, & fish not rising anyway. I took one. I tried to get her to bathe at Picnic Rock.

6/24 New York Miss Bryce & I took 9:00 for N.Y. Old man Channels met me at station, & wanted me to invest in his Grange Insurance Co. I refused, of course. Saw John Rogers, who went over me & said I was in good shape except too low blood pressure (about 100).

7/13 Grey Towers The humming bird was on his twig when I woke up, & the wren singing.

7/15 Grey Towers Emile came up early with an auto, & we went to Levi Lord's, saw the old man & had a nice talk (he said he could see the Pinchot in me, & that I looked like my Father & my Grandfather).

7/26 McPherson, Kansas Left at 9:30. Horner was on same train, & knew I was, for his men knew it. On reaching McPherson, as we got into the bus, one of his men started to introduce us. Horner held out his hand. I put mine under my overcoat & said: "Mr. Horner there are certain preliminaries necessary before you and I can have any intercourse of any kind whatsoever." He said, "Oh, very well," and that ended it.

7/27 Marion, Kansas Went to church…At R.R. station about noon Horner came to me & said: "What about those necessary preliminaries you spoke about?" I said: "Mr. Horner, you wrote me a letter which any man would take as insulting. I want a written apology, and until I get [it], I shall have nothing whatever to do with you." He said something about looking the matter up, and added that he thought he was the one to whom an apology was due. I replied that I declined to discuss that w. any other matter till the apology was received. He said, "You will get no apology, and I want to tell you you are acting in a very ungentlemanly manner." I turned then, walked up to him quickly, & said, "Mr. Horner, I take no back talk from you or any man. Is that sufficient?" He said it was. I replied Good, and turned my back on him.

8/4 Junction City–Ellsworth…Longstead told me here that Horner had sent him a copy of his letter to me threatening to sink me…

12/16 New York …Talk with George Woodruff in P.M. He thinks I can be elected if I run for senator for Pa.

1914

1/5 Cleveland Spoke to about 125 on Conservation & the Cost of Living, members of the Twentieth Century Club.

1/6 Pittsburgh Woman suffrage lunch. Mrs. Roessing presiding.

1/11 Washington Reading Lincoln-Douglas debates. Lunch with Bill Kent. Wild turkey soup & cutlets. Most delicious. Told Bill I thought he was making a great mistake staying out of the Progressive Party. Called on [McGee's] sister. A queer little old lady, for whom we can do little.

1/20 Washington …[was] advised strongly

I should make two separate statements, one of candidate & one of platform.

1/21 Washington …Wilson's message on trusts makes Amos program absolutely essential. It puts the Democrats in our hands. It will be taken generally as the first backward step.

1/22 Philadelphia Working on statement of candidacy.

2/10 New York Stopped at Dr. Curtis' office & had my uvula cut off to help my voice. At Amos' office—mail & preparing statement on my belonging in Pennsylvania. Harold Ickes came in…Throat painful.

2/27 Honesdale, Pennsylvania …Spoke to 550…The whole audience rose as we came in. I spoke an hour.

2/28 Milford …Uncle Jack died today.

3/14 Cleveland …Spoke to 1150…Spoke well, for me.

3/17 Huron, South Dakota ….Spoke Cons., & Vision & Will.

3/30 Washington …elected vice president of Men's Association for Woman Suffrage.

4/3 Allentown, Pennsylvania …Spoke to Women's Club on Conservation & Cost of Living.

4/26 Philadelphia …Amos has decided not to run for Senate. He says Mamee's letter settled it.

5/20 New York …T.R. just like his old self. Showed his pictures & talked about his river. Highly approved my plan of campaign. Like old times.

5/25 York County, Pennsylvania Spoke 8 times, last at York to 1500–1800 people from the court house steps.

5/26 York, Adams, and Cumberland Counties Spoke 8 times, last 2 at Carlisle.

6/30 Pittsburgh T.R. in town, Progressive conference. Spoke before T.R. at Exposition Hall.

7/30 Philadelphia …Leila came at 2:47 for N.Y. with Judge Carson. Met her & Miss Ruth Morgan at North Philadelphia, then to Diston Saw works…Then drive with Leila in the Park.

7/31 Roslyn, New York Met Leila…Lunch with Leila…& long talk with her…By motor with Leila…Spoke to Mrs. Bryce. Then a wonderful talk with Leila.

8/1 Saugatuck, Connecticut Leila and I to Saugatuck by the 1 o'clock ferry. I spoke to Mr. Bryce after lunch. Picnic just Leila & I, at Seaman's Rock.

8/2 Saugatuck Leila here.

8/3 Saugatuck Leila here.

8/4 Saugatuck Leila left at 8:15.

8/5 New York The Day of the Final yes.

8/7 Saugatuck The good morning letter from Leila. Also another.

1915

1/31 London …Leila's cold & mine about gone.

2/15 London Leila had her operation this morning 10:15. Came out of the anesthetic very soon and with little nausea. Operation very successful & very necessary.

2/18 London First day of German "blockade" of England. Tried to leave this morning for France on business of C.R.B. as to feeding the French N. of German lines. No trains running. Was very happy to get back to Leila.

4/8 London …Refused to add to my statement about expulsion from Belgium.

4/9 London Down to see Hoover. He was good & angry about the German action, & very nice. Hoped to have something to offer me in S.W. Belgium feeding 200,000. Delivered my pouch to American Embassy. Saw Davis with Leila. Not able to say positively but believe result of operation already serious. Gave strong instructions about being careful first & most. Leila not to go to Belgium, & to U.S. until June 5.GP

THE EDUCATION OF A FORESTER

"They resent as an insult to their profession my attempt to learn it quickly"

Conservation literature frequently refers to Gifford Pinchot as the first American forester, a somewhat puzzling statement in the so-called Land of Immigrants, where until recently the "melting pot" was a point of pride. In fact, the pointing out of birthright is part of a successful effort by his supporters to make the man stand out even more than he surely does from his apparent competitors—German-born-and-educated foresters Bernhard Fernow and Carl Schenck. Hands down, Fernow and Schenck were Pinchot's technical superiors, but forestry then as now was much more a political science than an application of natural sciences, and on his worst days the American politically outpaced the Germans by a mile.

That is not to say that Pinchot was a forestry illiterate. He earned a bachelor's degree from Yale University in 1889, and in the fall left for Europe with his father's watch in his pocket and a $600 allowance. He also left with an interest in forestry and his father's inspiration. Pinchot stopped first in London to become acquainted with the Indian Forest Service. There, he was given letters of introduction to Dietrich Brandis and William Schlich, German foresters who both had earned forestry prominence in India and in educating young Englishmen to manage forests throughout the Empire. Since 1875 this English program had been headquartered at Nancy in France as well as at the Dehra Dun school in India, started two years later. But the British wanted a school closer to home, and in 1885 Schlich was assigned to a forestry chair at Cooper's Hill College for Engineering, just up the Thames from London. Schlich would move the program to Oxford in 1905, where it remains.

Schlich and Brandis, especially Brandis, would become Pinchot's forestry mentors. It is fair to say that as a result, American forestry became organized along German lines, or rather German as developed for British India, Burma, and other lands seemingly so different from the United States. But in the nineteenth century the United States was also a rural, third-world nation that lacked the infrastructure to mount a management program for its vast forests. In India as in the United States, there was a strongly held belief that states' regulation of local resources was preferable; it was the ultimate dominance of the national governments over forestry that we look back on and call "conservation."

When Pinchot wrote Brandis's obituary in 1908, he stated that he had always believed young Americans interested in forestry should travel to India, as well as to Europe, to understand better just what they would be getting into. Even though that statement is no doubt the sort of generous hyperbole found in obituaries—there is no evidence that Pinchot had in fact literally felt that way—it does reflect the importance of the British-German-Indian forestry tradition to America. Today, the Society of American Foresters, founded by Pinchot in 1900, sponsors awards named for Pinchot, Schlich, and Schenck (whom Brandis had suggested as Pinchot's successor at Biltmore Forest); it is not clear just why Fernow and Brandis have failed to receive their much-deserved recognition by American foresters.

From London Pinchot traveled to Paris and made several tours of the forestry exhibit at the National Exposition. He noted for November 11, 1889, that Edouard Blanc, a French forestry student, "advised staying now and going through first year at Nancy. I so decided." He also arranged for Whitelaw Reid, family friend and minister to France, to write a letter of recommendation. On November 12 he was in Bonn, where he began his two-decade relationship with Brandis. Two days later he started formal study at Nancy with an eight-o'clock class taught by Professor Lucien Boppe, whose *Traite de Sylviculture* had been published earlier that year.

The French course for British students, like the program for French students, was a two-year mix of formal classes and excursions to French, German, and Swiss forests to see what forest conditions really looked like. It was on some of these excursions that Pinchot became close to Brandis. He was comfortable in French, and his German was better than that of the other students, so he became Brandis's assistant, at times dispensing discipline to what he saw as unruly and disrespectful young Brits. He participated in one year of the program, despite much advice to continue for at least an additional year.

The deeply religious and teetotaling Pinchot (two years later he recorded that he had drunk "some beer, being in Germany") had difficulty with student life outside class. He noted that a students' masked ball was "very rotten," and another time wrote, "I shall be glad to leave. All drink and no forestry is not my meat." This statement was a variation of an entry a year earlier at Yale, where he had written, "forestry is my meat."

Pinchot was also critical of the education program itself. After one excursion he noted, "I never spent time more uselessly than at Neupfalz." In a separate journal he kept at Nancy, he wrote of "dry lectures" and some professors' reluctance to field questions. In fact, he wrote that according to Schlich, one of the reasons for beginning the programs at Cooper's Hill was that the "English students from Nancy did not know anything when they graduated."

Nevertheless, it would be difficult to argue that Pinchot's abbreviated technical education of questionable quality hampered him later as he worked to shape American forestry. He well knew that European and Indian forestry practices could not be transplanted to the United States without being modified to fit New World conditions and culture. And growing up in this country, instead of entering as educated adults, as had Schenck and Fernow, no doubt made him more comfortable than they. Thus, there is some justification for calling Gifford Pinchot the first American forester.

1889

10/5 New York Sailed on North German Lloyd steamer "ELBE." Father gave me his watch and allowed me $600.00 for the trip. Only nineteen first-class passengers. Didn't miss a meal.

10/18 London To India Office where Mr. Sturt introduced me to Sir Charles Bernard, head of the Indian Forest Service in England, who gave me letters to Doctor Schlich and Sir Dietrich Brandis. I have never met such disinterested kindness to a total stranger before.

10/21 London I found the Cambridge students more hospitably inclined than any people I had ever met, cordial, polite, and in general very good fellows. Saw Mr. Sturt who gave me a lot more books.

10/22 To Cooper's Hill to see Doctor Schlich. Doctor Schlich gave me an autographed copy of his Manual of Forestry, kept me to lunch, and drove me through the park at Windsor. Doctor Schlich advised me to strike for reservation of national forests for he does not believe that Arbor Days, etc., are of any practical use.

As I learn more of forestry, I see more and more the need of it in the United States, and the great difficulty of carrying it into effect.

10/23 London Started second-class to Paris, via Newhaven and Dieppe.

10/24 Paris How glad I was to be in Paris again! It seemed like the good old times, almost, when I was studying at the Jardin des Plantes, and the family was here. We stayed at the Hôtel de l'Univers. Went to the Folies Bergeres.

10/29 Paris Studying forest exhibit at Exposition. Met M. Daubrée, Directeur des Eaux et Fôrets, who promised to write to Puton for me, and directed me to Nancy for all information. Supper at Café Voltaire.

11/5 Paris To see Pasteur inoculating Chalfant and others for rabies. Saw oak dug from bed of Rhône—31.60 meters long.

11/9 Paris Saw Maria Furman; Edouard Blanc, a forester. He advised staying now and going through first year at Nancy. I so decided.

11/10 Paris …Jim and Mme. deBury approved plan to stay and go to Nancy now. I had already got in touch [with] Brandis at Bonn.

11/11 Paris Arranged for letter of recommendation from Whitelaw Reid to Baubrée. Went up in captive balloon with Maria Furman. Started for Cologne to see Doctor Brandis.

11/12 Bonn …Arrived Bonn, and after supper at Golden Star to see Doctor Brandis. Doctor Brandis approved Nancy plan and wrote F.M. Meister. Doctor Brandis pleased because I could chop and plow.

11/13 Bonn–Nancy Took 6:45, first train, in morning. Arrived 4:19. Went to see Puton, who was very kind and made no difficulty. After dinner found Boppe.

11/14 Went to my first course at 8:00 A.M.—Silviculture under Boppe. Then saw Huffel. Got rooms at 13 rue des Champs at 40 francs a month. M. and Mme. Babel.

11/15 Nancy Heuffel helped me get maps. Ordered woods shoes.

11/16 Nancy First excursion to Fôret de Haye with Boppe, Heuffel, and Bartet. Lunched with them.

11/23 Nancy Botanical excursion—Professor Flische, also Boppe and Huffel. Then studying storied coppice.

11/24 Nancy Fôret de Vandoeuvres. Storied coppice. Later writing notes for Doctor Brandis.

11/25 Nancy Got news, Yale 36, Harvard nothing. Walked with a Roumanian, Vladoyano. Went to Berger-Levrault for Bagneris' Manual.

11/28 Thanksgiving Day. Made schedule of work covering every minute from 7:15 in the morning to 11:00 at night.

11/29 Nancy Solitary excursion to Vandoeuvres. Lunch with wood-choppers. Home in heavy snow storm.

11/30 Nancy Trouble with Sognet, shoemaker, about forest shoes. With Flische and Boppe to Rosiers-les-Salines with [illeg.] Liked them better.

12/1 Nancy Sunday. Writing letters. Heard Yale nothing, Princeton 10.

12/2 Nancy First met Joseph Hulot. Took me to his house.

12/13 Nancy To breakfast with Hulot, and then day in Forest of Vandoeuvres. Went to house of Gigou, fine old forest guard. Stopped at Brabois. Presented to Mme. de Brabois on way home. "She treated me just as if I had been clean."

12/14 With Gigou through Forest of Vandoeuvres. Dinner with Hulot. Excursion under Boppe. Walked well over twenty miles.

1890

1/1 To Bonn Dressed and saw Doctor Brandis, who corrected my notes on Forest of Vandoeuvre. Doctor Brandis arranged to dictate his ideas on the way to get at things in America. He believes that nothing general can be done till some State or large individual owner makes the experiment and proves for America what is so well established in Europe, that forest management is pecuniarily profitable.

1/2 Bonn Working with Doctor Brandis.

1/3 Walked with Doctor Brandis and his son Joachim. Saw for the first time Sequoia gigantea. Dinner with Doctor Brandis, and afterward finished report. Doctor Brandis said, half in fun, I think, that he was going to make me a sort of tutor to the English boys next summer. Here's where I try to be ready.

1/4 Bonn to Nancy Found box from home deCoubertin had brought over. I had my Christmas that night.

1/6 Nancy To library with Nesteroff. Walk with Hulot. Decided to cook my own breakfast hereafter with lamp Mama sent. Wrote Fernow and Meister.

1/7 Nancy Cooked eggs, small sur le plat. Worked 9¾ hours of 60 minutes each. Wrote to Fernow and read accounts of Fall of Empire in Brazil.

From the supplemental diary Pinchot kept at Nancy, France, in 1890:

Result of recent experience with French F. School is that the Fr. method of education has taken all enthusiasm from the fellows, and the teachers are at no pains to kindle it again. Mm. Henry Guyot & Petit Collot in the Alps were much better than the men we had in the Voges, especially than Huffel, who is generally useless as well as about to lose his temper. Dry lectures given after a thing has been seen, not at the moment of first seeing it, are not the best means to impress information about it. This was method used in Alps. [illeg.] we ascended to head of a torrent & there had a lot of statistics fired at us out of a note book whereas I was very anxious to hear about the dams, planting etc., on the spot. Profs very ready to answer, but occasion & skill to ask somewhat scarce.

Again, in Vosges we got only what we were able to dig out ourselves, very little being told us about what our work should have shown us fully. Boppe & Huffel did not like to answer questions and in gen. I did not get help from the trip that I ought to have gotten. I am not alone in my opinion of the French School, for Dr. Schlich told me (June 3rd) that the reason the Cooper's Hill School was started was at least in part because the English students from Nancy did not know anything when they graduated from there and a clamor was raised against it in England. Dr. S. says the school has de-generated markedly since estab. of the Republic. It used to be excellent. I agree w. him that it is not so at present.

1/8 Nancy Actually worked 10¾ hours.

1/9 Nancy Made engagement with Professor Henry. Walked with Nesteroff. Actually worked 10¾ hours.

1/10 Nancy Walked with Hulot. Called on Robinson, American medical student from Albany. Letter from Meister agreeing to take me as student at Easter. Finished Doctor Brandis's paper for Papa. Received fine lot of photographs from home. Eight hours' work only.

1/11 Nancy Getting my bag—knapsack— combination of tanned leather with brass hooks. With Professor Henry and Nesteroff to see tanning extract mill.

1/12 Dinner with the Clieszes, and walked to Maxéville and back after dark through the woods.

1/14 Nancy Am beginning to get hold of fencing a little. Examination in Aménagement [policy]. Did badly. Hulot for dinner.

1/15 Nancy Excursion to Petite Haye to see conversion of storied coppice into high forest.

1/16 Nancy Only about eight hours' work. Some trouble with my eyes. Good talk with Puton. I keep wanting to read home news, and it takes too much time. I can't read it on Sunday and write letters too.

1/17 Nancy…Cooked for breakfast broiled steak, scrambled eggs, with bread, butter, and jam. Called on Mme. Puton.

1/18 Nancy Breakfast with Hulot. Then walked to Clairlieu and talked with Gigou. Evening, dance at M. Paul's.

1/20 Nancy Young medical student named Wolff agreed to walk with me and talk German. Ten and one-half hours' actual work.

1/21 At Nancy Again walking with Wolff. Ten hours' work.

1/22 Nancy Between 11¾ and 12 hours of actual work. M. and Mme. Babel getting nicer and nicer.

1/23 Nancy Walked with Wolff, and preparing for trip into Vosges.

1/24 Nancy–Celles Up at 3:45—cooked breakfast—took 4:35 A.M. to Etival. Then through silver fir forest to Ravines, and on to Coichot and Celles.

1/25 Vosges–Nancy Talking with forest guards. To Bandonvillers. Express train to Baccarat—fourteen kilometers in forty-six minutes. Eight solid hours of walking, excluding stops on these last two days.

1/28 Nancy Reading again. A terribly useless day, but it put me in the mood to work again.

1/29 Nancy Eleven and one-half hours at least of actual work.

1/30 Nancy Gave Boppe American ax.

2/7 Nancy Went to Eden Cafe Concert, hangout of foresters of school. Rotten.

2/8 Nancy Into forest with Poncelet and got French woodchoppers to try American ax—of which they thought lightly.

2/10 Nancy Excursion with Bartet, to Tranchée de l'Ecole, and to Bellefontaine.

2/11 Nancy Have gone back to full board at Rocher de Cancale—and feel better. Ordered axes for Boppe.

2/12 Nancy Letter to Dr. Loring. Eight and one-half hours' actual work.

2/14 Nancy A kind of dislike for work bothers me.

2/15 Nancy Wrote C.S. Sargent.

2/27 Nancy Have not been done up at fencing by any of the students.

3/1 Nancy Excursion of whole school to Fôret de Haye. Martellange. Use of griffe. Evening read Ludovic Halevy's Notes et Souvenirs.

3/7 Nancy Ride with Hulot. Evening, Students' Masked Ball. Very rotten.

3/9 Nancy Dinner with Cleisz. Wrote Doctor B.

3/12 Nancy Only about eight hours.

3/14 Nancy …Got letter from Sargent, advising two years of study and one of travel before coming home, including India.

3/16 Nancy To church, Nancy. Wrote Doctor B. A couple of days before I got a letter from Professor Sargent advising two years in study and one in travel before coming home. India to be visited. My opposition scheme is this: Return in October, study and travel a year, and then get appointed to study and report on European and Indian forest management to our government. If the thing could be worked, it would give me a competence at once, a glorious chance to study, and a prominent position at once on my return. Wrote same in full to Mamee and in short to Dr. B.

3/17 Nancy Eight and one-half hours' work.

3/18 Nancy Fine talk with Puton, in which he advised a year's work and travel in the United States before taking up further European study (after next fall). Wrote to Fernow. About nine and one-half hours' work.

3/19 Nancy Twelve hours' work.

3/20 Nancy Stopped my German study. Only 8∫ hours' work.

3/21 Nancy Eight hours—and three more on American papers.

3/22 Nancy Ride with Hulot, and dance at his uncle's.

3/23 Nancy Sunday. Like every other Sunday, spent most of day writing letters.

3/24 Nancy Read Hulot's brother's book about America. Much mail from home. Best day since I left…Doctor Brandis advised most strongly that I should stay over here two years more, as does Professor Sargent.

3/26 Nancy Excursion with Boppe and Flische.

3/31 Nancy Villers le sec, with Hulot and deBrabois. Explored caves. A grand day.

4/1 Nancy Saying good-bye and getting ready to leave.

4/7 Zurich Arrived Zurich, 9:39 A.M. Tahlweil. Met Forstmeister, a little stumpy man in rotten jeans, but he does know his business. Wrote Doctor Schlich and Doctor Brandis.

4/8 Sihlwald Whole day in sawmill and wood-working plant. The Sihlwald sells no raw material. Consequently, the annual returns are from $4.00 to $8.00 per acre. Students at Silhwald are Siber, Garonne, and Haggar.

Forstmeister Meister runs the Sihlwald merely as a side show. He is head of the Liberal Party in Zurich; president of the biggest Swiss newspaper; president of a Silhwald Railroad (not yet built); president of the Board of Auditors of Zurich; president of the National Swiss Fishing and Piscicultural Society; boss of the Swiss "Anglers' Journal"; brigadier general in the Swiss Army; representative at Bern for the City of Zurich; and is writing a book. He must be a perfect marvel.

4/10 Sihlwald Up early fishing for trout in Sihl. Worked on diary in French for F.M. Meister. Tea with the Meisters.

4/11 Sihlwald Wrote Sargent. Walked to Birren-Boden, and to see timber chutes.

4/12 Sihlwald Walked to Albis Plateau and Burghen. Snow falling.

4/13 Sihlwald To Zurich to church. Called on U.S. Consul Catlin, Yale '60, who gave me his report on Swiss Forestry. Back in dark through Thalweil.

4/14 Sihlwald Woods all day. Glorious view from Albishorn. Snow Mountains—Rigi, Pilatus, Santis, etc.

4/15 Sihlwald Walked with F.M. Meister and read him my French diary, which he approved.

4/21 Sihlwald When I get along a certain way

in the study of anything, I seem to stick. That's my stage with the forest work now. I don't learn much additional every day.

4/22 Sihlwald Auction of fishing rights in the Sihl. Walk with F.M., who is a great authority on maps as well as on the rest of mortal affairs.

4/23 Sihlwald Forest statistics.

4/24 Sihlwald Sihlwald to Zurich and Lake Dwellers' Museum. Doctor Uhlrich. Siber's dog Luempli temporarily lost.

4/25 Sihlwald Have used ten francs in stamps on letters written since coming to Sihlwald.

4/28 Sihlwald Herr Oberlandforst Meister Coaz here to dinner, and showed him my photographs (which came yesterday). Said they were finest he had ever seen. Coaz a very quiet and affable man—an old gentleman, and head of Hunting and Fishing.

After supper with F.M. a long discussion on what I ought to do, in which F.M. paid me compliment of saying he thought me fit now to organize an administration in the United States. He said I must not lose any chance to get a good chance at home by staying here to study. He thought the Special Agent plan the right one.

Discussion with Siber at Restoration, Sihlwald. He thinks I ought to take four to six more years of study abroad. Rubbish!

4/29 Sihlwald Professor Buchler said, two years of study. So enough for him. Showed him my photographs.

To Zurich. Called on Landolt. Landolt was fine. A little bit of a man looking like a well-to-do farmer, but with the simplicity, the helpfulness, of a great man. He is the first Swiss forester by far, and has done pretty much everything that has been done in Switzerland in the last thirty years, law and all. Founded the Forest School and was for a while both professor there and head forester of Zurich.

He is, above all, a practical man and full of hard sense. About seventy now, and as lively and vigorous as a man of forty. Great power of concentration and steady work. But he has not the general grasp and versatility of the F.M.

4/30 Sihlwald To Zurich to meet Landolt, who showed me the collections at the Forest School for two hours. Asked me to his planting class in afternoon. He was mixing a mud bath for roots (in his hands), in shirt sleeves and bared head, and got down on his knees to plant.

5/1 Sihlwald …To see Landolt. Gave him photograph of Sentinels Calaveras Cave. Invited me to submit all questions in future to him by letter. Professor Landolt thinks one year enough. Go slow with forest organization in America. First mark out State forests, then protect them, then forest school. Two-hour talk.

5/5 Sihlwald…Excellent talk with Meister. Was very kind. Said now he had had chance to see me and know me, he thought with Doctor Brandis that I had splendid career ahead. Said I had clearness, insight, and zeal that were a pleasure to see. Said he would be glad to have me there all summer, and would be very glad to see me back. He has been very kind to me, and I did my best to thank him for it all. He then wrote his name in his book for me, and I went off feeling like a king.

5/6 Nancy Left Sihlwald and saw Landolt, and sent four photographs to Meister.

5/10 Vosges To Celles with Boppe and students.

Sihlwald, the town forest of Zurich, Switzerland, photographed by Arthur B. Recknagel during the 1911–12 European excursion by the Biltmore Forest School. Pinchot had toured the Sihlwald twenty years earlier. Forest History Society Collection.

5/12 Vosges In the woods. Working on plans for a series.

5/13 Vosges Morning in woods in pouring rain. Lunched in peasant's house. Fire simply built in one corner of the room on some earth. Much smoke. Blackened rafters, stone floor (rough blocks), meat smoking in chimney, just two rooms, a sort of story-book house.

5/14 Nancy As a moderate average I must spend $1.00 every two weeks for stamps. Fernow offered to look after me, and is generally very fine. Encourages me greatly as to prospects of work at home.

5/15 Vosges Spent day alone in the woods. Hulot came along afterward. He has a darn good heart, but he is an ass at times. A regular kid. Loves nature passionately, but can't get along with people in general. Don't ever quarrel, just don't have anything to do with them. Takes it for granted that we are a modern case of Orestes and Pylades and moons around when I'm not talking to him, and looks sad. Likewise doesn't give one solitary cuss for forestry. E.g., wants to set off red fire at night in the woods, ride a cow, etc., under the general impression that whatever is queer is hot stuff. Well, he has a darn good heart, as I said, and he is clean, so it doesn't matter much.

On Tuesday had a long discussion in the peasant's house with Critier and Gerard. Found both pessimistic. Gerard honestly, Critier because he thinks it's smart. But what struck me most is that neither has the least respect for his profession, calling it "fumistine" and "de la blaque," and asserting that there is no progress to be made in it, or any really scientific or exact or necessary work for a man to do in it. Anybody, they say, could do the work they will have, and they quote men in the service who have said that there was nothing in it. The curious part is that they refuse the testimony of men who praise it, asserting that their view is prejudiced by long service, that they would all lie to keep up the honor of their profession, or at least prevaricate, and that they, the young men, were far more capable of judging than their elders. It appears that this sort of ass is very common among French students, and it seems to be a logical result of their imbecilic system of education. A youth whose experience has been gained chiefly within the four walls of Lycée and Ecole, F., and in hole like the Eden Théatre, is about fixed to think he knows it all. I am told that pessimism is about universal among French students, and no wonder. As to these, it seems that Puton made them a speech to the effect that there was not enough for a man to do in the Service, and they must take up some outside brand of study, as botany, to keep busy. This would lead me to believe that Puton is either a liar or a fool, with the odds on the last.

5/24 Nancy Letters to Fernow and Sargent. Took Boppe some colored photographs.

6/1 London Have been perfectly useless all this week and am disgusted with myself.

6/2 London At Cooper's Hill, with lunch at Schlichs. He said, "Inspect and demarcate on the ground." Government forests are the most pressing.

6/3 London To Cooper's Hill to take photographs. Doctor Schlich extremely kind, offering to answer any questions.

6/9 Paris–Nancy Wrote Sargent.

6/14 Nancy From June 11–14, did little but write article for Garden and Forest, first of three on the Sihlwald.

6/16 Up at 5:00 to start with school for Grenoble at 11:00. Sent six California photographs to Doctor Brandis.

6/17 Excursion in charge of Professors Guyot, Henry, and Petitcollot. Guyot fainted on walk.

6/18 Started 4:50, A.M., for Grande Chartreuse. Drove from Voiron, and then 5-hour walk.

6/19 Grenoble Torrent of St. Eynard in morning. Afternoon to Bourg d'Oisans.

6/20 Grenoble Started at 6:00 for Torrent of St. Antoine. Evening, tried to write on second article on Sihlwald, but too sleepy.

6/21 Grenoble Started at 6:00 for Torrent of Manival.

6/22 Grenoble Dinner of French students to Gardes Generaux and strangers. Antonescou and I only strangers present.

6/23 Grenoble Nearly finished second article on Sihlwald. Left for Chambery.

6/25 Chambery Torrents of Saint Martin, de la Porte, Grollaz, and Grolle (?).

7/4 Paris Finished third article and sent it off. Evening, to Fourth of July Reception at Reids.

7/12 Paris All this work in morning is for examinations at Nancy. Up Eiffel Tower with Mother and Hod Walker, and to Mme. De-Bury's. Advised strongly against going back at all this summer, which Papa wants me to do. Personally I don't know what to do. Ought to stay through examinations with Doctor Brandis, and still must get a year at Munich.

7/15 Paris With Edouard Blanc to Ministry of Agriculture. Saw LaFosse and Daubrée himself. Daubrée said his way of tackling the problem would be to begin at once organizing and working comparatively small areas and trust that the plan would spread rather than to wait for action of a commission to decide which lands should be kept in forests, especially as the commission must be first appointed by Congress. This is just what is likely to happen, I think, in the Adirondacks. Daubrée invited me warmly to call again when next in Paris, and was generally very nice.

Much troubled because my father wants me to return, in summer or fall. Think best, in spite of pleasure of returning August 15 with Mother and Nettie, to finish with Doctor Brandis and go back in fall. Then get an

appointment if possible after traveling as much as possible.

7/16 Nancy Arrived 6:13, A.M., to call on my friends, and an hour for examinations. To Brabois' to dinner.

7/17 From Nancy to Aix-la-Chapelle, 5:10 A.M. to 5:48 P.M. Found Doctor Brandis and the Cooper's Hill boys rather young and green.

7/18 Aix–Roentgen Forest of Muelars Yhutte. Rode with Doctor Brandis. Incessant grumble of young Englishman, and disrespect to Doctor Brandis. Several times did I greatly admire the way Doctor Brandis treated this unruly mob.

7/19 Roentgen Am lucky enough to ride in carriage with Doctor Brandis and get constant benefit of talk. I speak best German of gang. Osmaston rides there also; and Foulkes, a dirty mucker, because he carries the maps. Other are Bryant, rather caddish; Henvey, young, green, but rather nice; McIntosh, with good instinct but bashful about owning them; Minges, stuck on himself but a worker; Hodgson, very nice perhaps next to Osmaston and Forreath, very young and inclined to appear tough; Burn-Murdock, sick so far; Coventry, quiet and nice; Messer, inclined the Foulkes-Bryant stripe, but much better. Most of them grumbled, and both this and their ungentlemanly conduct toward Doctor Brandis, who is of perfect kindness and courtesy, made me awfully tired.

7/20 Roetgen To church with Doctor Brandis and Oberfoerster Zebald and Osmaston. Prayers read by Doctor Brandis. Doctor Brandis's brother, wife, and daughters to dinner.

7/22 Roentgen–Aix–Geilenkirchen Willow plantations. Then to Julich. Osmaston sick.

7/23 Hambach Forest In Hambach Forest with Oberförster. Trip very hard work but extremely interesting. Omaston very much worse. Dr. B. not down to dinner because of taking care of him, and then the muckers of the crowd, Foulkes, Bryant, and McIntosh began to curse him for an old fool. I told them very plainly what I thought of their conduct and there has been no more of it since. That night Dr. did not know what to do about Osmaston. Could not explain high fever. Dr. B. telegraphed to his father and I offered to take the fellows on to Bonn and talk German for them. That night I saw Dr. B. really tired out, but was glad to find my offer to manage party made him cheer up. He could then stay with the sick man.

7/24 Morning in forest with O.F. Gehricke. To Bonn, where met Lady Brandis and F.M. Sprengle. Party in my charge. Great sport being in command.

7/26 Bonn–Bingen–Homburg Mother and Nettie there. Of twelve in Doctor Brandis's party, only four have had no sickness.

7/28 Up at 6:00, and with O.F. Loesch to see Oak Coppice in communal forest. Doctor Brandis advised me strongly again to leave State Service alone and make a name in some private forest first. He's one of the finest men I ever knew.

7/29 Bingen on the Rhine–Aschaffenburg Talked with director of Forest School.

7/30 Weissenstein Valuation. Riding as usual with Doctor Brandis in his carriage.

8/4 Homburg Rejoined excursion. Kloster Ebrach at night. Excursion around Kloster Ebrach.

8/5 Excursion around Kloster Ebrach.

8/22 Nuernberger …Von Dorrer said he thought forest organization in the United States must begin by the initiative of some single state.

8/25 Carlsheim–Rastadt In the evening continuation of troubles between Dr. B. and the students. Dr. B. has grown a little suspicious of their motives, having had ample provocation

thereto, and doubts their honesty even when there is only slight cause.

8/27 Town forest of Baden Baden. Long talk with Schoepflin about the marvelous energy of Doctor Brandis.

9/2 Herrenwies Went over the compartment described with Doctor Brandis and Doctor Schlich, who came Monday night. Pleasant dinner at night, and after it Dr. Schlich told me [he]did not believe in Dr. B.'s idea that forest conservancy in U.S. must be by large private companies.

9/6 Schoenmuenzach–Freudenstedt Rather long day. Before lunch at Valuation Survey got disgusted at the way Schoepflin was giving orders to me and others in my measuring area and told him so very plainly. Large excitement.

9/7 Doctor Brandis laid up.

9/8 To Rippoldsau O.F. Kneitel offered to let me work under him for a while.

9/13 To Schoenau Over the Belchen. No letter from Fernow.

9/15 Schoenau–Zell Conduct of Foulkes, Bryant, McIntosh, and Messer getting worse towards Doctor Brandis.

9/18 Todtmoos These last days many talks with Dr. B. about matters in U.S. His idea is that I shall have a hard time.

9/19 Todtmoos Group photograph taken. Thinning a quarter hectare. Fisher and Hutchins left.

9/21 Todtmoos …Shall be glad when excursion ends for me, useful and pleasant as it is. Want to rest a batch.

9/22 Todtmoos–St. Blasien Yesterday (Monday) spent afternoon having reached St. Blasien for mid-day dinner, writing article on Black Forest from Dr. B.'s dictation. Said article was dry as dust, but loaded with facts. To appear in New York, but will be revised first. Doctor B. offered to write a book on forest management in Germany, provided it could be published in N.Y. Told him would give opinion later.

9/26 St. Blasien–Rothhausen Met O.F. R. Krutina and his wife, a St. Louis girl. At dinner a grand farewell ovation to Schoepflin with any quantity of gaudy speeches—in which G.P. appeared.

9/28 Zurich Tea at Professor Landolt's with Doctor Brandis and Professor Buehler.

There are few men whom I admire as I do Landolt. He who has done the chief work in Swiss forestry is as modest and quiet and retiring and as ready to take off his hat as the humblest man in seven counties. He certainly is a great man.

9/29 Sihlwald Landolt went along. Meister was delighted to hear of my appointment. I had to lecture to the Englishmen on the forest. After dinner made French speech, telling F.M. Meister how much I thought of his kindness.

10/8 Munich Called on Professor Ebermayer, who was very polite, and on Hartig and Gayer. Delighted with Gayer, and as to Hartig, had the great pleasure of going through his collections with him.

10/10 Neupfalz Working on general account of Prussian Forest Service.

10/20 Neupfalz Day in forest, and evening on Doctor Brandis's notes of Black Forest.

10/21 Neupfalz …Yesterday letter from Stiles…of Garden and Forest, saying that a man in Tennessee wanted a young American to manage large forest. Wrote for a consulting place.

10/25 Bonn Neupfalz to Bonn to see Doctor Brandis. Long talks with Doctor B. and a most pleasant time. He spent this evening in trying to make out why it is that things don't prosper very well with me at Neupfalz. I think because

the O.F. and Referendars Reuter and Quint are much more interested in game than in forestry and talk of nothing but shooting. Hence they feel no sympathy for a man who wants to work nights…Doctor B. thinks they resent as an insult to their profession my attempt to learn it quickly. Anyway I am not getting what I expect out of my stay here.

11/2 Neupfalz Traced route of this summer's excursions on map with blue pencil.

11/3 Neupfalz Grand Hubertus hunt. Seventeen guns, ten beaters, and two dogs, from 8:00 A.M. until 5:00 P.M. Total proceeds: One fawn scared to death, not shot; one fox, and one woodcock. Whole company, but especially Frau Paulus, greatly surprised that I had never been drunk. In fact the congregation was positively shocked at such baseness. I shall be glad to leave. All drink and no forestry is not my meat.

11/4 Neupfalz Afternoon in the forest. I never spent time (since here in Europe) more uselessly than at Neupfalz, and all I have gotten from the O.F. could have been gotten from a man decently interested in his profession in less than a week.

11/21 Bonn …What I should be as a forester without Doctor Brandis makes me tremble. Got the paper pretty well done and left for Aix at 6:00 P.M.

11/22 Aix–Roetgen Talked with O.F. Sebaldt. He will take me as a student any time I can come—but preferably next spring. Shall probably get best from him the details of office business.

11/23 To Julich and to see O.F. Gerick. Better to work here than at Roetgen. Must be there in beginning of April to get benefit of spring planting. Left for Paris. G͡P

OUT WEST

"Who shall describe the Sequoias?"

Gifford Pinchot's first paying job was with the Phelps, Dodge Company, a Pennsylvania firm that owned timberland in Pennsylvania, New Jersey, Michigan, and Arizona. He examined its Pennsylvania stands and reported that still-young second-growth pine held financial potential. The company was satisfied with this information and asked him to examine the Arizona holdings as well. The trip would be his first to the American West, and it would add significantly to his perceptions about the complexity of forest management in terms of natural, as well as political, science. After packing a rifle and revolver in his luggage, he set out from New York City on March 20, 1891.

There is much in the diaries about the vast and awesome western landscapes. At the Grand Canyon he attempted, as so many visitors have done since, to describe its size and beauty and decided that "man can only wonder." Later in Yosemite Valley, which was at that time a California state park, he wrote that he "can't describe it at all" but wished he had seen it before the Grand Canyon, "because everything is tame after that." These are but two examples from many scattered throughout the diaries that reveal Pinchot's aesthetic sense, even though the man is generally remembered today for his utilitarian values and wanting to put natural resources to "use."

He traveled through California and north to British Columbia, meeting conservationists and lumbermen along the way. He was much impressed by the size of western trees and the huge sawmills constructed to turn them into lumber. In Canada he found what he saw as British reserve to be irritating. His trip of more than three months ended on June 3, as his train pulled into New York at 8:30 P.M.: "I was glad to get there." By now he had seen the forests of Europe, New York, Pennsylvania, the South, and the West. His next assignment would be at Biltmore Forest in North Carolina, as he continued to add arrows to his forestry quiver.

1891

3/16 New York Saw Mr. Dodge & agreed to go to Arizona & Southern California to study his land & the question of planting it, [only] payment expenses. No salary. Am to return by Canadian Pacific.

3/20 New York Deposit money at bank $250 from Mr. Dodge for travelling expenses… with rifle & revolver I am prepared for all events.

3/27 Dodge City–Kansas Went out & shot with new revolver with Arthur Jarvis. Out of about twenty shots hit a cow plat twice at 30–35 yards. Pistol a perfect dandy, all but the trigger. And that is the common fault of self cockers.

3/31 [Indian country]…Rifle & revolver along, but did not even see Jack rabbit.

4/3 [Arizona]… Most interesting day from variety of new trees seen. Am very deficient in U.S. forest botany.

4/4 [Arizona] Morning & P.M. till dark out collecting specimens for Fernow. Then started (after making bargain with a young man to finish the collection & after Hollenstine had agreed to pack & haul the specimens).

4/5 [Arizona] Up early & then finally got into the right place. Found Berner, the man we came to see, and got some breakfast. Berner an old soldier & a great talker. Well up on trees, too…Irrigation will do almost anything in this climate. Berner gets all sorts of fruit, beautiful flowers, & strawberries and the like.

4/6 [Arizona]…Shot a coyote running through brush at nearly 100 yards. Missed by about a foot.

4/7 Phoenix …Crossed the Gila in a row-boat, seeing some Pima Indians, notably one prize fat one & a lot of squaws. All well & comfortably dressed & looked prosperous, all but one boy with his head plastered with mud to kill the lice.

4/8 Phoenix Went about neighborhood of Phoenix on horseback & saw the wonderful effects of irrigation.

4/9 Phoenix–Gillet's & on Started 7 A.M. for Prescott, or rather the Boggs mine first. Drove four in hand myself about half way to first change of horses, & lunched from the driver's basket…Never heard such profanity as our driver's.

4/12 Flagstaff …Received batch of letters this night, among them one from Fernow with letter to D.M.R[ioden].

4/16 …the [Grand] cañon cannot be adequately described.

4/19 Grand Cañon …spent afternoon & till nearly 9 P.M. at edge of Cañon. Began to get some faint idea of its beauty and grandeur…It is so deep it masks the width & the width masks the depth, and a man can only wonder. At sunset it is magnificently beautiful & by moonlight magnificently terrible. But the great power of it lies in its serenity. It is absolutely peaceful.

4/21 Grand Cañon Hoar frost on blankets when we got up. Was ready to shoot those mules after leading them to water.

4/22 Flagstaff …Would have completed survey of Arizona timber lands. But too much snow still on the ground…took the train in P.M. for Los Angeles. Looked like an awful wreck, with holes in shoes & jeans & general appearance of dirt & dilapidation.

4/24 Los Angeles Read & fooled around on the idea of getting rested. Acted like an ass…a day I am thoroughly ashamed of. Expense at Hotel on me, of course.

4/25 Los Angeles …I am a good deal of a blanked ass when I get loose, it generally appears.

4/27 Los Angeles Saw Deubam at ten, & then packed and tried to find Lyons at Santa Monica Forest Experiment Station. He lives in Los Angeles. Had talk with his man at the station, found out something, and then back to Hotel Arcadia & had a swim, for first time, in the Pacific Ocean. Pretty cold & very dirty, but a good surf. Wrote up Cañon part of diary in spite of awful sleepiness. Bed early.

4/28 Los Angeles …Found Lyons & had talk…Found the trees we want in [San Fernando] Valley, I think. Also made plans for seeing California forests. Took measure of certain remarkable trees also…To bed tired but pleased to think chances of finding right trees good. Lyons says they will certainly do, and gives corroborating examples.

4/29 Los Angeles–Santa Monica & back Met Lyons at depot at 9:30. To Santa Monica to see Abbot Kinney. Found him, and had satisfactory talk, making date to see newly formed torrents tomorrow. Then to Station with Lyons & measure a eucalyptus Gwinn set out 2 yrs 3½ months ago, or 3 years old from seed next July, 45′ 4″ high by the Nancy dendrometer. Saw many others of wonderful growth…read up California in Sargent.

4/30 Los Angeles Met Abbot Kinney in A.M. & went to him to see torrents around Pasadena. Thence to his place, Kinnelva, where ate oranges from the trees & enjoyed the wonderful tropical vegetation…Mr. Kinney talks a good deal with his mouth, but is very kind indeed.

5/1 Visalia, California Met Dr. Powers on the train. Had been in to Grand Cañon with Fernow and the Raymond Party. Pleasant talk, but eventually somewhat wearisome…Much trouble en route to find where the big trees were & how to get there. Visalia from Execter by stage.

5/3 [Travel] Started, against habit & inclination, but forced by shortness of time, to the Giant Forest with Al Redstone as guide …Went along road built by Colony to the timber, an excellently graded highway twenty miles long. It is valued at half a million, they

say, though that seems to me very excessive. If the government takes the timber land over as a reservation the road will be nearly valueless.

5/4 Colony, California Started in fair season to Giant forest. Rough & steep trail in places, & in others a chance to fall several hundred feet…The timber so far was magnificent, but who shall describe the Sequoias? Their wonderful beauty is to me far more wonderful than their size. We saw a great number, of which the younger were the more beautiful, the older the grander & more imposing. The perfect shape, the massive columns, but above all the marvellous coloring of the bark make them surely the most beautiful trees in the world. When the black marks of fire are sprinkled on the wonderfully rich deep ochre of the bark the effect is brilliant beyond words, because it is at the same time so large.

5/6 [Travel] Tried to get to the Sequoia National Park, which is very different from Sequoia Reservation, but the river was too high, and we could not ford it. So came on to Visalia…There is a rather indiscriminate & unjustified enthusiasm of statement in the workers of the Colony, as when one said to me they had saved the big trees from destruction by fire 29 times (in 5 years). Also when Mrs. Redstone asserted that they only cut <u>dead</u> timber for their mill. But I suppose all enthusiasts of no great mental quality are that way.

5/7 [Travel] …advise to confide fact that I was correspondent of Dodge & Phelps to state agent at Raymond. Result. Fare in to Valley $15. Regular round $41. Pleasant drive in…At Wawona introduced myself to Thomas Hill the artist, and had pleasant talk. Splendid grizzly skin in his studio. Greatly impressed by magnificent forest growth on the way in. Very instructive drive.

5/8 [Travel] Made some reporter gag, which

Aftermath of logging and fire in the California redwoods, probably taken by Pinchot in 1891. This image was published in his *Primer of Forestry*, Part 1, 1899. Forest Service.

I took special care to explain was not the fact, but that I was simply an amateur correspondent[. G]ot fine treatment from hotel people, and offer [of] a horse free to Mariposa Grove. Shall pay for him. Took him for a day, & spent it in the grove. First impression less fine than in Tulare Grove. Color less brilliant & surrounding trees larger. But upper grove is magnificent. More large trees together than in Tulare. None so big as Karl Marx [later renamed General Sherman]. Largest—Grizzly Giant. Took lunch at him, and then measured him & a lot more. Saw & had long talk & trip about grove with Cunningham the old guardian. No vandalism that I saw but stumps of young growth trees cut should be removed. Greatly impressed by great height

& size of sugar pines, Pinus ponderosa & firs. A great thing to see in itself...Saw Mr. Hill & his magnificent bear skin again. Wrote up notes, cleaned rifle, wrote diary & to bed fairly early.

5/9 Yosemite On to Yosemite. Same splendid forest of pine most of the way, then Inspiration Point, which is well named indeed, and down into the marvellous valley. Can't describe it at all, but wish I had seen it before seeing the Grand Cañon. Everything is tame after that. Not that the alley is not wonderful & wonderfully beautiful, but it can't touch the Cañon...Nevada Falls most beautiful by far I ever saw. Nothing so fine, so graceful, so great & yet so delicate ever came in my way before. Splendid rainbow. View of whole falls from half way up the side is fascinating beyond belief. Wish I could spend a month in the valley.

5/11 Yosemite …Got good idea of general management of valley, and shall write against the vandalism changes in Garden & Forest. Had a Claude Lorraine glass along, and the pictures it made were wonderfully beautiful.

5/12 Travel …Rode with driver in from Big Tree Grove, which I saw again, and tried to go fishing but got wind. My dreadfully rough clothes beginning to bother me more or less. Met Mr. Hill again. Was most benevolently treated by Washburn of the Hotel & Stage Co., as being a member of the press.

5/13 Travel With the Moores all of today. Met a lot of Raymond excursionists at Grant's Springs. The way the drivers curse them is something awful. Rode with driver from Grants Springs in to Raymond. Same general impressions as before. It takes 40 horses to take a load of passengers to the valley & Big Trees & back to Raymond. Got talking about forestry with English bird named Crowe, Indian Civil, [who] was down [on] Indian Forest Service. Too hoggish with land according to him. Thought nothing of driving out the agricultural population. Should not think forestry only thing on earth. Mistake may be avoided here.

5/14 San Francisco Arrive in San Francisco about 12…Finally got a wash, a bath & some clean clothes. They did feel good…Interesting visit, especially that to the [Chinatown] opium dens. Very tired.

5/15 San Francisco Hustling most all day. Breakfast at Wilson's Restaurant, on Post Street. Cheap & A1. Saw Alvord, Earl, Burgin, Mrs. Brandegee and Forman. Also Dr. Powers. Got along fairly in forest work with them all.

5/16 Cazadero, California Off early to Cazadero by way of Guerneville to see the redwoods…Much impressed by wonderful shoots of redwoods on the way to Cazadero.

5/17 Cazadero No church in the place. Read & wrote & went to the Bohemian camp where the Bohemian Club of San Francisco have their annual Jinks. Wonderful trees.

5/18 Travel Called on various birds, got packed up, and finally blew off at 9:30 for Portland, with design of stopping at Sisson on the way. Sands Forman, who was slightly jazzed when I first saw him, said he was going to dinner & could not call me when I called today. Probably jazzed again. Is enthusiastic for forestry, however, and a good man to help. Has been at it ever since first Forest Board estab[lished] in California.

5/19 Shasta Delightful trip up valley of Sacramento, one of the most picturesque large rivers I ever saw. Reached Sisson at 12 something. Went to Sisson's & tried to get into woods that P.M. Too late to see what I wanted & get back. Fishing poor…Glorious view of Shasta from the hotel. Most impressive single snow mountain I have ever seen. Uncivil conductor on train. Told him my opinion.

5/20 Shasta Breakfast at six & off with young Sisson to find Abies nobilis which Mr. Sisson said lived on the foot hills of Shasta. Young Sisson a fresh kid whom I had to sour on. Forgot to take lunch. Sent young Sisson home about 2:30 he being too fresh, and traveled slowly back, counting stumps on the way…Abies nobilis turned out to be merely magnifica, which I had seen at Yosemite.

5/22 Portland Reached Portland about 9:30…filled up on ice cream. Got lunch, saw Harry M., went with him to Albina & saw sawmills, then to Portland Heights after seeing big mill in Portland…Had already got $150 from the bank, drawn on father, so did not need to draw on grandfather. Took 10 P.M. train for Castle Rock, where they had arranged for an old timber man to meet me.

5/23 Portland Up about eight and off to the

woods with George F. White, an old lumber cruiser. Most magnificent timber I ever saw… White agrees with me in general about [need] for reserving government lands and as to use of forest management. He believes fires may be prevented by annual burning…Fooling with yearling bear named McGinty, got slightly bitten in the left thumb.

5/24 Tacoma Reached Tacoma about 6 A.M. To sleep & then to church…Evening walked about & read Taine's article in National Review on Napoleon's views of religion. Was very glad of the rest. Simply howling to get home. Tired of solitary travel…

5/25 Tacoma A.M. Found Schultze, head of Land Dept of Northern Pacific R.R. & found him rather given to brusqueness too. But got what I wanted from him & an invitation to lunch at the club besides, which I took. P.M. visited Tacoma & St. Paul Mill. Two band saws. Capacity of mill 150,000. Superintendent has idea that forest legislation will meet with favorable reception from mill men. Took 4:35 for Wilkeson, & saw Mr. White there. Tacoma new & raw but with a decidedly [illeg.] look. The Tacoma Hotel easily the best on my trip so far.

5/26 Tacoma Up at 3:30 A.M. & went with a small kid to see the most splendid forest I ever looked at. Then took 7 A.M. train to Tacoma, and saw Schultze & Rankin, his timberman.

5/27 Vancouver Reached Vancouver about 4 P.M. On boat watched scenery & read Paradise Lost. Finally found the tideland spruce in Stanley Park. Greatly pleased. Vancouver a place of 20,000 but decidedly dull. Awfully English. Hotel good.

5/28 Vancouver Stanley Park in A.M., where saw the great tideland spruce & measured & counted rings. I never saw so large a river

[Fraser] so swift before…Car full of English, all full of reserve & mannerisms and clad in wonderful jeans. The general impression they create when they look at a fellow is "Why the devil are you travelling in my car?" They made me tired, and I suppose that they saw it, as such people usually do.

5/29 On train Out of the Gold Range into the Selkirks and Rocky Mountains. A day of magnificent scenery. Passed the great glacier of the Selkirks about noon…Spent all day nearly on the back platform or in the observation car. Would have enjoyed it hugely had there only been one single companionable person on the train. But they were chiefly English, and we had not been introduced. At Field found disk of cedar 6¼ diameter & 347 years old.

5/30 On train Caught myself again & again looking out of window [at snow and fog] with the impression of being at sea…Spent much of the time making a system of conventional signs for our trees…Not so easy since the signs are to give habitat & kind roughly.

6/1 On train Winnipeg toward Minneapolis in the middle of the day…Same flat country. Difference between U.S. & Canada apparent at once as soon as you cross the line. Glad to get back to U.S. Dakota looked prosperous.

6/3 New York …Reached Port Jervis at 5, but found all family in N.Y. So went on & got home at 8:30. And I was glad to get there.

8/11 Bar Harbor Worked on report for Dodge Phelps & Company in the morning.

8/28 Simsbury, Connecticut Corrected report to Phelps Dodge & Company and submitted it to father & grandpa.

8/29 Simsbury Made tables for my report in the A.M.…Saw Stewart Dodge to whom showed report. GP

BILTMORE FOREST

"Vanderbilt's place just right for forest managment on a rather intensive plan"

In his diary entry for July 28, 1890, Pinchot quotes a portion of a letter from his German mentor Dietrich Brandis: "Doctor Brandis advised me strongly again to leave State Service alone and make a name in some private forest first. He's one of the finest men I ever knew." No doubt this advice was central to Pinchot's decision to forgo the opportunity afforded him by Bernhard Fernow to work for the U.S. Division of Forestry as assistant chief. Harvard's Charles Sargent had also urged Pinchot to find something other than the Division of Forestry, because he felt that neither Fernow nor the division had good standing in the Department of Agriculture. Pinchot noted on August 1, 1890, "What I want most is charge of the Adirondacks. To manage a forest area is the right way to begin." The only opportunity to "practice" forestry was on privately owned land: it would not be for another decade that federal forest management would begin.

Pinchot notes in *Breaking New Ground* that his father and Frederick Law Olmsted had been good friends and in that way he became acquainted with the renowned landscape architect. In fact, the diaries show that they first met at the family home in Milford, Pennsylvania. At the time, one of Olmsted's clients was railroad fortune heir George W. Vanderbilt, who was constructing a vast estate in the mountains of North Carolina. Olmsted advised Vanderbilt to include a model farm, arboretum, and game preserve and to "manage" the forests he had acquired. Vanderbilt agreed with his architect on all accounts, and it is no surprise that Pinchot was invited to be the estate's forester.

Biltmore Forest was a tract of a hundred thousand acres that Vanderbilt had purchased near Asheville. The first block of twenty thousand acres was the site of the mammoth house and elaborate grounds; the second and much larger tract, a bit to the south, was the Pink Beds area, named for its abundance of rhododendron and azalea. Much of the land had been logged and poorly farmed, but there were also stands of valuable timber. Thus, its management would entail both long-term programs of rehabilitation and short-term opportunities to generate revenue. With no American models to serve as examples, Biltmore Forest presented Pinchot with a rare opportunity and major challenge.

There are several threads to Pinchot's Biltmore story: his relationship with Vanderbilt, Olmsted, Carl Alwin Schenck, and others; work at the estate; purchase of the Pink Beds; the 1893 World's Fair in Chicago; and in some ill-defined way Laura Houghteling. The diary entries from Strawberry Hill (the Houghtelings' summer home across the French Broad River from the Biltmore estate) tell us that Pinchot visited and even stayed with Laura's parents long after her death in 1894.

In *Breaking New Ground* Pinchot writes about Vanderbilt with admiration and friendship, calling him "George." But others he saw frequently were always addressed more formally: Mr. Olmsted, or Mr. McNamee. G.W.V., as Pinchot usually refers to Vanderbilt in the diaries, responded in kind. In a scrawling hand, Vanderbilt wrote from New York on April 12, 1892, "Dear Brother Pinch," reporting that he was homesick for Biltmore and looked forward to summer when he could return. Even though the Pinchot family was wealthy, the Vanderbilts were more so, and as he traveled with G.W.V. and Olmsted to Biltmore on Vanderbilt's railroad car, Pinchot noted that "traveling on private cars is something almost too good for words." They also rode horseback together and played whist in the evening. Their friendly relationship notwithstanding, Pinchot was shy about asking Vanderbilt for money and struggled with how much to charge for his services. Olmsted smoothed the way by suggesting a range to consider, and after much thought and discussion with others, Pinchot asked for $2,500 per year, to which Vanderbilt agreed. The deal was struck, and Biltmore would become the site of what can be fairly called the nation's first working example of practical forestry.

The forestry exhibit for the 1893 World's Fair became a major effort for Pinchot. The project was jointly sponsored by the state of North Carolina, through its geological survey, and Vanderbilt. To learn how to prepare exhibits, Pinchot traveled to England, Germany, and France, consulting with the more experienced Europeans, many of whom he had met earlier when he had studied forestry abroad. His chief mentors were Brandis in Germany and Schlich in England, as well as Sargent at Harvard's Arnold Arboretum. He also purchased many botanical books for the Biltmore library. The diaries provide us with a detailed account of his preparations. However, the Chicago event itself is scarcely reported, although we know that Fernow also had an exhibit for the Division of Forestry, and Pinchot helped him by collecting wood specimens.

A young history professor from the University of Wisconsin, Frederick Jackson Turner, was also in Chicago at the time of the fair to read his paper on the closing of the American frontier to an assembly of historians. The condition described by Turner, or at least its perception, was a driving force for the just-emerging conservation movement that looked squarely at how best to protect nature while using finite resources. There is no evidence that Pinchot ever knew of Turner, but his work in conservation can be seen as a response.

Carl A. Schenck was Pinchot's successor at Biltmore. As old men, both wrote memoirs based upon their diaries. Reading about their relationship in *Breaking New Ground* and *The Biltmore Story*, one might not guess that Pinchot and Schenck were writing about the same events. No doubt their eventual falling out colored their ultimate recollections of a distant time.

Pinchot wrote that "Schenck came in the spring of 1895. I did my best to break him in, but never quite succeeded." As Schenck remembered it, "Queerly, the task awaiting me at Biltmore was scarcely touched in our conversations, which were restricted rather to discussions of hunting and fishing." According to Schenck, Pinchot told him, "you will be forester and I shall be chief forester" at Biltmore. Schenck further recorded that Vanderbilt said "Pinchot's connection with the Biltmore Estate had ended and that I was in no way subject to his orders or to his supervision." Pinchot's version was that he remained on as technical adviser, and his diaries show in some detail that he was involved with the Biltmore Forest while Schenck was there.

The splash dam on Big Creek was also an issue. Schenck remembered that Vanderbilt pretty much gave him a free hand, except that he was to finish the dam that Pinchot had started. Schenck complied but felt strongly that the dam was a mistake; that the money would have been much better spent on a road system. Moreover, since a log drive would move only logs that were buoyant, logging would be limited to poplar, which would be overcut to justify the cost of the dam. In his autobiography, Pinchot remembered differently, proudly describing the dam's success and emphasizing just how well the poplar had been handled.

It's probably not worth the effort to sort the various stories out, except to note that Pinchot did not get along with Fernow, either. Others have suggested that Pinchot's French heritage caused him to dislike Germans and the English. He certainly did not care much for the mannerisms of the English and their Canadian cousins, but he revered Brandis and respected Schlich. Perhaps the simplest explanation is good enough: three was a crowd in America's early forestry days.

In April 1937 Pinchot returned to Biltmore to refresh his memory as preparation for writing *Breaking New Ground*. Many of his associates from the 1890s were still around, and he much enjoyed recounting times past. He drove over Forest Service roads (Vanderbilt's widow sold most of the estate to the government, and it is now part of the Pisgah Ranger District) and proudly noted the results of his work. He hiked to see the Big Creek splash dam and found that the "spillway and the rock piles of the cribs were still there. On the way down in the coves the Poplar reproduction was superb." He wrote his memoirs after seeing how his forest plan had turned out by 1937, but we remain uncertain about his thinking in 1895.

No doubt his work at Biltmore, as well as other consulting assignments in the forests of New York and New Jersey, plus his travels through the South and the West, enabled Pinchot to judge both similarities and differences between American forestry and what he had studied and observed abroad. Volume 1 of his *Primer of Forestry* appeared in 1899, shortly after his Biltmore experience had ended. The opening page, in which he characterizes the diversity of the forest ecosystem, holds up even under today's harsh glare. He knew a lot about both forests and forestry and was well prepared for what lay ahead.

1891

2/20 Asheville Up early & out on horseback with a guide to see Vanderbilt's place, which was object in coming here. Mud in Asheville worse than any other place, by a good deal. Vanderbilt's place just right for forest management on a rather intensive plan. Hilly, but regeneration of conifer & deciduous both excellent and his house & grounds will be absolutely gigantic.

10/12 Milford …Found telegram fr. Vanderbilt asking me to come down Wednesday instead of Thursday. Answer, I would, although had engagement for Tuesday afternoon. Reason, to meet Mr. Olmsted who left on Thursday.

10/14 Biltmore Read Forestry magazine & Montagne all day, bored myself stiff with useless thoughts & wishes. Am an ass. Reached Biltmore 5:55. Mr. Olmsted met me at the station.

Had delightful talk with him on the way up the Approach Road. Found he had advised forest management & it was decided upon. Was much delighted naturally. V[anderbilt] & young Barker met up on horse back. Was amazed and charmed by situation & scale of new place. Found Mr. Hunt here. Had more talk w. Mr. Olmsted who asked me to come & see him in Boston. I "yeaed" with alacrity.

10/15 Biltmore Rode up to new place in A.M. & saw Mr. Olmsted again. House is 367 feet long, 150 wide. Terrace 320 x 120. Esplanade 900 feet long. Walled garden a little over 400 feet square. View is gorgeous. Then took a ride. P.M. another ride. More I see of the timber, more sure I am forest management will be a success. Evening talk with V. about forest management in which he seemed to consider it certain it would be introduced, & spoke of building a distillery for wood acids etc. Has big ideas, anyhow.

10/17 Biltmore Went through V's nursery (40-odd acres w. <u>4200</u> species of trees & shrubs) and then lunched w. Mr. & Mrs. MacNamee. Met Miss Houghteling after lunch. Capt. V., G.W.V., young Barker & I then drove to & through Asheville, and I managed to get a sore throat.

10/18 Biltmore …Walk w. V. who is a simple minded pleasant fellow, full of his place. P.M. read & wrote back diary. Evening played proverb & other similar games.

11/4 New York …Met Mansfield White on Forestry Committee of World's Fair Commission. Sprung forest management idea on him for forestry exhibit…

11/12 Brookline, Massachusetts …Mr. Olmsted met me in Boston, drove me along new Parkway & about the Fen, explaining his plans. Met Mrs. O., Miss & John O. Also Miss Chatfield of Brooklyn, N.Y. Mr. O. asked many questions about forestry, especially at Biltmore, but went no farther. Kept my tongue still on subject of doing working plan. Not wishing to seem eager or pushing. Bed late.

11/20 New York Worked A.M. on scheme for exhibit of forest management at Chicago for Fernow…[letter] to Fernow expressing willingness to make collection abroad, & enclosing scheme as above for illustration only…

12/6 New York—Sunday Heard Dr. Parkhurst on the value of suffering in forming character. Call at Grandpa's, noon. Wrote diary, then to Communion Service with Father, and then to call on Geo. Vanderbilt. Had not expected to talk forestry, but he introduced subject, and it was decided that I am to make his working plan for Biltmore. Spoke also of 100,000-acre scheme, and arranged I am to go to Biltmore with him & a party including Mr. Hunt & Mr. Olmsted about New Years. Object, to get opinion about feasibility of handling big tract profitably.

12/20 New York At 11 P.M. met Vanderbilt, Mr. Hunt, Mr. Olmsted, Burnett, Dick Hunt on G.W.V.'s car.

12/31 Biltmore …Long & pleasant talk w. G.W.V. Also talk w. Mr. Olmsted. Reached Biltmore about six thirty, & dined about nine. Very pleasant time. This traveling on private cars is something almost too good for words.

1892

1/1 Biltmore Mr. Hunt stuck his head in at my door & wished me Happy New Year. So 1892 opened. Went up to Esplanade, saw Thompson, the engineer in charge, about maps of the estate, & he agreed to have blue print made of one of them. Rode down the approach road w. Mr. Olmsted. Talk about the time for making the working plan, etc. We agreed, of which I was very glad…Evening talk with Mr. O. about exhibit at Chicago.

1/2 Biltmore G.W.V., Baron de Lange, Dick Hunt, Burnett & I rode to sheep farm & back by way of the ferry. Fine view of snow covered mountains. Got blue print map at Esplanade.

1/4 Biltmore The man Thompson said he would send to guide me did not show up, so I got one at Esplanade, & went off about 10 A.M. Got back at three, having been over whole north end of the estate. Saw Mr. Gall then & had talk with him. Precise old person without much knowledge of trees & none of forestry. Mr. Olmsted came up & then Gall & I traveled through woods above the lake & beyond, he on horseback I on foot. This day's survey showed sad lack of middle ages.

Eve. Dick & I played against G.W.V. & Burnett, the experts at whist, & beat them. Good sport. Then sat up & talked w. Mr. O. about terms of my future contract. O. said $1,000 to $3,000 for Biltmore Forest & the Pisgah tract together. Advised to have it all down on paper, more to avoid conflict of authority than anything else. Bed at 2 A.M.

1/5 Biltmore Up at 7 o'clock. Gall came with Miller at 8 and we went over south part of estate east of the river. Lost lunch, so had only crackers & cheese from Miller's lunch. Gall went back about 1 o'clock. Miller & I went over more land, & I got back about 2:30. Lunch. Then to nursery to find Beadle. Out. Esplanade to see Thompson about a surveyor to help. Said he could spare me one. Evening more whist. Dick & I on top again.

1/6 Biltmore Off with Miller to west shore of river. Very cold with occasional snow squalls. Had no overcoat & the wind blew very hard. Back about 2, lunched, packed, rode with Burnett over to see Beadle. Out again. B. gave me some facts about heads of Departments at Biltmore & how things are managed. Met the car at Biltmore Station, and so off. Blinding snow as we rode over.

1/9 Natural Bridge–Hagerstown, Maryland Breakfast at Natural Bridge Station. Took four-horse wagon ordered by telegram & drove to the Bridge. Cold clear weather & smooth time. Snow on ground. The Bridge itself magnificent…Long talk w. G.W.V. about general matters in P.M. Evening Mr. Olmsted left us at Hagerstown. Whist. Dick & I won, making a tie for the whole series of evenings. G.W.V. bored, I think. Long talk with Burnett about what I should ask G.W.V. Said about $2500. Told me he got $2000 & Mr. O. $3000. Was very nice about it indeed.

1/11 New York Wrote up notes of trip on cards & then had long talk with Father about work for next year. Decided to ask $2,500 a year for five years to make plan & run Biltmore Forest, spending all the time necessary for that end. Also to require clerk & surveyor for three months so as to get ready for Chicago. To go down in February probably and cut European

trip short if necessary. To require good young lumberman for assistant, & have him right away.

1/30 New York …Lunch w. G.W.V., and talk over agreement, which was quite satisfactory to both. Then to hear Paderewski with him. Gorgeous. Left early. Almost dead for sleep, & much to do.

2/3 Biltmore To office to see Mr. McNamee, with whom good talk, then to see Thompson at esplanade, stopping on way to see Beadle. At esplanade met Beadle, and got method of desc. of forest (by sections) settled with him. Then arranged for maps with Thompson.

2/4 Biltmore Began work of describing sections. Each 500' square. Topographic map made & stakes set. Work came hard. Much systematizing necessary. Spent evening getting description blank into shape. Things necessary to be known hard to decide & define. Work well started & with good prospects.

2/5 Biltmore Start late. Vigorous day's work. 34 sections. Arrowhead perimeter. Back at four. Read & rested. Work evening at overseeing, etc.

2/6 Biltmore Start at 8 sharp at last. Feeling rocky. Put up horses in abandoned farm house, then to work. Cold & raw. Back to Buck Farm House after exhausting day's work at 4:30. Got little done before dinner. Wrote letter home on typewriter. Work hard, very trying in field. Described today 35 sections. But assistant willing & good and prospect good too…Work on Arrowhead perimeter.

2/11 Biltmore Morning saw Mr. Bushee at the office. Talk about getting up exhibit for Chicago by cooperation of state & G.W.V. Said there would be no difficulty—gave me letter to Mr. Wilson, chief of Commission. Afternoon in woods…Evening wrote Mr. Wilson, Prof. Sargent & Mr. Olmsted.

5/31 Bern–Geneva–Zurich Found F.M. Meister there, after waiting a while at Bernerhof, and had shinning time with him. Talked over whole Biltmore matter, and he approved course so far. Had no photos with me. Then also talked over North Carolina Chicago exhibit. He did not think models of treatment for Fair practical, & suggested photos or photochrom Zurich. In a word, bully talk with him.

6/1 Zurich–Basel Orell Fussli first to see about photochroms of Sihlwald. Large size would cost about 800–1000 franks each to produce. Hence out of question. Photos colored by hand suggested. Then to Ganz to see about Sihlwald photos already taken…Then to see Prof. Landolt. Very pleasant talk. Most kindly offered to criticize Biltmore management later on, & gave me catalog of collections of forest school.

6/10 Hann. Munden …very pleasant call on Weise, Director of Forest School. Old bird said he would come around after supper & see photos, which he did. Also brought list of German forestry books for G.W.V.

6/14 Aschaffenburg–Bonn Had very satisfactory but short talk with [Furst] there, showed him photos & offered to send him a few. He said he would complete Weise's list of books.

Dr. B[randis] took me to Coblentzerstrasse, & there spoke of Biltmore & list of forest botany works for G.W.V.'s Biltmore library.

6/15 Bonn Went around to Dr. B's rooms in Coblentzerstrasse at nine & then he came. Had long talk about list of forest botany books, which he completed, then read part of book [*Biltmore Forest,* written for the World's Fair], which he thought would be useful, but found many mistakes in, & then talked over collection for Chicago & Biltmore working plan. A most interesting & instructive morning. Introduced me to Straus' bookstore.

6/20 Aix-les-Bains Got up early & went to fruit market. Then worked all morning on lists

of books for G.W.V. Sent list of forestry books to Dr. B. & to Straus.

6/30 Zurich–Sihlwald …F.M.'s carriage met me there. Most delightful to be in Sihlwald again. Had long talk w. F.M. about the photochroms of succeeding ages of regenerated plantation crop, and other facts of Chicago exhibit. Walk in the forest. Then met Herr Siber & showed them photos & map. As usual, S. much struck with card catalog description, had some idea of squares for Sihlwald. After capital dinner at the Forsthaus, during talk after which I struck idea of new way of cutting logs for exhibit. Then walk over Hockwacht with S., who told me of difference of opinion between him & F.M. & how he would like to go to America. Also told me many interesting things about E Coast of Africa. Shall try to get him for Biltmore game preserves. Another talk after supper. The F.M. intends him (S) for his successor in spite of differences. Both agree w. Biltmore working plan as outlined. A big day. Much learned.

7/1 Sihlwald–Zurich Drove in w. the F.M. & Siber & then w. S. to see Gang & Orell Fussli. These last wanted me to pay for experiment to see if they could make picture of Sihlwald in photochrom. Simple steal. Then to Polytechniceum for suggestion for forest exhibit at Chicago. Got none. Then saw & said goodbye to F.M. & after dinner at S's, where met his brother in law Lumpli again, to see Professor Landolt, who approved of Biltmore working plan and was much interested in map & photos. Also went over list of books given me by Weise & Furst & marked the most important. Very pleasant talk…

7/4 Munich Called on Dr. Gayer in the morning & had smooth talk. He was most kind, & much interested in the photos. Gave good lot of advice. Then tried to find Dr. von Tuboeuf & got left. Called on Hartig & had an hour's talk with him. Seemed very much interested, & gave me much help about models, of which he thinks very well. Date with him tomorrow & to see Tuboeuf, who has photographed a great deal…Called on Ehenneyer, who was kind enough to say he would answer any questions I might send him from home…bummed around & got tree for sample for models.

7/5 Munich–Augsburg Met Professor Hartig at nine o'clock, & had splendid talk of 2½ hours spread through the morning. Also w. his assistant, Dr. Karl von Tuboeuf. Saw von T. again in P.M. Results. Prof. H. will give numbers & dimensions of tree…for models. Dr. T. will see that the trees are rightly made & shipped in time. Will also make a series of photos to represent same condition of growth as each model. Dr. von T. will be paid, Prof. H not. Also shall get for myself series of photos of spruce w. nounenfrass etc. Pay for printing. Prof. H. charming. Promised to send him Biltmore photos & tree pictures later.

7/8 Paris Bankers's after getting prices for brown (bistre) photos for forest pictures at Chicago, then action to get some books out (awful red tape), then to Byron Library & Louvre about books…

7/11 London Went to Quantch's & looked at bot. works. Then to Price Whittaker & Co., then Wesley & Dulan. W. impressed me best of all the bookmen…

7/13 London–Hampstead & back …Paid Wesley & Dulan for G.W.V.'s books & then took bus for Hampstead…But finally found Mr. Olmsted & had good talk. Spoke of Siber; & found that he approved of my buying the forest botany books. They amount to something over $300.

7/14 London–Coopers Hill & back Took 8:17 to Coopers Hill. Had good talk w. Dr. Schlich. Asked him a lot of questions & got a good deal of satisfaction, especially as to books.

7/26 New York …Met [McNamee] and G.W.V. at 640 Fifth Ave at 9:45. Smooth talk. G.W.V. approved all I had done & wanted to do. Has decided to get the Pink Beds…

7/28 New York–Albany …Forgot pocket book. Got money from Prof. Sargent at Albany. Long talk with him. He strongly advised giving up collection of logs & getting large planks, or else, still better, taking photos & making no log exhibit. Time for big planks very short. Log collection not representative of North Carolina forest in size. Photos best. Not having heard from N.C. Commission, telegraphed Brunner from Rochester…thought over changes of plans. Decision probably lies with Vanderbilt.

7/29 Chicago [en route] Long talk with Sargent. His photo scheme seems capital. Also much talk about Biltmore. He advised planting chestnut strongly. Was rather skeptical about forest management there.

7/30 Chicago Off to the Fair right after breakfast. It is magnificent. Sargent [et al.] & I went over it…Smooth time. The most impressive buildings I ever saw.

7/31 Boston Found Buchanan after breakfast. Good talk. Photo exhibit allowed. B. inclined to the pleasant & obliging. Has little idea of forests, I judge. Said he presumed that all states making exhibits would show logs. France had asked for 3000 feet. Virginia & Michigan & N.C. biggest forestry exhibits…Took 12:30 for Bar Harbor to get G.W.V. to accept photo plan.

8/2 Bar Harbor Arrived at ferry, found G.W.V.…Delightful sail over. Then talk with G.W.V. about new plan, which he fully approved & continued his contribution. G.P. delighted clear through…Wrote Brunner about new plan for N.C. exhibit at once on getting G.W.V.'s approval.

8/11 Biltmore Saw Whitney for a moment at Hoisting Engine, then to office, where saw all but McNamee, & saw also to sending

Hammond [typewriter] for repairs. Then went over area cut with Whitney, & was very much pleased with the way he had done it. Slashes very small, good judgment used, & great economy. Meantime Colwell had arrived & was looking for me. Came for lunch, & then had talk & dictated. Greatly pleased with him also. Then saw McNamee & had very pleasant talk. Pink Beds scheme doing well. Then long talk with Whitney. His accounts, etc. Counting out his salary & mine we are about $330 dollars to the good. Perhaps $350.

8/12 Biltmore Met Whitney & Mr Gall at 10 & had a walk through the woods & a talk. His idea of preserving trees for effect fits in fairly with aims of forest management. Then Beadle was here to lunch & had love feast over forest botany books.

8/14 Biltmore …In P.M. scheme of my going to see the new tract [Pink Beds] was started & partial arrangements made.

8/18 Biltmore–Asheville–Mills River Finally got away…In the morning had been at work getting things straightened about the Biltmore & North Carolina work, & fixing things to leave. Stayed at Mrs. Johnsons at Mills River & had good grub & a bed to myself.

8/19 Mills River–Pink Beds …At night slept in room w. three beds & a shake down, P & I in one & the others full of women & children. This is part of being in the mountains. The people are very like Miss Mumfree's characters, only not quite so much so.

8/21 Kings'–Pink Beds–Transyl Got up at daylight after a fairly comfortable night, considering, thanks to the things I had brought,

Biltmore House near Asheville, North Carolina. Forest Service.

especially chocolate & rubber blanket...ate blackberries for breakfast...If Plumadore had been a little less of an ass we should have found the road easily. He said he knew it. After second breakfast took a wash. Clothes have not been off for 4 days. King looked on & remarked he hadn't "had a bathe in 12 years."

8/23 Kings'–Biltmore ...Mr. McNamee telephoned as soon as I called him up that G.W.V. wanted me to start at once on another trip over big tracts other side of Pisgah. I said all right, & started right in to get ready. Stipulated to take Whitney. To report on one tract of 94,500 acres Sept 1, & another of 62,500 Sept 7.

8/24 Biltmore–Asheville & back All day getting ready to start. Interview with Carter, Asheville lawyer, who had the options & then hustled to get things in order. Bought tent, ordered provisions, got shoes, etc etc, & got back here about 3:30 very much used up. Evening, dictated long letter about Pink Beds to G.W.V. & was awake till about 1 o'clock.

8/25 Biltmore–South Fork Hominy Mr. Aston came over & helped us pack up. Otherwise goodness knows when we should have gotten off. Did at length about eleven o'clock. Then made a long detour & finally struck Hominy. Got to place about three miles below Densmore & camped. Got some milk, eggs, I believe, & roasting ears. Rained at night but the tent held tight. All going well so far.

9/1 Three Forks to Francis Cove, Haywood Co., N.C. ...Went to beautiful spot to camp, in some of the finest timber I ever saw. Sent Whitney to Waynesville with telegram containing favorable report on 94,000 acres. He also took list of supplies to get. I wrote long report to Mr. McNamee...Had a camp fire very largely made of Black Walnut...

9/2 Francis Cove, Waynesville, North Carolina Mr. M.P. Francis came up in A.M. & showed us some magnificent trees. Chestnut 20'...& a walnut stump said to have measured 9' diameter.

9/6 Denton's Mt. Starting Haywood County—to Boyd's Jonathan's Creek Got up very early feeling very old. Rain about over...Climbed two balsams & got a capital view of nearly whole tract. Delighted I had come...had to wait till about 8 o'clock for supper. Awfully long time.

9/7 Boyd's–Jonathan's Creek–Biltmore Packed the mules & got away about 6:45...Got to ferry at 4:10 P.M. & were very much pleased to be there. At Biltmore farm house unpacked stuff, read mail, got a bath, & was pretty happy, though very tired. Got to bed rather late.

9/8 Biltmore ...At lunch got word to meet Prof. Holmes on train & talk over North Carolina work. Did so, & found Sargent plan approved in a provisional way. Had long talk & will go ahead with the work on the new basis. Prof. Holmes very nice indeed about it. Will do my best about making it as they wish, but part of their specifications cannot be carried out with any sort of economy. Then good talk with Mr. McNamee on way back. He had been to Chicago. Said there was good chance of G.W.V. getting the big tract, which was good news.

9/10 Biltmore Spent the morning marking trees near Approach Road with Whitney. Saw Mr. Gall, who spoke about our delivering wood contracted for under him. At a necessary loss, too. Told him I declined. Then saw Beadle & the plantings of white pine, etc. All [illeg.] looking well, but deciduous very poor compared to his own magnificent showing. Saw black walnut less dense one year old & about 3 feet high. Also splendid tulip [poplar]. Then back & went on with letters, etc.

9/12 Biltmore Saw Mr. McNamee & arranged about 50 cords wood Mr. Gall wanted us to deliver in Asheville at $2.50. Refused to do it…Afternoon spent mostly getting up list of questions for Caldwell to compile information for Sargent, Curtis, Chapman, Hough, Fuller & Newhall for N.C. pamphlet.

9/14 Biltmore Working with Whitney in A.M., & then met Prof. Holmes here, & had long confab w. him about forest exhibit. Later went with him & Whitney to Approach Road & got Mr. Gall to go over our marking. He did not reserve a single tree we had marked…Prof. H. said he would send Mr. Ashe free to us & offered much other assistance. He is very kind. Saw Beadle in A.M. & had good talk over kinds of trees to plant.

9/15 Biltmore Prof. Holmes left early. I was pretty used up, because he had talked very late…A.M. saw Mr. McNamee about changing to Hale House. He was very nice about it. P.M. went over it w. Whitney & looked at house near it. Hale house too small for three, & other place pretty awful. Evening did little.

9/26 Biltmore So far & including today have 28 days to charge against N.C.

10/26 Biltmore …Sent in application for space for G.W.V.'s exhibit at Chicago.

11/4 Biltmore Up at the sawmill in the morning. Back to house about noon, where I found notice that Wheeler had had no wood since the first, and what he had then was bad. Found at Biltmore that fault lay with Herndon, who had not sent cars asked for.

11/5 Raleigh At Raleigh met Wilson & then Holmes, & went with latter to meeting of Committee on Collections, which was over an hour late. Did not discuss past action, by my request, but went straight [to] consideration of my conditions. Spent pretty much all day at that. Substantially carried as I wished, except that the committee had no power to advance as much money as I asked. Took 6:15 train for Biltmore. Prof. Holmes going part way…Well satisfied with result of committee meeting,

except that there was not time to have corrected copies of agreement made & signed.

11/7 Biltmore Up to sawmill with Post in A.M. & to Whitney's house…Evening began what I intend for a regular thing, that is, a talk over a certain amount (say 15 pages) of Boppe's Traite de Silva. Post to read them & recite and theme to be generally discussed. Seems promising.

11/8 Biltmore …Dictation in A.M., then work on meteorological record of estate for pamphlet. Ride to pick out trees for derrick shafts for Mr. Gall…Whitney came in & we had second evening of talk over Boppe. Works very well so far.

11/10 Biltmore At work in house all morning. Biltmore pamphlet etc. P.M. walked over with Post to Approach Road & marked on both sides of it. Evening school about soils.

11/11 Biltmore Marking all day: Had four men with hammers, & Post recorded for Whitney & myself. Stopped work before three, when we had marked 820 trees…Got back to mill & found some fool had tied horses badly, & they had got loose. Had to walk back.

1894

4/11 Biltmore …Whitney came to dinner, & we talked over at length the cutting on Arboretum Drive, going over the map with Mr. Olmsted's notes.

4/12 Biltmore To Mr. McNamee's in the morning to see him about methods of getting stumps out of Arboretum Drive route. Then went over Forest Acres species for a while with Beadle. After lunch marking on Arboretum line near 420.

4/13 Biltmore Forest Acres species with Beadle in the morning, and in the afternoon marking, also near 420. After very early supper went to see Weston about stump pullers.

4/14 Biltmore Marking on Arboretum at about 410. Saw cutting begin. P.M. to Biltmore about camping outfit, which took some time.

4/16 Biltmore Marking on Arboretum line in A.M.…After lunch to Biltmore about a cook & the camp outfit. Then to Asheville on various errands. Got Harvey as cook.

4/19 Biltmore–Pink Beds Started at seven with Whitney & took early dinner at Mrs. Rickman's. Had a very pleasant ride, reaching Sorrels' at 3:15. Fished a little, but had no luck.

4/24 Davidson's River–North Fork French Broad River Broke camp & packed mules and then with Whitney to see young poplar under Cedar Rock and on Laurel Fork. The last most interesting…Went a way up stream to see the country, & fished back.

4/26 In camp Up Second Fork where we are camped to Tennessee Bald. Most interesting results of erosion from heavy week's rain last fall.

5/1 French Broad to Sorrels', Pink Beds …found young poplar in quantities in old lumbering, & chiefly on bare soil. Same also in unbroken forest…

5/4 Taylor Trail & Slate Rock Creek …Tramping…Decided to try camping alone to study the regeneration of poplar. I work better when alone, & I want the experience & the chance to think.

5/8 Chestnut Flats To Pisgah over Little Pisgah & down Mill Shoals Creek which has five falls. 7:30 A.M. to 3. P.M. Magnificent view from the mountain.

5/9 Chestnut Flats Bobbie's Cove etc. The best run of trees seen yet. In all Big Creek Country will probably cut 3,000 easily. Saw good young growth in open where cattle could not go.

5/12 Cantrell Creek Fished after breakfast …Cutting so much wood with my little axe is hard work. Sleeping on the ground & waking so often to mend the fire is hard work also. Midges very bad at times.

7/17 Milford …Letter fr. G.W.V w. check & confirming reduction in price of cordwood.

8/28 Biltmore Marking in A.M., and P.M. to Nursery to see Beadle about collecting seed for Forest Acres.

9/12 New York In the morning to see C.F. Squibb, who offered to superintend the wood alcohol plant at Biltmore. A very generous offer.

10/9 Sorrels' House, Pink Beds Raining hard, so I stayed here. Shot a good deal, & found my rifle excellent. Spent the day in shooting & making final preparations for my trip.

10/24 Pink Beds–Camp Joree Squirrel hunt in A.M. with Case up Thompson Cove. Two only. One got away. Afternoon ditto on Rich Mountain. Eight, & one got away. Very much delighted w. my Stevens 22-20. Four misses in 20 shots at very shy squirrels.

10/30 Richman's Up Big Creek & look [at] dam site. Out in the rain…

11/9 Pink Beds, Sunfish Cove–Sorrels' Cold morning. Packed in by Rich Mountain & found only one squirrel on the way. Dinner at King's, with the coon as pièce de résistance. Very good, considering the cooking.

1895

1/23 New York …In the afternoon long talk with G.W.V. about the scientific aspect of Biltmore, and replacing me in part at least by a resident German forester. He followed my recommendation in this latter matter.

3/4 Strawberry Hill Getting ready to plant. All day nearly, on the estate.

3/5 Strawberry Hill Arranged about planting and inspected I.C. & mill. Lunch with the Whitneys.

3/12 Strawberry Hill Planting. F.R. Mill was bought yesterday. Beadle, Rick Olmsted & I had conference about arboretum w. Mr. O. for about four hours this afternoon.

3/23 Strawberry Hill Planting. Long &

successful talk from 3 to 7:30 nearly with Mr. Olmsted, his son, Beadle & Manning.

3/30 Strawberry Hill After packing in the morning took eleven o'clock car, and met Roseveer at twelve. He said: Sawing $2.25, total cost say $7. Weight poplar per M 27,000 lbs when dry. Ready sale for all chestnut at $7.00 in Asheville, & better grades go North. Freight to Phila—$6.50 +/– per M, N.Y. $7.25 Boston $8.25. Price Boston 1 & 2 $31. Dined Roseveer, & took train. McNamee on it. We had the stateroom together.

4/4 New York …After lunch cabled Schenck…

4/19 New York …Schenck arr. at the house. Good talk. Pleased with him…

4/20 New York …Talk & lunch at Century w. Schenck…

4/22 New York …Lunch w. Schenck at W.J. Schieffelin's, & with him also to Natural History Museum.

6/15 Biltmore Talk w. G.W.V. after which he decided to lumber Big Creek next fall. Saw Schenck & Whitney, and found plantations doing admirably. Went to the F.B. Co. & saw cordwood from Arrowhead. Also inspected the boom.

6/17 Strawberry Hill Early start, met Whitney & Dr. S[chenck] at the planting, & gave directions for cutting back some plants. Got started from brick farm house about noon. Dinner at Moore's & reached Rickman's about 5. Fished, & caught little.

6/18 Rickman's–Chestnut Flats, Big Creek Spent the morning on Rocky Fork verifying Whitney's estimates. Afternoon went on in to camp, fishing some.

6/19 Big Creek Down stream with Schenck. Long talk. Whitney came in at night. Had a little fishing in the afternoon.

6/20 Long discussion with Schenck & Whitney. Schenck rather rash in statement & conclusions, but improving.

6/21 Big Creek–Rickman's Left camp early, went up Bee Tree Branch with Schenck. Whitney going straight back. Chased poacher. Dinner at Jones's & a little fishing. Got to Rickman's at dark. Dr. S's arm (boil on right wrist) getting to look serious. I have been dressing it.

6/22 Rickman's–Brick Farm House Breakfast 6 o'clock, & then started after dressing Dr. S's arm …Talk with George McNamee in the afternoon …Beadle to make arboretum list…To Biltmore & back via Whitney's. Schenck to dinner. Lockwood did not appear.

6/23 Biltmore W. Schenck who spent the night at the B.F.H. to his place, where I dressed his arm & missed church…Took 4:40 train North.

9/14 Strawberry Hill Whitney & Schenck met me in Asheville, & I spent the afternoon at the mill, reach home only just before supper, for the cars were running only occasionally.

9/17 Brick Farm Talk w. G.W.V. & Schenck, defining my sphere to lie wholly in the technical work, & not at all in money matters, of which I am very glad. Whitney to lumber at my suggestion, in his own way on Big Creek. Shooting after lunch. Peninsula with Schenck to see contractor, etc.

10/5 Biltmore After lunch to nursery with Ribbentrop, G.W.V. & Schenck, & with R[ibbontrop] & S. to sawmill.

10/6 Biltmore …Afternoon ride with R., Schenck & Olmsted. R. said of the work here that it was "a wonderful good operation," and also that it was a perfect piece of work, or words to that effect, referring to the silvicultural treatment. Not meaning that it couldn't be improved upon, for he said the only improvement he could suggest was that the cutting might have been a little heavier the first time.

10/20 Spartenburg–Biltmore…arr Biltmore at eleven. Ride through the woods with Schenck, who approves silvicultural treatment. After dinner to Schenck's to see Fernow, who approved plan suggested by himself of getting Secretary Morton to invite Ribbentrop over, & pay for it from contingent fund. Von Hermann, Leupp, Weston, & Olmsted there.

10/21 Biltmore Nursery w. Sargent & Schenck. List for Forest Acres. Lunch at Oldford. Then to see planting, and Sargent's portrait of M. Olmsted & Mr. Hunt. George came in A.M.

1896

3/9 New York …to see G.W.V., who agreed to houses for Malley & Foster, and was entirely in accord with me as to my directing the forest policy at Biltmore, and not Schenck.

1897

2/17 Biltmore Over to Biltmore at once after breakfast and after seeing G.W.V. to nursery to see Beadle, who was much in favor of board of trustees for arboretum.

2/18 Biltmore Ride with Schenck & G.W.V., after 1 Schenck had narrated his woes to me…P.M. went about with Schenck. Fight with the buck in his enclosure.

2/19 Biltmore Left the house before seven, met Schenck across lower ferry, & up Bent Creek. Left horses, & across Bent Creek Gap to Big Creek. Long talk with Schenck, explaining to him how foolish he had been. Back to Biltmore House via Upper Ferry. All alone in the grandness. Dismal. This day 20 miles on horseback. 18 miles on foot.

2/20 Biltmore Left after breakfast. To nursery. Talk with Fritz Olmsted, whose expenses agreed to pay on the spruce work next summer. Talk with Beadle about the board of trustees. Then to Biltmore Park Hotel.

11/28 Biltmore Reading on the train, and at Biltmore talk with the Olmsteds and Schenck. Then also with McNamee. Then to Biltmore House. The McNamees here, & a lot of others.

11/29 Biltmore Talk with George & Schenck, arranging basis for next years work. Then ride with Schenck. After lunch to nursery…

11/30 Biltmore Talk with George, McNamee & Beadle about Arboretum, and then w. Field & Schenck to Buck Spring. Met Case on the way. Arrived 7:30 P.M.

12/1 Buck Spring Lodge Left the Lodge at 6 A.M., found & photoed fine poplar reproduction in Big Creek Valley. Reached Biltmore House with Field at noon, and took the train north with the whole party. Ǥ

BERNHARD E. FERNOW AND THE DIVISION OF FORESTRY
"A fair man, as far as his intentions go"

There is rather skimpy mention of Bernhard E. Fernow, chief of the U.S. Division of Forestry, in Pinchot's diary, except when the two worked together. Thus, it is apparent that Pinchot kept close track of Fernow and the division only when he was directly involved. Too, he makes little mention of the forest reserves, which began appearing in 1891, until his participation in the National Academy of Sciences Forestry Commission began in late 1894.

In early 1889, while he was still a student at Yale University, Pinchot traveled to Washington, D.C., and visited Fernow. He offered, and Fernow "gladly" accepted, his offer to work for free the following year. A year and a half later, while Pinchot was in Europe and well along in his study of forestry, Fernow wrote and offered him the position of assistant chief, it would seem for pay. Pinchot quickly regretted his prompt acceptance, as both Dietrich Brandis and Charles Sargent strongly urged him to decline.

In December 1890 Pinchot returned to the United States and met with Fernow. He judged Fernow to be "of sterling worth" but noticed he was "unhealthily apt" to take offense. As they worked together during early 1891, Pinchot recorded more and more that Fernow's temperament was difficult to take. While they traveled through the South, Pinchot gathered tree specimens and made judgments about the lives he saw. When he and Fernow parted company, Pinchot anticipated he would begin full-time with the Division of Forestry in July 1892, despite his reservations about Fernow's personality. As we know, Pinchot accepted the Biltmore Forest assignment instead.

Pinchot's youthful intolerance is evident from his disgust with the "bad" coffee and "poor white trash" he encountered on his southern travels with Fernow. Although we know that Pinchot was later an advocate of racial equality, we see him approve Cullman, Alabama, as a county with "no negroes." Several times he also recorded his delight with botanist Charles Mohr. To this extent at least, Pinchot shared Fernow's trait of strong likes and dislikes.

As chief of the Division of Forestry, Fernow contributed substantially to the body of forestry knowledge and was a central player in the American Forestry Association, a citizens' conservation group whose advocacy was respected by Congress. Forest science, especially the linkage between forests and water supply, was of great interest to congressional members as they deliberated the role that the forest reserves might play. Thomas McRae, chairman of the House Public Lands Committee and ultimately a major figure in the 1897 Organic Act, explained that initially he had opposed timber management as a proper function of the reserves but that Fernow had convinced him otherwise. Although we cannot know what Congress might have done without Fernow's presence, we do know what it did because of him, and the Organic Act would be the Forest Service's primary mandate until expanded upon in 1960 by the Multiple Use Sustained Yield Act.

Fernow left the Division of Forestry on June 30, 1898, to become founding dean of forestry at Cornell University. In 1907 he founded the forestry school in Toronto, thus becoming an important figure in Canadian forest history as well.

Each year, as part of the appropriations measure, Congress routinely asked the secretary of Agriculture for a report on forestry investigations. Secretary James Wilson asked Fernow to prepare a final report covering his twelve years as chief of the division. The resulting 401-page *Forestry Investigations and Work of the Department of Agriculture* (1899) is impressive even today for its scope and depth. But Wilson could not resist a jibe at the already-departed Fernow in the official letter of transmittal to Congress. Pinchot was now chief, the secretary reported, and the Division of Forestry was moving in "distinctly different channels"; Pinchot's plans "meet with my full approval."

1889

1/5 Washington A.M. went to see Fernow & made him provisional proposition about coming to work for him next year free. He accepted gladly. First he advised not to study forestry as principal but as secondary. Then he seemed to think that there would be a show for me.

1890

5/14 Nancy, France ...Fernow offered to look after me, and is generally very fine. Encourages me greatly as to prospects of work at home.

8/1 Lohr Kitzingen, Germany Letter received on Wednesday from Fernow offering me post of Assistant Chief of Forestry Division. After very much talk with Dr. B[randis], confirmed by much more with Mamee, I telegraphed him on Sunday (August 3) as follows: "Yes, await letter before answering." Monday got letter from Sargent advising strongly against taking position since general standing of Agriculture Department, Division of Forestry and Fernow were not satisfactory. But thank heavens, though I telegraphed "yes," I sent letter after at once asking leave to begin work only after Christmas holidays; and did not say or imply what would happen if it were not granted, nor consider that it might be refused. By advice of Dr. B. will back out if Fernow refuses delay. If he does, I will go and make a good thing out of it in one way or another. What I want most is charge of the Adirondacks. To manage a forest area is the right way to begin, says Dr. B., and I'm with him. Only took Fernow's offer because saw no way to get said forest.

10/10 Neupfalz, Germany …Yesterday on arrival queer letter from Fernow, who O.F. Paulus used to know (and whom he thinks queerly of), in which he assures me that he wants only to see me get on and assures me that I will one day be at top, but advises against accepting his offer, though he has no one for the place. Either wonderfully kind, or hides something. Believe the first.

10/21 Neupfalz On way met postman with letter from Fernow, offering me time to complete studies and then the place of the chief assistant. I may say I was somewhat pleased.

12/20 New Haven to Boston Dinner with Sargent, who sees needs and difficulties, both most vividly, but will do nothing himself. Is at odds with Fernow and present Forestry Association and wants another founded. Discovered after that he is not thoroughly up to the situation nor in touch with the movement.

12/31 Washington …to Fernow's to dinner and to stay…A fair man, as far as his intentions go, but unhealthily apt to take up any real or imaginary slight or offense. Not a man to make a cause popular, but of sterling worth. Got at Fernow's personal history.

1891

1/1 Washington …to Fernow's & with him to Secretary of Agriculture Rusk. Uncle Jerry cordial also…Fernow says he can't do the diplomatic work necessary to get forestry legislation & believes that with my connections & acquaintances I can. Would prefer, he says, the charge of a scientific bureau to that of Inspector General. My place held for me but

without obligation on either side. Fernow disposed to be fair & very liberal. Evidently wants me there very much.

1/2 Washington To Department with Fernow, where saw Ayers with whom I was very pleased. Then to Department of the Interior & saw General Bussey & got introduced to Dr. Ames with whom made arrangements to get a lot of reports.

1/19 Memphis Found letter from Fernow at Post Office, saying he would not reach Jonesboro till Thursday, & asking me to go ahead with the inspection without waiting for him. Shall do so.

1/20 Jonesboro, Tennessee Memphis to Jonesboro ($2.40). Pleasant trip, with great interest watching the forest. Saw cypress & its knees for first time in a satisfactory way. Had roast 'possum for dinner. Very fat & good. Also sweet potatoe pie…Mr. Krewson & Col. Markle came in about 9:30. Talked over situation with them & decided to start early. Bought hip boots.

1/21 Jonesboro Luck in finding horses & guide. Mud simply awful. Horses had to walk all the way…Shook a 'possum off a grape vine & killed him with a club. Did not play possum, but showed fight.

1/22 Jonesboro Mr. Fernow arrived about 4:30 A.M., so we got little sleep. After breakfast went to hotel to see Col. Markle…Ride altogether of 15 to 20 miles. Not stiff at all from any of this riding.

1/23 Meredith, Tennessee Early to Meredith, Woodruff Co. with Krewson & Col. Markle. Object: Fernow to inspect Markle's land. Saw another mill, and then Fernow & I took ride with a guide. Tried to scare us about wild horses, wherein he fell in the soup.

1/26 Paragould–Harrisburg, Arkansas …the driver stuck Fernow $9.00 for the trip, which was wicked.

1/28 Memphis–Jonesboro Fernow sick with lumbago. Krewson & I back to Jonesboro. Fooled away time after 4 P.M. in tracking & seeing the 140 acres which I want to join Fernow in buying. Krewson to pay interest (6%) & the principal of 1/3 of purchase money (total about $5,000) out of proceeds of his third interest before taking anything himself. Jonesboro growing very fast & investment likely to be very good, I believe. Wrote Papa about it. Land is just east of last houses of town between two railroads & on each side of them, & will make available mill sites if the English syndicate buys the land. Fernow will report favorable & some mills at least will come to Jonesboro.

1/29 Jonesboro …The coffee is awful in this country. After breakfast only two saddles to be found, so Will Beasley & I took inspection tour on Fernow's account…Collected fine specimen of hackberry & some cypress knees.

1/30 Jonesboro Col. Markle got me passed to Pine Bluff on Fernow's pass…Country generally uninteresting & the people, while very kind & entirely friendly to strangers, very coarse & rough. On the "chaw terbacker" order.

1/31 Pine Bluff, Arkansas …Met Fernow & Mr. Leak at A[rkansas] City. Crossed Mississippi.

2/2 New Orleans–Mobile Bought a Marlin safety rifle .32 for $14.55. 26 inch barrel…To Ocean Springs, meeting Fernow on the way. Arrived in Mobile at 11 P.M. To Dr. Mohr's house. Delighted with him. Bed, very tired.

2/3 Mobile Dr. Mohr showed us a lot of oaks from his herbarium & made plain how almost impossible to distinguish certain oaks by their leaves…Walk in P.M. with Fernow about the city of Mobile. Dr. Mohr getting more & more delightful. Much pleased with his sons. He is an old lover of nature, sincere & enthusiastic, simple & very learned. Am getting pretty weary of Fernow. Hear nothing from him but endless

self appreciation at the expense of others. Runs everybody down with tiresome uniformity.

2/4 Mobile Out to Spring Hill & in the woods. Saw Georgia & other pines for first time. Dr. Mohr wears finely…Getting more weary of Fernow's endless detractions. Said he did not want to seem fault-finding, but he has been at it ever since we met in Arkansas. Was likewise at it all the time we were in Washington. Got in discussion with him about meaning of bonitary [aspect of property law], wherein he tried to crawl, but may be partly right. Assumes simply that he knows it all.

2/6 Mobile …I am staying with Dr. Mohr who is a typical old botanist. With his dressing gown, blue velvet skull cap & specs & white beard he looks the character completely. And so good a man one seldom sees. Simple as a child & certainly wiser than any serpent.

2/7 Mobile …Picked over & sent off specimens of winter buds collected on Thursday to Sudworth, Sargent & Miss Price.

2/9 Mobile Early start with Dr. Mohr for Spring Hill to see small area (1 section) of virgin Pinus palustris. Put off trip to Apalachicola till Wednesday. Made two volume surveys & had fine instructive time. Much struck by awful shiftlessness & poverty of the Piney Woods natives, the Poor White Trash. Also by the good prospect for a regeneration of long leaf pine provided fires & cattle are excluded. After return Dr. Mohr according to letter received decided to go to Cullman tonight to estimate & report on timber lands. Will give up trip to Apalachicola & go with him, starting tomorrow.

2/10 Mobile–Montgomery Chased around in A.M. & got a specimen of Juniperus virginiana with female flowers for Dr. Mohr. Packed valise to go by express to New York & saddle bags to take with me. Also made arrangements for specimens of woods to go to Fernow. Each is

26" & I get ½ made into a specimen to pay for sending them to him, which is smooth.

2/12 *Cullman, Alabama* Drive to northwest of Cullman with Mr. Henderson, a Scotch speculator, & Fuller of Cullman. Timber rather poor, & Henderson always trying to influence my measurements & judgment. I went in Dr. Mohr's place, as weather was bad. Roads simply awful. Such mud I never saw, or such reckless driving as Fuller's.

2/13 *Cullman* West from Cullman with Dr. Mohr, Henderson and Fuller. A fairly good day. Roads bad, but not like yesterday. Colonel (by courtesy) Cullman, who found the German colony did so on the lands of the L & N Railroad as their agent. He got an awful wound in the forehead from an American in the early part of his work because the natives objected to the German immigration. The result is admirable. No negroes in the county & only two men in jail. No stealing at all. Everybody prosperous.

2/16 *Cullman* Rainy. Dr. Mohr did not go out. Fooled a good deal in A.M. & P.M. went with a wagon & collected sections of small trees for Fernow. Am to get half of each stick as pay for collecting. Hence cut them 26" long.

3/14 *New York* Fernow and Charley & Mrs. Dodge to dinner. Delighted with Charley and his charming wife. Long talk with Fernow. Result: I go to Europe in October, compiling book first. While there may or may not be delegated to make collection for World's Fair. Pay probably only travelling expenses. Then return in June & enter Department under Fernow in July 1892 if he wants me to. His desire for credit for everything still very strongly apparent in what he says. He may have wanted to write the book himself. A very queer man.

3/16 *New York* …Proctor to dinner. Is very modest and quiet. Told us of killing his first bear & first elk on same day when only 17 years old. Saw Stiles. He had a jag letter from Fernow

Bernhard E. Fernow, chief of the U.S. Division of Forestry, 1886–98. In 1915, when this photo was taken at Bow River Forest, Alberta, Fernow was dean of forestry at the University of Toronto. National Archives of Canada.

demanding more credit for the Division in Garden & Forest. A fool letter. He got all due credit in the article that he kicked about.

10/13 *Washington* Saw Fernow at Washington, had good talk with him in a general way. He hinted that European collection would not amount to much.

11/20 *New York* Worked A.M. on scheme for exhibit of forest management at Chicago for Fernow. Letter to Fernow expressing willingness to make collection abroad, & enclosing scheme as above for illustration only.

12/30 *Washington* Read paper at National Museum, "Notes on the History of Forest Policy." Vote of thanks moved by Dr. Lendy was feebly assented to. Other papers followed by Mr. French of Boston, President Adams of Cornell, and B.E. Fernow. Meeting good. Met Governor Hoyt of Wyoming, etc, etc. Long talk with Fernow afterward. He insisted on need of action before people are educated. Not let legislation wait for them to know what is best.

1892

2/5 Biltmore ...Letter from Fernow in a very pleasant spirit, saying I had made a mistake in giving up government work.

1895

10/20 Biltmore Breakfast at 8 & arr Biltmore at eleven. Through big house with Sargent, Edward Atkinson, Fernow, and others. Ride through the woods with Schenck, who approves silvicultural treatment. After dinner to Schenck's to see Fernow, who approved plan suggested by himself of getting Secretary Morton to invite Ribbentrop over, & pay for it from contingent fund.

1911

12/28 Washington ...Meeting S.A.F. Fernow spoke on Canadian condition. I introduced him as having honorable part in forest history of U.S. He said at end what Canada needed was a Roosevelt & a Pinchot. G℘

THE FORESTRY COMMISSION
OF THE NATIONAL ACADEMY OF SCIENCES
"Sargent utterly wrong on all points, as usual"

On January 15, 1896, Secretary of the Interior Hoke Smith signed a formal request to the National Academy of Sciences to establish a forestry commission. The purpose of the commission was to examine the western public lands and make recommendations for areas to be set aside as forest reserves under the 1891 Forest Reserve Act. The academy's president, Wolcott Gibbs, responded favorably and appointed a distinguished panel: Charles S. Sargent, Alexander Agassiz, Henry L. Abbot, William H. Brewer, Arnold Hague, and Gifford Pinchot. Pinchot was the only one who was not a member.

Gibbs named Sargent commission chairman. Head of Harvard's Arnold Arboretum, he had compiled a major volume on trees of North America for the tenth Census and was putting together a multivolume work on trees. He had known Pinchot for years and had advised him on his career as well as offered technical advice for Biltmore Forest. Although they began the National Academy of Sciences assignment as friends, ultimately they had a falling out, and angry letters continued long after the commission disbanded.

The forestry commission comprised an interesting mix. Like Sargent, Agassiz was a scientist from Harvard. Brewer was a botanist from Yale, who had compiled a report on trees similar to Sargent's but a decade earlier, for the ninth Census. Abbot had just retired as head of the Army Corps of Engineers; widely recognized as a leading authority on flood control, he brought useful skills to a commission charged with recommending creation of additional forest reserves for watershed protection. Hague was with the Geological Survey, and he had been assigned to the examination of Yellowstone National Park. He had drafted the language for the president's proclamation declaring the first forest reserve in 1891, thinking it would be an addition to the park. He and Pinchot would become good friends and found themselves assigned the task of drafting the commission's report.

There were important linkages. Sargent and John Muir were friends and mutual admirers; Muir was enthusiastic in his praise of Sargent's first volume on trees. Robert Underwood Johnson, publisher of *Century Magazine* and Muir's writings, was also close to the naturalist; most historians see Johnson as an important participant when Muir founded the Sierra Club in 1892. Johnson was close to Sargent as well, and Pinchot was close to all three. Muir had written to Pinchot in 1894, thanking him for his gracious hospitality in New York and saying, "you are choosing the right way into the woods. Happy man. Never will you regret a single day spent thus." As the diaries show, Johnson was helpful in getting the forestry commission established, and Muir joined the commission for part of its mission.

Armed with a $25,000 appropriation, the commission headed west in the summer of 1896, with Pinchot going ahead on his own accompanied by his good friend Harry Graves. Once they all met up, it did not take long for Pinchot to find fault with Sargent, who did not support the proposal that the final report include specific recommendations on managing whatever forest reserves would be established. Too, Pinchot favored more acreage than Sargent; as the young forester jotted his diary entries, he was not charitable toward the great man from Harvard.

Pinchot, who had paid for a portion of his trip west, hunted and fished along the way, and a selection of entries on such pursuits have been included to provide a sense of landscape. We can also see Pinchot's sense of humor in the names of his camps, such as "Misery" when they ran short of food and "Plenty" when the larder was full. His references to old forest fires—fires before white settlement— are of special interest today as we strive to define just what a "natural" forest is.

As the commission report took shape, there were internal debates over whether an agency would be necessary to manage the reserves, or would the Army with its various western detachments suffice. After all, the Army was already "protecting" Yellowstone National Park, and some—notably General Abbot—saw little need for anything more. Pinchot disagreed: no surprise here. The report itself began with a summary of European forestry policies and practices, to give Congress some sort of a model. In the end, however, the final report was submitted to Congress after all the important legislative decisions had been made. There is no evidence that the report itself influenced Congress, but there is ample evidence that the commissioners themselves did.

Secretary of the Interior David Francis, Smith's successor, forwarded to President Grover Cleveland the portion of the preliminary commission report that contained recommendations for 21 million acres of new forest reserves. He suggested to the president that he proclaim these reserves on February 22, 1897, as a fitting tribute to

George Washington. Cleveland followed the suggestion but without consulting with a Congress that had been routinely assured that the reservation program would not proceed as a purely executive action. In the furor that followed, Congress attached a rider to the appropriations bill that would rescind all forest reserves. Cleveland vetoed the budget measure on the last day he held office, and newly inaugurated William McKinley began his term by calling a special session of Congress to end the impasse and fund the government that would otherwise run out of money on June 30.

Pinchot was called back to Washington on March 1 to help the academy's forestry commission with its salvage operation. Since the special congressional session was to deal with budget only, the trick was to get the forest reserves considered at all. Whereas until then the Public Lands Committees had led the debate on reserves, now it was up to the Appropriations Committees to set the agenda. Thus we see William Allison, chairman of the Senate Appropriations Committee, appear again in Pinchot's diaries. Congressman John Lacey, chairman of the House Public Lands Committee, whom history remembers primarily for federal legislation to protect wildlife, had urged an amendment to the budget bill that would provide for the reserves, and the House concurred. The Senate needed to agree but first had to mollify South Dakota Senator Richard Pettigrew, who insisted that nothing could pass that would hurt the Homestake Mining Company, a South Dakota enterprise. The specific portion of the appropriations bill that treated forest reserves was the allocation to the Geological Survey, and Director Charles Walcott is both visible and influential. By the middle of April the major compromises had been struck, and Pinchot turned his attention elsewhere. Congress approved a measure that contained a statement of purposes for forest reserves (since 1907 called national forests) in late May, and McKinley signed the bill into law on June 4.

Important pieces were now in shape for the Conservation Movement to unfold, except it would take Pinchot until 1905 to be given charge of the forest reserves. By 1910, when Pinchot was removed from office, the system of national forests had grown to 150 million acres, and the Forest Service—the agency that manages them still—had taken the form that we would recognize today.

1894

11/26 New York Long talk w. R.U. Johnson in the afternoon. There seems a chance to do a good deal with Congress now...

12/16 New York Long talk w. Sargent & Stiles, & later R.U. Johnson, in which the details of the proposed bill to appoint a commission to report on the public timber lands were settled...

12/17 New York Prepared outline of bill for commission to study forests and submitted it to Windmuller. Then saw R.U. Johnson & slightly altered my letter for February Century. After lunch submitted draft of bill to Committee of Chamber of Commerce, wanted more information. Then saw Johnson again. McRae bill passed House today.

1895

6/5 Boston Sargent's place about nine thirty. Found Stiles, Harvard & Geard also...Dr. Gibbs there too, coming a little later...Dr. Gibbs and Stiles both for having Commission of National Academy of Sciences study public timber lands & report on them. Also for expression by commercial bodies...More talk about public forests...

9/4 Springfield, Massachusetts ...Forestry Association meeting in A.M. P.M. Fernow, Johnson & I read about national forestry matters. Johnson & I favored forest commission policy & carried vote of convention in spite of Fernow. Long talk with Newell on way back.

11/6 New York Up very late, and to Century Magazine, where Mr. Gilder gave me excellent news of the National Commission matter...

11/18 Ringwood, New York. Call on W.C. Whitney, & prepared letter for him to sign to Hoke Smith regarding National Academy forest commission plan.

11/30 Brookline, Massachusetts ...Sat up till after 12 talking forest commission with Prof. Sargent.

1896

2/3 New York Letters, saw R.U. Johnson who had good news from Bowers as to prospects of commission...

3/2 New York No letter from Gibbs. Took 10 A.M. train to N.Y. [from Brookline]... Saw Johnson at four about going to Washington concerning money for National Commission.

3/10 New York ...Eve saw Stiles at Century about editorial on forest commission...

3/16 New York To Sportsman's exposition ... Spoke about trip to St. Mary's this spring. Talked with Father about it & about Sargent's delay. Also saw Johnson about the letter...

4/29 Washington Called on Dr. Schott, then to Geological Survey, & had talk with Newell, then with Hague, then with Newell to Department of the Interior. Tried to see Secretary, but he was busy with Indians delegation...then talk with Hague & then with Walcott, & to see Allison to try to have appropriation made avail at once. Too late.

4/30 Washington Map work. Steele of Oregon came in. Met Silas McBee. Saw Secretary Smith as to date. He said "anything we have got you can have." Lunch at the Hagues. Met Emmons of the 40th Parallel Survey. Dinner with McBee. Long talk with him tonight. He is a splendid fellow.

5/1 Washington With McBee. Pleasant talk with Secretary Smith. Odds & ends. Very satisfactory time with Jones of the Land Office...

5/2 Washington Forest Commission work. Topographer assigned to map work. Talks with Newell & Griswold...Am to see the President on Wednesday next.

5/4 Washington Saw Perkins last night about map work. Got Griswold started on Oregon report. Long & most interesting talk with Gen'l Scholfield, who outlined what seems to me the best practicable scheme for forest management yet. Talk with Weed after lunch. Then with Bowers. Then Churchill Satterlee. Dinner with Newell & to Cosmos Club. Met Greeley, Coville, Carroll, Wright...

5/5 Washington Talk with Steele, then with Randle to see Secretary Herbert, who took us to see the President, who was very cordial, especially as to forest work & reservations. Met also Carlisle and Wilson. Then Gen'l Schofield again. Land Office after lunch...

5/6 Washington Survey, Bowers, Land Office, Anizi Smith, the President, who spoke most encouragingly of the forest work.

5/7 Washington Survey, talk w. Steele about his paper, part of which then finished he read to me for suggestions. Then to see Coville, who promised much help on Idaho, & suggested going along. Talk with Dr. Merriam, & a most useful one. Weed ditto on N. Montana…After dinner to see Emmons & then talk with Hague.

5/11 New York Forest Commission work mainly, preparing report to whole Commission. Intensely hot till night.

5/13 New York–Washington …Forest Commission work. Took 3:20 train to Washington and had long and very satisfactory talk with Hague.

5/14 Washington Forest Commission work. Saw Hoke Smith, who agreed to get back through Congress money advanced on the work now, total to be within the appropriation. Lunch with von Herman.

5/15 New York Committee (Hague & me) report for tomorrow. At it all day & till 10:30 tonight.

5/16 New York Satisfactory talk in morning at Century with Gibbs and Hague. Meeting at 3 P.M. Sargent opposed to all real forest work, and utterly without a plan or capacity to decide on plans submitted. Meeting a distinct fizzle. Dinner at Century with commission & Stiles. Talk with Johnson after dinner. He takes the right view.

5/17 New York …Lunch at the Century with Brewer, who advised me to write to Sargent a letter giving my reasons for thinking work in forestry required as part of the work of the commission, and Hague, who advised me similarly, & also to send copies of the letter to each member of the commission.

5/21 New York Errands. Read to Father letter to Sargent; he approved it. Decided Graves to go along West…

6/1 New York Various preparations. Said goodbye & took 4:30 train with Harry Graves. 8 pieces checked, 200 lbs. excess.

6/4 St. Paul–Minneapolis Tickets etc. Saw Whitney of the Great Northern Railroad, then Lee McClung. Found Judge Newell, who introduced me to Kendice, Bunn & McHenry of Northern Pacific R.R. At lunch…other Yale men. Then a very useful talk with McHenry. Then a talk with J.J. Hill, & to country club on bicycle with a lot of Yale men…

6/5 Minneapolis–St. Paul With Ed Dwart to mill of Shevlin Carpenter & Co. Harry Graves along. Talk w. M. Shevlin & Mr. Clark. A most interesting mill…Conrad of Kalispell also on the train.

6/8 Fox's–Fort Lowe–St. Mary's Lake, Montana A stormy day. Reached camp about 2:30 & Harry & I went with Bill to see bait. Bear had dragged horse away & we waited about four hours at 15 yards from bait. Heard bear, but he didn't come. Very cold, & at times very exciting.

6/9 St. Mary's Photos & vol survey in A.M. To bait again in P.M. Thought we heard the bear nearby & crawled up. Intensely exciting. But he wasn't there. Birds made the noise.

6/10 Kootenai Mt., Montana Harry & I left camp about nine with Billy Jackson for the sheep lick on Kootenai Mt. Left horses about two thirty & went over snow up a spur. Waited on top in shelter for wind to fall. Blowing fiercely, with frequent snow squalls. When we got to the lick Jackson looked over the bank & was seen by a ram which ran at once. I hit him once at 100 yds & once at 150 out of five shots. Fired three more at very long range. Second hit broke its hind leg. Waited an hour, tracked & shot him dead. Got to horses about 9 & to camping place at

10:10. Mare bucked pack off just before we camped, & we had to repack.

6/11 Camp Breakfast about ten. Studied forest & made notes. Reached camp again about five, after seeing that bear had not visited the bait. Stories from Billy in the evening.

6/12 The Narrows S.E. slope. Flat Top Mt. studying fire slash. Late in P.M. came on up, Harry & I, with Billy Jackson, & camped near the Narrows…

6/13 The Narrows–Upper St. Mary's Lake Fishing before breakfast. Harry got 2 brook trout…I two lake trout…

6/14 The Narrows–Upper St. Mary's Lake–Goat Mt. Climbed Goat Mt. from the Narrows almost to the top with Harry & Fox. Saw, stalked, shot at &, I am glad to say, missed a goat. Back rather tired about 8:30, after a 12 hour trip.

6/15 The Narrows–Camp Foot–Upper Lake Found Monroe & Flinch at camp, or near it. They had just crossed the range from Lake McDonald, a feat never performed at this season before. Arranged next trip. Loafed & packed.

6/16 Upper St. Mary's Lake–Jackson With Fox & Harry through the timber to Fox's ranch on foot. 5 hour trip of fast walking. Much snow. Mail there. Then to Jackson's Ranch, & spent the rest of the day writing letters.

6/17 Jackson's Ranch–Blackfoot Started for Blackfoot after packing, and wrote letters there all day, waiting for a freight. Hired a stock car & put our things in. Slept beside the track, expecting to leave at 6 A.M.

6/29 Swan Lake–Camp Armour Left head of Swan Lake with Jack Monroe at 2:10 P.M. We were on foot, & carried about 30 lbs. (27 for me). Intensely hot…

6/30 Camp Armour–Louis Simons' Left camp at 7:30, and arrived at cabin of V.C. Wood at 11:30. We helped him get a deer out

of the river & he gave us some venison. Good dinner & bath. Then on to Louis Simons' place. A dirty but kindly Dane.

7/3 Camp Misery–Camp Plenty Up about 6:30. Breakfast a little leaf tea, the last, & a little bit of salt pork, mostly rind…At Wood's Jack made bread & I fished…

7/5 Camp Plenty–Bear Bait Breakfast 7:30 & to the lick. Bait visited, hams shaken out of tree & two gone, & part of doe carried off. Jack trailed it up splendidly, & we dragged it back to lick. Back to camp at 1:40.

7/16 Col. Falls–Belton–Lake McD. Commission. John Muir along.

7/20 Kootenay–Spokane Left Casts early and reached Kootenay about ten. Interesting ride there on Spokane & Northern Railroad, crossing into U.S. again about Northport. Then down the Columbia to Spokane. Arrive about 7:45. Talk with Gen'l Abbot on the way. He takes same ground as Sargent about any real forest work. Evening wrote home, & wire to ask for funds to take Graves with me at my own expense.

7/21 Spokane–Missoula …John Muir left the party & plan was suggested by him, & approved by Sargent, of my making short trip with him to Alaska. Plan objected to by Hague. Very interesting ride. Accounts on the way. Enormous burns.

7/22 Missoula–Hamilton Lieut. Ahern called & we all had good talk. He is very sensible. I wired Harry to come on & wrote Father about it. Took 2:45 train for Hamilton, & after long talk first with Bishop & then with Prince, it was decided that I should make the Clearwater trip. Spent evening looking over the big mill (Anaconda Copper Mining Co.) with Bean & —— Dr. said matter w. my knee was rheumatism. Not serious.

7/23 Hamilton–Missoula Bean very kind indeed about helping get information. Talked

Sawmill near Custer, South Dakota. Report on Black Hills Forest Reserve by Henry S. Graves, published in the Nineteenth Annual Report of the U.S. Geological Survey, Part V. *Forest Reserves*, 1899.

with several men about Clearwater & Salmon River regions. Commission came back by afternoon freight Hamilton–Missoula, & with the rest. Stopped at Fort Missoula. Dinner at Lieut. Ahern's…Colonel gave permission for Ahern to go along on Clearwater trip.

7/24 Missoula–Hamilton Saw the commission off from Hotel, & then spent morning over accounts with Shuster. Came up on 2:45 train. Evening talking with Mitchell & others about Salmon & Clearwater regions.

7/25 Hamilton Letters & preparations of various kinds. Harry came in about 5 with cook & outfit. Evening over his Michigan report etc.

7/26 Hamilton—Sunday Tried to go to church. Failed. Tried to get a swim. Failed. Packed & worked on different things.

8/22 Portland Work on train. Arrive Portland about noon…

8/26 Ashland Reached Ashland about 1. Read Pike's Barren Ground book & in evening had talk with Sargent & Hague about forest policy. Sargent utterly wrong on all points, as usual.

9/3 San Francisco Arrive 10:45 Palace Hotel. Saw McAllister, secretary Sierra Club, & Alvord. Various errands. Wasted evening reading.

9/24 San Bernardino–Hemet Packing & errands. Arranged to send penner & telescope home by express…

9/25 Hemet To Hemet Lake & back. Very interesting day.

10/1 Flagstaff To Agassiz Peak with Sargent

& Abbot. Marvellous view with horizon of over a thousand miles. Drove back in the dark.

10/3 Colorado Springs …interesting scenery. Col. Ensign called in the evening. Then I had pleasant talk with Sargent.

10/4 Colorado Springs—Sunday To church w. Col. Ensign, & then met Pres. Slocum.…Then went over cones etc. with Sargent.

10/21 New York …Dinner with Reynolds at the Century. A lazy day. Stiles was at Century, and explained about Fernow's article on The White Pine.

10/22 New York Office work. Dinner with the Stimsons, and work after.

10/24 Newport Reached Fall River early, & thence to Newport by train. Mr. Hague met me. P.M. Full meeting of commission which decided not to try for legislation from the present Congress, wrongly in my judgment. Lively discussion over Sargent's proposal to recruit forest officers only from West Point. Dinner at Agassiz.

12/28 Boston Talk with Sargent at the Arboretum about proposed reserves. Telegraphed Secretary Francis.

1897

1/7 Washington Met Sargent & Hague at the Arlington at ten. Later long talk with Secretary Francis (we three & the Secretary) and after lunch at the Hagues' we began work with Hiram Jones to assist.

1/8 Washington Work at the Interior Department in the morning and at the Geological Survey in the afternoon…

1/9 Washington Morning at the Department Interior. Hard work keeping my temper in the face of Sargent's blaze way of dealing with great interests. Also with his desire to throw out the whole St. Mary's country. Read Peter Stirling in one sitting at night.

1/11 Washington Breakfast with the Satterlees, and then to the Department. After lunch there again, when we decided to try to have the St. Mary's country reserved…Dinner at the Hagues'. Secretary Francis there. He said title to Indian reservations always rests in the government. Also that our appropriation probably does not expire July 1. Pleasant time with him.

1/15 New York Finished (mostly) revision of Swan River trip.

1/16 New York Swan River trip, etc., etc. Evening Boone & Crockett Club dinner. Low spoke on Labrador & Thompson on Wolves. A very interesting dinner. Wasted several hours.

1/25 New York Forestry Commission nearly all day…

1/26 New York Forestry Commission all day & eve…Harry Graves came back from Adirondacks.

1/27 New York Forestry Commission all day and in the evening. My answer to Sargent's proposal to defer beginning a permanent U.S. forest service about ready.

1/28 New York Final preparations for Forestry Commission meeting. Took 1 o'clock train to New Haven. Saw Amos there & met the Hagues' later on Colonial Express. Long and satisfactory talk with Hague, who agreed wholly with my position. Heavy snow, & much delay.

1/29 Boston …Meeting at Boston Atheneum at ten thirty. Sargent read his capital descriptive paper of the proposed reserves, and we discussed minor matters. After lunch to see Brewer with Hague. Brewer expressed himself as much dissatisfied with Sargent's plan, & uncomfortable over the tone of it. Evening dinner at Sargents'. Mrs. Sargent, Mrs. Hague, & myself, all of commission but Gibbs.

1/30 Boston Meeting ten to one about organization and after lunch again till nearly dark. We carried our most important points…

1/31 Boston …Back to Boston and talk with Hague.

2/1 Boston–New York Took 10 o'clock train, and worked somewhat on Forestry Commission matters on the train. All well here.

2/4 New York Forestry Commission all day hard. Complete first draft of proposed bibliography.

2/5 New York Forestry Commission all day hard. Very tired tonight.

3/1 New York–Washington At 2:15 got telegram from secretary interior calling me to Washington because of the Senate attack on the reserves. Left 3:20, found Ernest Howe at the train, and then to Department of the Interior & to Capitol after a talk with the secretary. Saw Senator Allison. Back to the Hagues' about 12.

3/2 Washington To Department Interior & to Capitol, where I saw Senator Hale & got copy of the Lacey amendment. Then saw secretary, & then at Geological Survey, with Hague, Brewer & Abbot. Wrote the commission's statement about the amendment. After a talk with Sargent, who objected to the Lacey amendment, and Hague, saw the secretary (all 3 of us) & met Brewer & Abbot at Capitol. Then all five saw Allison & Gorman. Sargent opposed Lacey amendment. Evening Sargent & I heard debate in House. Kept secretary posted all through the day.

3/3 Washington Watching matters at Capitol & seeing secretary about them. Evening went to Capitol with Sargent & Brewer, & when they went home stayed till 2:45 & then walked back.

3/4 Washington With the Howe boys to the Capitol. Saw McKinley take the oath. Then to Aunt Nettie's window in the Hotel Regent. Saw the parade from there. Evening called on Mrs. Satterlee & R.U. Johnson.

3/5 Washington Talk with Johnson & Hague,

& others to see Jones, & to Capitol to get Congressional Records with statement of attack reserves. Dinner with Aunt Nettie & to see interior of Pension Building.

3/6 Washington–New York …Evening over Congressional Records…

3/9 New York Forestry Commission all day. Saw Stiles & Johnson & wrote interview for Stiles. Dined at the Hewitts, and found Mr. Hewitt strongly in favor of having our bill ready at once. Spoke of it as being of the first necessity.

3/10 New York Forestry Commission all day. Finished "interview" & gave it to Stiles. Saw Johnson, and spent evening going over proposed laws with Stimson.

3/11 New York Forestry Commission all day. Saw Stiles about editorial. Dinner with the Hartshornes. Fear I have made a bad mistake in giving out that interview.

3/12 New York Went to New Haven to see Brewer, who thought I did right in the interview…

3/13 New York Forestry Commission all day nearly. To see Alice in Wonderland at the Waldorf…

3/14 New York Stayed in nearly all day & did nothing…

3/15 New York Book for an hour in the morning. Forestry Commission rest of the day. Evening to Sportmans Exposition with Harry. Have wasted an hour today.

3/16 New York …Forestry Commission.

3/17 New York …Forestry Commission afternoon and evening.

3/18 New York Forestry Commission all day, & some after dinner.

3/19 New York Forestry Commission all day, and in the evening. Saw Roosevelt, who said the president could classify offices made by secretary of the interior to carry out object of an appropriation. Saw Stimson evening who gave me the riders after criticism by Mr. Root (both) and Mr.

Clark (survey) and much work by himself.

3/20 New York Forestry Commission meeting at 10:30, which lasted, with a recess for lunch of something over an hour, until 6:30. One of the hardest days work I ever did, but we got a great many concessions from Sargent's original plan. Century Club. Century again in eve.

3/21 New York Forestry Commission till 11:30 (meeting at 9:30) & calls in P.M. I voted against Sargent's bill, the others for it, except Hague, who did not vote.

3/22 New York Got little done today… Forestry Commission. Talk with Hague about a possible minority report.

3/24 New York Letters in the morning, & Forestry Commission mainly until 6:30. Met Austin Wadsworth & had a good talk with him…

3/25 New York Forestry Commission all day. Statements of forest administration abroad Sargent.

4/4 Philadelphia–Washington …Evening talk at Hague's, where I am staying with him & Brewer. Also Mrs. Hague.

4/5 Washington With Hague to meeting with Sargent, Brewer & Abbot & Walcott in Hague's room, at which Walcott explained the situation. Then to meeting with these and Secretary Bliss, Commissioner Hermann, & Senator Wilson. Sargent & Abbot against suspension & McRae amendment to Sundry Civil Bill, the rest for. Bliss for forest protection. Then coming to see McKinley. Talked with him for nearly an hour, sitting around Cabinet table. Sargent & Abbot for suspension, against amendment. President strong for the reserves. He impressed me very favorably. P.M. saw Walcott with Hague, & at my suggestion he made changes in amendment

to exclude mineral land from recession after survey, permit secretary to "oblige" forests. Evening Cosmos Club.

4/6 Washington Saw Walcott, then Senator Hale…Evening talked with the Hagues.

4/7 Washington Pettigrew's amendment all day. Dinner with Walcott, who had many of Geological Survey come in after.

4/9 New York Letters etc., in part Forestry Commission…(the situation when I left Washington was: Pettigrew agreed essentially to all amendments proposed to his amendment except the last, "for mining or" which he struck out, and Allison agreed to hold the amendment in committee till it was satisfactory to Walcott. Bliss also agreed to the amendments. Walcott brought all this about.)

4/10 New York Forestry Commission: French Forest Service statement for Sargent in A.M.

4/11 New York Largely a wasted day.

4/12 New York Forestry Commission. (Indian statement) nearly half the day. The rest chiefly wasted.

4/13 New York Account of forest organization in India for Sargent in A.M. & P.M. & Pettigrew amendment with Stimson in evening. Forestry Commission all day.

4/14 New York–Washington Forestry Commission etc., etc. After lunch to see Stimson about bills in Congress. To Washington at 3:20 to see Mrs. Hague who asked me to stay with them.

4/15 Washington Good talk with Hague, & then with Walcott.

4/19 New York Letters & Forestry Commission all day…

4/20 New York About 1/3 Forestry Commission. Rewrote Swan River trip. ⅁

CONFIDENTIAL FOREST AGENT

"Much evidence of old fire"

On June 4, 1897, President William McKinley signed the appropriations measure that included language on purposes of the forest reserves, and funded their survey by the U.S. Geological Survey. (Much later the portion of the appropriations measure that stated reserve purposes would be dubbed the Forest Service Organic Act.) On the same day, Pinchot received letters from Survey Director Charles Walcott and his associate Arnold Hague, inviting him to Washington, D.C., to talk with Secretary of the Interior Cornelius Bliss.

Pinchot caught the 3:15 train from New York. After negotiating the terms of the assignment, as well as his title, he became Confidential Forest Agent for the Department of the Interior with the task of examining the 21 million acres of forest reserves proposed by the National Academy of Sciences Forestry Commission, which had been suspended for nine months by the Organic Act as a sop to western members of Congress. When Commission Chairman Charles Sargent learned of Pinchot's assignment, he felt that the young forester had betrayed his trust and "gone over to the politicians." Angry letters were exchanged, as a somewhat bewildered Pinchot failed to understand the intensity of Sargent's feelings.

In July Pinchot headed west with his brother Amos. In *Breaking New Ground*, he devotes ten pages to his time as confidential agent, and he uses much of the space to recount camping tales. There are general observations about widespread evidence of fire and meetings with local newspaper editors and politicians, but few specifics. About the Washington Forest Reserve, he asserted that his survey was the "first time any forester had ever looked this region over, and the same was true of most of the country I saw that summer." A few months earlier, while furiously lobbying Congress to save the reserve system from what seemed certain demise, Pinchot and the other members of the NAS Forestry Commission had given their assurances that the recommended reserves had been properly examined.

As is generally the case, segments of Pinchot's autobiography mirror his earlier diary, and the following entries for his time as confidential agent, which are a substantial sample of the whole, are largely about hunting and camping. Although they tell us little about conservation specifics, the entries provide a good flavor of Pinchot's life in the field and his impressions of the sheer beauty of western landscapes. This experience as confidential agent, when added to his NAS adventure and the western trip in 1891, offer convincing testimony that Gifford Pinchot had more hands-on experience with the full range of western forests than any man living. Too, he gained the reputation as a "field man," a major plus in subsequent years as the Forest Service evolved.

After he returned to Washington, D.C., Pinchot prepared *Surveys of the Forest Reserves* (1898), a 159-page document that contained the specifics that are missing from his diary and autobiography. He reported a favorable shift in western public opinion about the reserves, and toward that end he recommended excluding agricultural and mineral land; that exclusion had been a point of substantial contention, and a promise repeatedly made as Congress considered the Organic Act. Good forest management, he explained, required continuity of ownership and management, and good forest management required technically trained foresters. Without trained foresters "the high standard of fidelity, honesty, and ability" that was necessary would not be available. His report is dated March 15, 1898, yet it would not be until the fall of that year that formal forestry education began in America at Cornell University under Fernow and at Biltmore Forest under Schenck. Thus, not only was he proposing technical training that did not yet exist, he was also suggesting the sort of high-minded qualities that foresters should have—an image that he would foster for the rest of his long life.

At Bliss's request, Pinchot also described the bureau needed to take charge of the reserves; at that time, they were loosely administered by the General Land Office. He proposed regional management because of the wide range of market and natural conditions—a decentralized model suggested by Brandis. A decade earlier, Fernow had also proposed decentralization for the same reasons; it is fair to say that this German model, honed in India, is the form that would be adopted after 1905, when we can first see outlines of the modern-day Forest Service.

The final months as confidential agent were hectic for Pinchot, as he pushed himself to near exhaustion to complete his report. A parallel situation, and one that would turn out to be the bigger story by far, was his day-by-day consideration of becoming chief of the still ill-defined federal forestry agency. In the diaries the two themes overlap and intertwine; in this chapter and the next, the two have been separated.

1897

6/4 New York ...Letters from Walcott, calling me to Washington, & Hague asking me to come. Took 3:15 train. Hague said he understood Secretary Bliss wanted me to examine reserves to decide what land should be given up.

6/5 Washington–New York Talk with Walcott at Survey, then with him to see Secretary Bliss, who wanted me to make exam & report to him on suspended reserves, and offered me place as Special Agent at $1200 a year, saying he could not legally make any other appointment. In interview in P.M. I said I would like to do the work, but would not like…to take a place as special agent. He said he would see Walcott about what could be done.

6/15 New York …Got back about four & found telegram from Hague to come to Washington at once.

6/16 Washington Breakfast with Hague. Saw Walcott, who had asked Hague to call me down to Washington. Walcott said matters were taking shape in mind of Bliss. In suggestions I wrote out, with Hague's advice, memo of duties I would like to have assigned me, which Walcott approved. I also suggested title Confidential Forest Agent. Walcott went to secretary, got him to approve instruction, name, & $10 a day, & also saw attorney general for Interior & Procter of Civil Service Commission & got everything arranged. Bliss said it would stand that way unless something unexpected came up. Talk with Gannett. Dinner with Hague at the club.

6/17 Washington–New York Long talk with Gannett. Talks also with others—McChesney, Willis etc. Saw Schuster. Got account for over seven hundred dollars. Walcott said no further obstacle whatever to appointment for three months, & then for three more. Better defer exam till next winter. Better obey all civil service rules, & by all means appoint only that way when service is made…Took 4:00 P.M. train.

Secretary has asked to use funds left from Forestry Commission in his own forestry work (Deficiency Bill, & also for $100,000 for forest surveys). If so, I shall have charge according to Walcott, who advised me to have outlines of main papers for subordinates ready.

6/18 New York Various matters, mostly government forestry (schedules etc. for Gannett). Drive with Father, & dinner with him at the Century. Then to see Stimson, & later worked in my room till midnight.

6/29 Washington–New York Saw Coville, Gannett, Willis & Hague. Talks with each. Talk with Bliss, who said he intended to have a separate bureau of forests as soon as he could. Also found through Evans, Acher, & Schuster, that the accounts prior to July 1 that Sargent won't approve can & will be paid through the secretary.

7/9 New York Packing etc. Worked late. Harry Graves came down & had talk with him. Stimson came in in evening.

7/10 New York Left New York 10:00 for Chicago, just catching the train.

7/13 On train Read and worked a little. Not very profitable.

7/14 Blackfoot, Montana Arrive 5:20 A.M. Jack Monroe at the station. Drove to Agency. Saw agent McLaughlin & then to Billy Jackson's ranch. Fished & sighted rifles, etc. Billy can't go now, but will in September. Bought some grub, & arranged with Monroe to go.

7/16 Priest River–Priest Lake, Idaho Arrived about six, after rain, & camped…

7/17 Priest Lake Lower end Lake Kaniksu to upper end Priest Lake. Up about 3:30 & got away at 8. Many heavy showers, Jack & Amos in the canoe, Corlin & I in his boat with the baggage. Much old burn. Clouds low. Camped at Corlin's camp on upper lake. Fishing poor.

7/18 Priest Lake A quiet day. Took a few pictures; after church tried to get some fish, but failed. But for the fires this would be an exceptionally beautiful place.

7/19 Priest Lake–Lake Kaniksu Up at 4. As I was going down to the boat about 5:30 some fool in a camp across the lake shot apparently at me. Shot hit water & then into bushes less than 10 feet away. Started up mountain south of lake at 6, & reached top at 10. On top killed large buck (mule deer) & helped Corlin pack meat down. Descent 2¾ hours very severe work. Took many pictures. Amos & Jack went ahead on steamer with baggage. Corlin & I came after, reaching camp about 9 half way down lower lake at Chimney Creek.

7/20 Priest Lake–Kaniksu Chimney Creek to Corlin's. Up at 3:30; & pulled down the lake with whole outfit to Corlin's. Lunch, & then got away at 11 & climbed mountain west of mouth of river. Back to camp about 6:30, with a few fish. Took many pictures. Leiberg was at camp in evening talk with him.

7/21 Priest Lake Up late & did little beyond photographing & making a four hour trip through the woods. Hit turkey buzzard or raven flying.

7/23 Spokane Saw about repairs to kit & development of photos. Gave interview to Durham of Spokesman Review, and got check for $250 cashed.

7/24 Spokane After breakfast numbered photo films, and gave directions about them …Dr. Merriam turned up in course of afternoon. Had dinner with him & Amos… Interview of column & a half, editorial favoring reserves.

7/27 Watson's–Lake Chelan After breakfast Amos, Jack & I started up the brook and spent the day looking about. Shot some grouse & had them for lunch.

7/28 Watson's–Stehekin Took Steamer Stehekin & after a beautiful trip up this most lovely lake reached Stehekin…

*7/29 Stehekin–Bridge Cr.…*Photographed & then took skin of a small rattler. Very beautiful rough mountain, & much ice high up.

7/31 Twisp Pass Lake to Camp on the Twisp Up to the summit on foot. Killed whistling marmot off hand 200 yards.

8/1 Twisp–Williams' Ranch above Winthrop …killed 8 or 9 grouse, shooting heads off. Total 25 miles.

8/2 Williams' Ranch–Early Winter Creek Got away in fair season & made 22 miles before lunch.

8/3 Early Winter Creek–Camp on Bridge Cr. Started at 7 A.M. & traveled without stopping for lunch until 6:40 P.M. Through Racing Pass, but had no time to go to Rainy Lake. Found Newell & Gannett in camp…Made about 31 miles, much of it without trail except a line of blazes, & some without that. Hard traveling.

8/4 S. Fork Bridge Cr.–Park Creek Started after early lunch, the horses being tired, & made only ten miles.

8/5 Park Creek–Horse Shoe Basin Breakfast 5:30. Horse fell. A mare back over back trail & Gannett & I started ahead on foot. About ten Newell, Gannett, Field, & I had some lunch at the state road camp, & then went with the others to the summit on foot. Left Gannett & Newell there about 2 P.M. They got through to Marblemount that night about 10:30. Back to road camp, another lunch, more grub bought, & then to the basin. Reached camp about 6:30.

8/6 Park Creek–Horse Shoe Basin Left camp soon after 9 A.M. and shortly after saw a goat on west side of lower basin. Made fair stalk, Field with Amos (his shot), Monroe with me. Amos hit him first at about 175 yards & I killed him at 125. Skinned him & went on. From upper basin saw another on the divide of peaks south of saw teeth below middle one of three slight rises. In 2¼ hours got near enough to shoot. 250 yards. Head showing first shot. Missed. Hit in shoulder second, missed third. Then crawled up & broke his back. Goat fell, still living, & I had to shoot him again. Had good views of headwaters Park Creek & glacier at head. Camp about 8 P.M.

8/8 Horseshoe Basin Quiet Sunday. Service in the morning. Stomachs of Amos, Jack & me upset by eating dried peaches cooked in graniteware dish mended with copper rivets.

8/9 Horseshoe Basin—Leach's, Cascade Creek Got away late, about nine, & crossed Cascade Pass. Made about 9 miles down North Fork Cascade Creek to Leach's ranch. All tired & hungry, & all helped get supper.

8/10 Leach's—Marblemount Horses took back trail...I went ahead on foot to take pictures.

8/11 Marblemount–Hamilton–Seattle ...We arrived in our woods clothes, but the [Hotel Butler] took us in.

8/12 Seattle Haircut & shave, & then to see Judge Burke. Got him to introduce me to Mr. Graves, of _____ National Bank, & got necessary money. Talks with various men about the reserves. Judge Burke came again in evening & took Amos & me to Rainier Club.

8/13 Seattle–Everett, Washington Various errands. Accounts for July. Renewing outfit...no train goes to Monte Cristo till Monday. So I had to wait.

8/14 Everett Wasted the whole day reading, except that I finished & forwarded my July accounts. Then I read till nearly 2 A.M., fool stories of no account in magazines.

8/15 Everett To church to hear a man preaching that Baptists were outside the communion of God's people. I wish I had spoken to him about it afterward.

8/16 Everett–Monte Cristo ...reached Monte Cristo about 2. Left again at 7, with 20 lbs. pack & went on to pass toward Index. Missed trail, but reached pass about 8:30, the regular time for the trip, and camped there after dark. Good wood & bad water.

8/17 Camp–Columbia Peak–Galena ...too smoky to see much.

8/18 Galena–Index–Seattle Rose 3:20, & left at 4 on foot with pack. Walked to Index, 9 very long miles, in 3 hours, got some more breakfast there, & took at 7:25, Great Northern train to Seattle. There bath & errands. Saw Judge Burke, who in evening took me to see Mrs. Burke. Went to bed very tired about 10:30.

8/19 Seattle Letters & errands. Called on Judge Burke twice & in the evening he came around & took me to see editor Seattle P.I. & we talked about forestry. Editor came to right view.

8/20 Port Townsend–Lake Crescent ...Smoky, but beautiful sail along coast.

8/21 Lake Crescent ...made trip to Section 16, T 30 R 9 W. In all about 2 to 2½ miles going & coming & it took from 10 to 7. We traveled with many stops, but prob were going not less than six hours, & part of the time working hard in spite of the heat. A wonderful forest...

8/22 Lake Crescent Reading, writing, & late in P.M. tried to catch some fish. Poor success.

8/23 Lake Crescent Went back along road about four miles—spent whole day taking pictures. Evidence of old fire (charcoal under a cedar 4–5' DBH) shown me by lumbermen. Back about six, after most interesting day.

8/24 Lake Crescent–Hurricane Place Dr. Merriam came last night. We got away about 8 ...much evidence of old fire on the way.

8/25 Camp in basin below Hoh River Divide Via Hot Springs. Dr. Merriam & I took baths there: the water's very hot...took pictures of Olympics etc.

8/26 Close Call Basin As I was dressing Dr. Merriam saw a big black bear at about 500 yards. I went after him, but some men in another camp began chopping, & I did not find the beast…Saw another bear & got within 50 yards, but could not shoot. Wonderful views of Olympus & of whole region to N., W., & S. from top of ridge.

8/27 Close Call Basin Not working. Up on ridge to watch for bear. Saw none. P.M. went again to look where we saw the bear last night. Nothing.

9/4 Port Crescent–Seattle …Reached Seattle [by boat] about 6:30, & was much delighted to get into clean clothes again. Found I had just missed Walcott, but found Holmes at the Rainier Grand. Long talk with him.

9/5 Seattle Rose late, met Holmes, & we went together to Port Blakely & saw the great saw mill. Lunch with him at the Rainier Grand, & after it met John Muir in the lobby. Spent the afternoon with these two. Much delighted to see Mr. Muir again. Dinner with them at the Rainier Grand. Church in the evening with Holmes & then dictated interview for the Post Intelligencer, & gave it to Mr. John W. Pratt, editor of the same. Dictate to his stenographer. Then more talk with Muir & Holmes.

9/6 Seattle Errands etc. Met Bailey, of Mr. Merriam's staff. Got outfit repaired in part, & took 4 P.M. Great Northern train East. Met Professor Holmes of Edmonds, & was with him all the morning. He got off at Wenatchee in the night. Wonderful cloud & mist effects in the moonlight as we crossed the Cascades.

9/7 On train [to Montana] Rainy. Read & posted back accounts in A.M. Slept in freight house by courtesy of the night operator.

9/11 Camp Going to the Sun Up Going to the Sun till we reached the high benches, & along them westward, getting good view of whole lower North Fork country. Killed two goats on way home, & reached camp about 10 P.M. With Harry & Jack. Amos went after a white goat, & almost climbed Going to Sun after it, but did not get a shot. The party was Stimsons, Mis, Amos, G.P., Jack, Fox, & a cook.

9/13 Camp Going to the Sun Wrote report to secretary, and in late afternoon went down to mouth of Berings Creek & brought back three trout weighing together 8 lbs.

9/14 Camp Going to Sun Rain…Harry, Amos & I went down & caught six trout…

9/15 Camp Going to Sun–Camp Reynolds …Camped on plateau without blankets. Magnificent view down in to the valley.

9/19 Glacier Camp Before breakfast to look for bear east of camp with Harry. Saw three, probably silver tips…

9/20 Glacier Camp Up late, & with Amos & Harry to gap just east of Jackson…

9/22 Glacier Camp–Camp No Rain …Red Eagle Basin, which is the most magnificent one I have ever seen.

9/24 Glacier Camp–Camp Doughnut Early breakfast, & after Harry's wounded bear…Harry stayed at bait but saw nothing.

9/25 Glacier Camp–Camp Slide Rock Trouble in catching horses, & so left camp about 10:30. About dusk Amos missed his rifle, in going back lost the camera.

9/26 Camp Slide Rock to Forks Left camp at 6:30 and back after camera, which we found about 8:45…Waited at Morris' for Jack, who went back after tent pole.

9/29 Blackfoot To look for ducks while breakfast was being cooked. Found none. Overhauled—repacked outfit, and then went to work on papers. Telegram from…Davis asking for reports of work done.

9/30 Blackfoot Loafed. A wasted day. After ducks etc.

10/1 Blackfoot Reports & accounts. Over to

wait for the Stimsons, & talked after one A.M.

10/2 Blackfoot A wasted day. The Stimsons came, & Harry had killed his bear, probably the one Amos & I saw.

10/3 Blackfoot A quiet morning…In the afternoon I rode to Agency with Boak but failed to see agent.

10/4 Blackfoot–Camp Boak …Started at 1, & made about 24 miles. Camped near a lake…

10/5 Camp Boak–Steel's Ranch Boak & Jack started about daylight, & found Jack's two [runaway] horses.

10/15 Middle Fork Sun River …followed around in densest kind of young growth lodgepole pine [illeg.] after fire.

10/16 Middle Fork Sun River–North Fork Up before sunrise, and hardly up when Jack …found a big bull elk on the hillside watching Dan, Doody & Ronny.

10/21 Edgemont–Custer, South Dakota Train late. Left Edgemont about 9:30. Found Harry waiting for me at Custer. Also much mail, official & otherwise…

10/22 Custer–Eighteen Mile Left Custer shortly after 7, & to top of Herney's Peak. Excellent view.

10/23 Eighteen Mile–Hell Canyon Got away about 8, & after shooting some prairie dogs came on across the divide.

10/24 Smith's Ranch–Hell Canyon Loafed, read, & rested.

Old burn near Stehekin, Washington. Report on Washington Forest Reserve by H.B. Ayers, published in the Nineteenth Annual Report of the U.S. Geological Survey, Part V. *Forest Reserves*, 1899.

10/28 Calvert–Bear Gulch–Spearfish …traveled 37 miles…

10/29 Spearfish Left at 7:30, & up Crow's Peak. Harry went on to Beulah en route to Bear Lodge Mountain, & I came back. Wasted P.M. & evening reading.

10/30 Spearfish–Tery[?]–Lead–Deadwood …Wasted most of the day & evening reading trash [while traveling].

11/1 Deadwood–Hill City Telephoned & met Dr. Carpenter, and went with him (he is Sup't of the Deadwood & Delaware Smelter, the second largest concern in the Hills) to the Union Shaft, others to see Given, Sup't of the Homestake, with whom I made an appointment to meet Moody & Carpenter on Wednesday.

11/2 Hill City–Rapid City Up about 5:30, & got away in the wagon at 7. Reached Rapid 12:50, and at dinner met C.W. Green, the special agent. Went over various questions with him, & to see Warner, receiver of Land Office, & Myron Willsie, a U.S. deputy mines surveyor, who was most interested about the Homestake lode locations for timber. Evening with Green.

11/3 Rapid City–Deadwood Took F.E. & M.V. R.R. at 8:45, & marked timber on map. After dinner met Moody at his office, & Grier soon came in. Carpenter & one or two others were to have been there. Had a talk for three hours, at the end of which they had arrived, in words at least, at my own position regarding the reserves, including the desirability of including all the area of the Black Hills. Wrote down account within an hour after interview ended. Call on Dorr in evening.

11/4 Deadwood–Custer Called on Mrs. Ware, and to Lead to find Mr. Ware. Saw Grier, & got from him statement of wood consumed by the Homestake & allied mines. Then found Mr. Ware, and had a good talk. Back to Deadwood, & short talk with Carpenter before the train left. Also with McPherson, cashier 1st National Bank.

At Custer talked with Dunnington all evening to about midnight, & worked out a practicable scheme on lines I had already thought best. A good fellow.

11/5 Custer–Edgemont Talk with Dunnington & work on report for October. Took train at 5:29 for Edgemont & on by B & M to Chicago. Met a man on the train who had hunted with [illeg.] & was just back from a trip in the Shoshones with Salons.

11/10 New York Various odds & ends. Long talk in P.M. with Father about Sargent's letter to Dr. Brandis. Evening over the summer's negatives.

11/11 New York–New Haven Letters, photos, etc., etc. Took 4 P.M. to New Haven & had long talk with Professor Brewer over Sargent's letter to Dr. Brandis. He thought I ought to write Sargent a general letter offering information, but not fight him on his accusation. Capital talk with him.

11/12 Washington Arrive 10:42, & to Survey Building. Short talk with Hague, and to Interior Department. Secretary out. Met Captain Redway & Mr. Mankin, then back to Geological Survey & lunch at the mess with Gannett et al. Gannett spoke very highly of Graves. Work on accounts with Mankin, short talk with secretary who wants reports early, & then received $469.60, in full for July. Short talk with Hermann, and dinner & long talk with Walcott, who will help to get a separate bureau for the forests. Says be very careful to Mr. Hermann the right way. Then to Cosmos Club. Was elected last Wednesday.

11/13 New York Various errands & letters. Talk with Hague at Century in evening.

11/15 Washington Work on report, & getting matters in order. Took room in Cosmos Club. Evening regular weekly meeting. Mr. Riodan, Fernow, Gannett & others.

11/16 Washington The morning with Coville

about sheep in Oregon. Afternoon various errands. Evening talk with Bowers, who says the way to get a service is to put it in the Land Office, but make its head practically independent of the commissioner, thus securing permanent officers & making the commissioner think he's founding it.

11/19 Washington Report etc. Dinner at Gannett's with the Walcotts & Merriams.

11/20 Washington Report. Ride with Willis before dinner. Sat up & read till 2 A.M. like a fool & worse.

11/22 Washington Report all day. Ride before dinner. Long talk with Coville in the evening.

11/23 Washington–New York Report, talk with Coville, and talk with Secretary Bliss, to whom I explained situation in the Black Hills, and that part of my report was ready. Did not hand it in.

12/7 Washington Report. Called on Hague, & after supper with the Walcott's to Professor Eastman's. Met a lot of scientific men. Doll, Gill, Hall, Pritchen, Galleindet, Cross, & many others.

12/9 Washington Report. Called on Hague.

12/10 Washington–New York Report. Talk with Binger Hermann about sheep in Oregon mainly. Took 4 P.M. train to N.Y., to get note books I could not get them to send. Tired.

12/11 New York Work in A.M., P.M. golf with Amos.

12/13 Washington Office at nine, & work on report till after four. Then to the Hagues. Long talk with Bowers, to whom I told the facts between Fernow & me.

12/15 Washington Report etc....to secretary's office with report. Too busy to see me. Call tomorrow. Dinner at the Walcotts'. Fred Kellogg there. To bed early.

12/16 Washington Report. Unsatisfactory talk with Bliss when I handed in first part of my report.

12/17 Washington Report. Tried to find Hanna Dunnington, back from Black Hills, says Moody will fight the reserve. Prospect rather dim, with the Civil Service fight & all.

12/18 Washington Saw Hanna, who said he would help whatever was for public good, and said I might call again when he got back, if he came back. Consulting with Coville, Fernow & O'Brien about The Forester [magazine]. For dinner to the Willis' & to spend a few days there. Wise talk with Mrs. Willis after dinner.

12/21 Washington Finishing work till after holidays. Drew salary for self ($230) & signed for August ($250), which was sent later. Talk with Coville & Fernow about The Forester for February & March.

1898

1/3 New York ...Talk with Harry Graves about forestry. The two-year forest fire study plan, with a book to follow, struck me today. I am much delighted with it.

1/4 New York ...Very busy all day with various small things. Government accounts etc. Took late train for Washington. Exceedingly tired.

1/10 Washington Reports all day. Office till nearly six. Annual meeting of Cosmos Club. Staying at the Satterlees.

1/11 Washington Reports & accounts. Got reports of Ormsby & Allen through Hermann from Jones, & after & before dinner at Cosmos with Bowers & Coville went over them with the latter. Good advice from Bowers about making the secretary put himself on record for or against the plans I propose. Office till 10:30 P.M.

1/12 Washington Reports. Gave Coville copy of Ormsby on sheep.

1/15 Washington Reports. Dinner with Hermann at Met. Club (Hague, Bowers, Fernow) to consult about forest description of the world.

1/17 Washington Reports. Paid by government to January 1, $1571.03.

1/20 Washington Reports. Dinner at the Walcotts. Meeting with Fernow & Coville about the paper (The Forester).

1/21 Washington Reports. Bicycle ride. Satterlee's to dinner. Very tired.

1/22 Washington Reports. Work in eve. Like a wished fool read till very late.

1/24 Washington Reports till 5:30 & 7 till 11.

1/25 Washington Reports 7:50 to 7:15 & 10:50 to 2:15. Almost done. Harry helped me very much. Dinner at the Hague's.

1/26 Washington At office 8:10 A.M., handed in report 9:30. Lunch with Hague, Hermann, Fernow & Bowers to talk over forest description of the Earth. Decided to act as a self appointed committee & address circular giving plan to various bodies, & attempt final action through International Geographical Congress Berlin 1899. Saw Secretary Bliss. Went over report hurriedly & commended it highly. Would not believe Redway right about funds being still left. No more work for the present…Finished editorials for The Forester at 10 P.M. A very busy day. Tired.

1/27 Washington–New York Saw Acker and explained to him in part about the Special Forest Agents, and made small correction in manuscript. Saw Fernow, and resigned from publication committee of The Forester. Told Coville in confidence about the forest fire study plan. Various errands.

3/22 Washington Correcting proof of my report to Secretary Bliss. Walcott said a bill had passed Public Lands Committee of House to suspend reserves for another year, but it would be killed in the Senate. Said Hermann had tried to stop him from continuing surveys of reserves, but had failed.

4/21 New York–Washington …Took 3:20 train & Senate passed provision in Sundry Civil bill practically abolishing the reserves suspended till March first. GP

THE FOREST SERVICE
"Western men will object"

On April 22, 1898, Charles Walcott, director of the U.S. Geological Survey, told Pinchot that he would recommend to Secretary of the Interior Cornelius Bliss that the forester be named head of any new forestry agency. A few weeks later, Walcott suggested that Pinchot take Bernhard E. Fernow's place as chief of the Division of Forestry in Agriculture. Judging from his diary entries, after Pinchot had talked with both Secretary Bliss and Secretary of Agriculture James Wilson, he concluded that being Fernow's successor was the more attractive offer. The diary also reveals that he was urged by his close associates to accept it.

Typical of Pinchot, he consulted with his family as well. He even went so far as to check with his mother's physician for assurance that her health was adequate to withstand whatever stress might accompany their move from New York to Washington, D.C. Finally, his very good friend Henry S. "Harry" Graves agreed to become assistant chief "if I go." Although it is not clear on exactly which day he decided, on May 28 he noted in New York, "Division work in A.M." He continued working from New York and Grey Towers, and then went to Washington on June 30, Fernow's last day in office.

Pinchot officially began the next day, but there is no entry. For July 2, which was a Saturday, he noted, "Division all day." Working on Saturday, or even Sunday afternoon following church, and during evenings throughout the week was typical of Pinchot, and by default of those who worked closely with him. He wrote in *Breaking New Ground* that Secretary Wilson had agreed in advance to his irregular schedule, which by any form of arithmetic would add up to much more than forty hours per week.

A niggling point perhaps, but on July 5 the secretary agreed that Pinchot's title would be Forester instead of Chief. To Pinchot, the capital was full of chiefs, but there would be only one forester, and in that way he could stand out. Since then historians have had to fiddle with language to be certain that their readers were not confused that just any forester headed the Division of Forestry, which itself had a confusing succession of names, becoming the Bureau of Forestry in 1901 and the Forest Service in 1905. Many have resorted to referring to Pinchot and his successors as chief forester—technically incorrect but at least less confusing. Forester Ferdinand A. Silcox became Chief Silcox in 1935; the title has remained Chief, at long last making the writer's lot an easier one.

Fernow should be given much credit for leaving a solid base for Pinchot to build upon, and build upon it he did, with gusto and skill. Already in place was the forest reserve system and the so-called Organic Act of 1897; it was due to Fernow that language for timber management had been added to that for watershed protection, a fact of great significance to the future of the agency. Too, there was a network of scientific collaborators, so necessary to an agency with a very modest budget. In fairness, though, one is compelled to add that Secretary Wilson must have been relieved to see the prickly Fernow go off to be founding dean of forestry at Cornell University; perhaps that made his welcome of Pinchot even broader and more generous than it might otherwise have been.

Even before he was on the federal payroll, Pinchot sought to expand the division's network of collaborators. The effort resulted in Circular 21, *Practical Assistance to Farmers, Lumbermen, and Others in Handling Forest Lands* (1898), which described the availability of technical assistance to be paid for by landowners. Through this program, millions of forested acres were brought under management; the following year a companion program focused on assisting those seeking reforestation following logging. For initiating these seminal efforts, Pinchot relied on James Toumey, who shortly would move on to be a distinguished professor at the Yale Forest School.

To augment his meager budget, Pinchot hired student assistants for little more than expenses and honoraria. In addition to obtaining work in the field for modest cost, he groomed future employees: many who were prominent in the Forest Service during its early years had begun while still students and had been imbued with Pinchot's sense of mission. Those who would be hired on a permanent basis, whether former student assistants or not, had to demonstrate a proper level of initiative and skill, as Pinchot vigorously declined to accept political appointees. In the diaries we see the name John R. Procter, president of the Civil Service Commission, who worked with Pinchot to set the higher standards.

Much is made today about a supposed split between Pinchot and Sierra Club founder John Muir, a split that "explains" the divergence of preservation from its conservation roots. The two men got along famously during the 1896 National Academy of Sciences Forestry Commission tour, and when they spent most of a week together in 1899, they once again very much enjoyed each other's company; Pinchot recorded that it was "wonderful" to travel with Muir. To the extent there was a split, it began at the end of

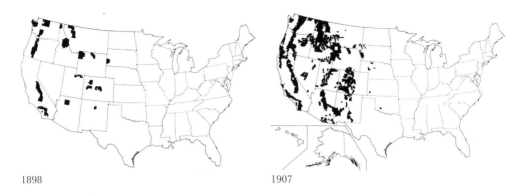

1898   1907

Pinchot's tenure as chief, during the debate over damming the Hetch Hetchy Valley in Yosemite National Park. With Muir, it was always difficult to tell how he really felt about something, as he routinely used grand language. Once he wrote to Pinchot to encourage his efforts in forestry: "radiate, radiate, radiate far and wide as the lines of latitude and longitude on a globe."

A major diary theme until 1905 was Pinchot's tireless and surprisingly patient campaign to have jurisdiction of the forest reserves transferred from the Department of the Interior to Agriculture. Often he uses the term consolidation—that is, consolidate forestry under his bureau. It is interesting to see that not only President Theodore Roosevelt concurred, but also Secretary of the Interior Ethan A. Hitchcock, who might well have seen the transfer as loss of turf. But Congress, at least House Speaker Joseph Cannon, was opposed, and his opposition was usually enough to prevent a measure from passing the House. Perhaps the real reason for delaying the transfer until 1905 was that Roosevelt was a cautious president during the term he inherited from the assassinated McKinley. After the 1904 election, he was president in his own right, and we see him adopt the aggressive posture by which he is remembered. Unfortunately, Pinchot was so busy in the final months of achieving transfer that he failed to keep his diary current. Thus, we are not able to read of his long-sought victory.

In 1902 Pinchot traveled across Europe and Russia en route to the Philippines, an adventure that is treated fully in another chapter. The point to be made here is that he felt comfortable about leaving his agency for an extended period, in large part because he was confident that Overton Price, his associate chief forester, could handle its affairs more than adequately. Throughout his Forest Service tenure, Pinchot was frequently absent from Washington, D.C., tending to issues out West or elsewhere. The name of Price deserves an asterisk on the roster of Forest Service staff who made a difference.

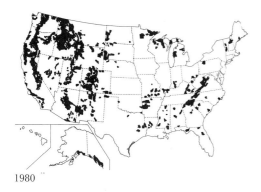

1980

The extent of the national forests in 1898, when Pinchot became chief forester; in 1907, when Congress rescinded presidential authority to create forests by proclamation in six western states; and in 1980. Except for addition of the national grasslands, little change has occurred in the West. National forests east of the Mississippi River were purchased after 1911, under Weeks law authority. From *Encyclopedia of American Forest and Conservation History,* Richard C. Davis, editor, Macmillan/Forest History Society. Reprinted by permission of The Gale Group.

Roosevelt appointed Pinchot to be secretary of a Public Lands Commission, which made a western tour in early 1904 to learn and to report. In his diaries, Pinchot demonstrates just how he could trumpet perceived support for federal forest and irrigation policies in Oregon, for example, and then ignore or dismiss disagreement a bit later in Wyoming. He often found it difficult to believe that westerners in general did not fully support him and the Forest Service.

Weldon Heyburn, U.S. senator from Idaho, receives a few diary entries and a few lines in *Breaking New Ground.* Generally, Pinchot dismissed him as part of the "states' rights fetish" and remarks that he published their correspondence, adding to Heyburn's hostility. What he fails to explain is that Forest Service Bulletin 61, *Forest Reserves in Idaho* (1905), included statements by Roosevelt justifying not consulting with Congress in advance of creating new national forests. Yet the legislative history of the 1897 Organic Act, which placed limitations on reserve creation, clearly promises prior consultation. In fact, it was lack of such consultation by President Cleveland in withdrawing the so-called Washington's Birthday reserves in 1897 that came within a whisker of spawning congressional rejection of the entire reserve system. Perhaps Heyburn had a measure of the last laugh when he cosponsored the 1907 measure that rescinded presidential authority to create national forests in six western states, including Idaho. If one looks at a map of the national forest system in 1907 and compares it with a current map, it is immediately obvious that there has been essentially no overall addition in the western part of the nation.

On occasion Pinchot jots that he ate at the "lunch mess." This was the Great Basin Lunch Mess that John Wesley Powell had begun as an informal meeting vehicle for his scientific associates. Powell named it for the Great Basin of the Intermountain West, where the U.S. Geological Survey had made so many significant advances. The tradition continued, and regular attendees included WJ McGee, Arnold Hague, Frederick Newell,

Charles Walcott, and Karl Gilbert, as well as Pinchot, in yet another way demonstrating the personal and professional linkages between forests and water.

In June 1905 Pinchot notes that the attorney general had decided that the secretary of Agriculture had the authority under the 1897 Organic Act to charge for the use of forest reserves. Enabling regulations were forthcoming. There was immediate western opposition to the levying of fees; permits for use were one thing, cattlemen argued, but the forage ought to be free. The Organic Act specifically stated that timber was to be sold at auction, so timber sales were not controversial from that point at least. Led mainly by the state of Colorado, the issue worked its way through the courts, and in 1911 the Supreme Court decided in favor of the federal position.

From time to time we see reference to an Appalachian Park/forest reserve, which had been advocated since 1899. The result would be the 1911 Weeks Act that authorized federal purchase of land to protect watersheds of navigable rivers. These purchased acres would become national forests, all in the East. Today, there are twenty-four million acres that were purchased under Weeks law authority and subsequent legislation. Speaker Cannon had been opposed. "Not one cent for scenery," he asserted, meaning there would be no purchase of land for national parks. The ensuing debate filled hundreds of pages of the *Congressional Record* and evolved into a volley between the Corps of Engineers and the Forest Service, General Hiram Chittenden and Gifford Pinchot, about whether forests effectively prevented floods. The foresters "won" the debate (Fernow scoffed privately over Pinchot's use of "buncome" when testifying to Congress), and Cannon withdrew his opposition. By 1911 Pinchot was out of office, but the Weeks Act and the eastern national forests are part of his legacy.

1898

1/5 Washington Reports all day. Talk with Hague, who advises strongly that I abandon any attempt to influence formation of a forest service, and let matters simmer for a while. Walcott says Pettigrew says western men will object to forest service being made vehicle for Republican political jobs, & fight vigorously. Hague believes there is no chance of my having any part in the forest service under Hermann. I agree with him.
1/13 Washington Walcott told Bliss today of the opposition in the Senate to a political forest service.
4/22 Washington …Talk with Walcott, who

said he would suggest to Bliss that I should be made head of a bureau created to manage the reserves, if the attempt to put them under the Survey failed.
5/2 New York …Fernow came in in P.M. & told plans. 4 year course [at Cornell], very exhaustive training, more money needed to begin real work in the woods. Objects to contracting. I predict a very serious failure.
5/10 Washington Talk with Walcott, with practical offer of Fernow's place in Agriculture Department. Refused. Hague thinks I should reconsider.

5/11 Washington Walcott saw Bliss, who said he would manage the reserves with Hermann, & put some good man—it didn't matter much whom—in charge of separate division of the Land Office. Then to see Wilson, who said, if I would take Forestry Division I could run it to suit myself & appoint my own assistants, do what work—kind of work—I chose, & need fear no interference from him. Said I could also run Adirondack work. Said he would keep the place open three years for me. Couldn't have said more. Walcott, Hague, Newell, Willis, Gannett all in favor of my taking it.

5/12 New Haven Talk with Brewer, who was very strongly of opinion that I should take the Division.

5/13 New York Dinner with Stimsons… Harry believes I should take the Division.

5/14 New York …saw Dr. Dillingham, who said there was no reason on Mamee's account why I should not take the work in Washington.

5/15 Garden City To [army] camp. Found Amos well & brought him back to lunch. He thought I ought to take the Division of Forestry. Back to camp with Amos in P.M. & long walk after, trying to get division of work in Division clear, in case I take it.

5/17 New York Talk with Graves & Reynolds about Washington. Harry will take assistant chief's place if I go.

5/18 New York Question of taking Division of Forestry.

5/19 New York …Practically decided to take the Division of Forestry.

5/28 New York Division work in A.M.

6/1 New York …Letters & Division work.

6/6 Washington Conference w. Coville & Gannett about cooperation.

6/8 Washington Long talk w. Riordan in evening. Told me about chance to make working plan for Santa Fe Railroad.

6/9 Washington Walcott did not believe Coville's proposed transfer of reserves possible. Arranged with Gannett for cooperation with Ayers' field work.

6/11 New York Long lunch with Lyman & Chisholm at lunch at the Lawyers Club. Chisholm agreed to have working plan made for some forest of the International Paper Company.

6/13 New York Page agreed to let Division have management of his land as a woodlot. Long talk with Harry about spruce book and Division work. Lawson was to come to the office but did not.

6/15 New York Bowers on the train coming down. Thought timber test work should be continued. I don't.

6/17 New York Griffith came in & said International Paper Company people want him as a professional forester, with the idea that their mills are to be supplied for a hundred years. They have from ½ to ¾ million acres. General studies of these lands his first work.

6/18 New York Griffith came in & said International Paper Company was still undecided about engaging him.

6/21 New York Chisholm said I could quote intention of officers of International Paper Company to engage Griffith and give me area for working plan.

6/26 Grey Towers The conference reports against abolition of Forest Reserves.

6/28 Grey Towers Long talk with Ayers, who is to take notes this summer. Joe & Flathead Reserve & in winter to begin study of white pine in Minnesota, after writing out report.

6/30 Washington Getting ready to begin work. Talks with Fernow & the Secretary. The latter agreed with me not to discuss work of Division yet.

7/2 Washington Division all day [Saturday]. Haas transferred, and arrangements made for John Foley to come down (at this end only). Talk with Coville about forest fire study. Dinner with him. Arranged that I pay nothing now but get even later, that I take Sudworth again to bring back Omaha exhibit. Also that my men in little-known places collect specimens of trees & shrubs.

7/4 Washington At Department arranged to get a stenographer in place of Haas.

7/5 Washington Getting in order. Secretary agreed to give me the name of forester, just as Coville is botanist.

7/6 Washington Walcott telephoned he has had boundaries for forest reserves referred to him by Bliss. He is to take my boundaries so far as I have recommended any. Reuss nearly all day on Black Hills lines, for difference in location of township lines on map. Have new information made slight changes necessary.

7/7 Washington Drew line of Washington Reserve with Gannett & Walcott. Routine work at Division. Ball game with Walcott. Talk with Keffer in which I set $4000 as the limit for expense of tree planting experiments.

7/9 New York All the morning in small matters, except that Harry Whitney came in about Adirondacks & authorized preparation of a work plan for his father's land.

7/12 Grey Towers Long talk with Father, Burns & Graves about probable Adirondack purchase. Father in the end thought favorable of it, but no final decision was reached.

7/14 Washington Letters, etc. Talk with Cutter, & thought it better for him to take over the whole forest library. Luebkert much encouraged about fire history.

7/15 Washington Division work. Finally have an idea of western planting experiments. No plan, no results. Utterly vague. Good talk with Sudworth, whom I have recommended for Gannett's work in Colorado.

7/22 Washington Division all day.

7/23 Washington Father came to Division in A.M. & met Secretary Wilson.

8/18 Washington Letters at office. Hard day's work, but wasted evening.

8/19 Washington Office routine, etc.

9/12 Washington Got my estimates finished for 1900. $69,920. A good day's work.

9/14 Washington Letters etc. Secretary Wilson agreed to my estimates without change! $69,920.

9/27 Grey Towers P.M. Exam papers & ride on Jim.

9/29 Grey Towers Discussed matters with Harry. Sent Exam papers to Luebkert. Shot with Harry.

9/30 Grey Towers Work & letters. Harry left to prepare papers for Whitney interviews. Golf & ride in P.M.

10/10 Washington Long talk with Whitney (W.C.), who applied for examination of Lenox lands, and said he would reconsider application of working plan to Adirondack lands now, and would write to Moynehan to see if he would agree to take my marking as equivalent to a 10-inch limit. I rather think the working plan will go through.

10/11 Washington Circular 21 in hands of printer—1500 copies. Graves' appointment secured. Also arranged for Griffith & Ashe. Talk with Arthur Hill of Saginaw, a white pine operator. He applied for working plan, 10,000 acres in California. Saw Radin & later dined with him & he will apply for working plans in Oregon. Corrected Spruce proof.

10/12 Washington Lots of letters. Proof of Circular 21 & Spruce book. A busy day.

10/14 Washington Whitney accepts working plans, which is to go into effect immediately. Letters. Names for Circular 21. Meeting executive committee Forestry Association. Decided to employ a secretary, keep on publishing The Forester. Send a circular to lumberman in re forest fires & membership & see that miners know substance of forest reserve regulations. Spruce proof. Agreement proofs. Preface to Spruce book.

10/15 Washington Letters & distribute Circular 21, which appeared this afternoon. Took 4 P.M. train to New York. Worked till nearly midnight on proof. Ferris decided to delay application for working plan till after sale of his land to Cornell completed.

10/16 New York Preface of Spruce book. Took 10:25 train for Ringwood. Mr. Hewitt decided to put Ringwood tract under the supervision of the Division. Also asked me to visit 20,000 acres in West Virginia & probably 260,000 acres more there. Long talk with him.

10/17 Ringwood, New York Talk with F.R. Meyer, who agreed fully with plan to put Mr. Hewitt's land in charge of the Division. Has made far too minute work, as I think. Mr. Hewitt agreed to sign application for working plan for Ringwood, & said he thought he could get enough more from Sterling Company, Mr. Harriman, Tuxedo Jack, etc. to make 60,000 acres in one body.

10/18 Highland Falls, New York To his farm with Mr. Bigelow & Grace Bigelow. Caliper some SC[?],—40 years +/−. Very poor & short mostly. Yield 40 cords in 25 years according to Miller the farmer…Thought I had lost our badge this morning, but found it tonight.

10/26 Washington Spruce proof. Various small matters. Some work on annual report, but little progress.

12/12 Washington Letters. Leiberg came in & suggested we make working plan for school lands of Idaho. Saw Secretary & later Senators Shoup (with card from Secretary) & Hatfeld. Both heartily in favor. I said I thought it could be done without expense to the state. Hatfeld said he would be in favor of giving the Division

2 or 3 times $70 thousand. Arranged with Hill to write bulletin for $200 Puerto Rico & with Gannett to get bulletin from Leiberg on North Idaho.

12/20 Washington Arranged with Hill for Puerto Rico bulletin for $250.

1899

1/2 Washington Letters etc. Call from Theofilbus Tunis, who is in charge of the forest statistical matter for the lumber people.

1/4 Washington To the Survey to see Hillers about photos & evening. Long talk with Alexander T. Biltue about Northern Pacific Railway & its lands inside reserves. He wants A.F.A. to memorialize Secretary of the Interior that N.P. can exchange its lands inside for lieu lands. Talks with Coville, Newell, Leiberg, Ayers…Long talk with Harry about forest statistics afterward.

1/7 Washington Consulting with Ayers & Schwarz. Suggested to Britton American Forestry Association would answer questions of Secretary of the Interior regarding forest reserves.

1/11 Washington Lost the morning with the lumber people, who were not very courteous.

1/12 Washington Routine. Gannett, Newell, Coville. Harry and Elwood Mead to dinner.

1/13 Washington Routine. Treadwell Cleveland began work today.

1/14 Washington The Adirondack Spruce came from N.Y., where the edition is finished.

1/17 Washington New system of accounts in effect in the office. Haas in charge of book keeping & computing for some time back. P.M. saw Shoup about appropriation & Senator Berry about his objections to title of forester in appropriations bill. He thought it sounded like aping foreigners.

1/18 Washington Routine, with a little time on book. John Norris in charge of legislation

Gifford Pinchot, *A Primer of Forestry*, 1899, pp. 7–8:

…The forest is the most highly organized portion of the vegetable world. It takes its importance less from the individual trees which help to form it than from the qualities which belong to it as a whole. Although it is composed of trees, the forest is far more than a collection of trees standing in one place. It has a population of animals and plants peculiar to itself, a soil largely of its own making, and a climate different in many ways from that of the open country. Its influence upon the streams alone makes farming possible in many regions, and everywhere it tends to prevent floods and drought. It supplies fuel, one of the first necessaries of life, and lumber, the raw material, without which cities, railroads, and all the great achievements of material progress would have been either long delayed or wholly impossible…The forest is as beautiful as it is useful. The old fairy tales which spoke of it as a terrible place are wrong. No one can really know the forest without feeling the gentle influence of one of the strongest parts of nature. From every point of view it is one of the most helpful friends of man. Perhaps no other natural agent has done so much for the human race and has been so recklessly used and so little understood.

---

for free paper & pulp came in…Chapman, U.S.G.S. to dinner. Letters after.

2/25 Washington Some office work. Showed Secretary statement of work done—budget for next year.

3/4 Washington…wired Toumey to see if I can get him to look after the tree-planting.

3/6 New York Saw Ferris, who applied for working plan for 150,000 in Adirondacks, or said he would.

3/7 New York Talk with Mr. Boardman of the Railway Gazette, who agreed to make application for Adirondack League lands. Good talk with Miss Hewitt, & agreement to visit Fingerwood & finish working plan.

3/11 Washington Attack on Olympic Reserve by Cloes, [f.?] superintendent. Thoburn demonstrating his incapacity some more.

3/13 Washington Decided to make establishment of forestry in relation to the farm in consultation with Dodge & the Secretary. Toumey accepted position to take charge of tree planting work.

3/30 Washington Gannett decided to take the North Carolina forest census (eastern half of the state). Professor Graves here to stay a few days. Everything all right at the Division.

4/7 Washington Toumey arrived. Most satisfactory talk with him.

4/12 Washington Routine. Harry Graves left for trip in the South. Toumey to dinner. He is a first-class man.

4/13 Washington Routine. Decided with Toumey to offer assistance in planting woodlots along line of Circular 21.

4/19 Washington Addressed National Academy in P.M. on work of Division of Forestry.

4/25 Washington Routine. Dodge told me finally we are to have forest exhibit at Paris under Beau.

4/26 Washington Beau approved plans for exhibit at Paris.

4/27 Washington Finished last of Part I of my book. Prepared & sent in estimates for Paris exhibit in forestry. Routine. Golf with Harry. Dinner at Satterlee's with assorted chief justices.

5/1 Washington Binger went for information

as the best boundaries for the Rainier Reserve. Long talk with Willis, then with Gannett.

5/4 Washington Routine. Sent Binger at his request new boundaries P.R.F.R. Also did more final touches on book.

5/31 Washington Routine. Decided on student assistants for the summer.

6/1 Washington Routine. Ten exams for assistant forester came in the mail. Also half time for my book.

6/15 Washington Routine & proof. Plan of work for next year approved by Secretary. Toumey's plan approved by me.

7/9 Kansas City Last night forwarded Toumey's circular with corrections & tonight my last revise of Part I of Primer.

8/3 Ashland, Oregon On the train. Good talk with Merriam. Evening long talk with Orestus Perce, who has been planting cotton-wood for paper on islands in the Willamette. A very interesting man indeed.

8/4 San Francisco To the Occidental. Met with Dr. Merriam at California Academy of Science…Evening meeting at Press Club. Congressman Kahn & others. Admirable sentiment, & immediate result a meeting arranged for 7th with lumbermen.

8/5 San Francisco Took 9:30 train to Tamalpais with Miss Eastwood & Dr. Merriam. A capital trip. Much redwood young growth and Douglas-fir doing well on north west slope under dense shade. Came down through cataract canyon.

8/7 San Francisco Spent the day seeing people. Meeting at Chamber of Commerce at 4 to discuss work on growth of the redwood. Final result that, as proposal of Mr. Dolbeer, another meeting should be held to raise money. Dolbeer and Dollar a committee to get it up for next Monday at 2. Herbarium man from Stanford offered work on cork oak in California. Long talk with Adams in evening, agriculture writer for Chronicle.

8/8 San Francisco–Sonora …Took 8:30 train with Muir & Merriam, & (via Niles & Stockton) reached Sonora about 6:30 P.M. Hot. Last part interesting. Saw Table Mountain where Truthful James lived. Interesting talks and things to see.

8/9 Sonora–Calavaras Big Trees Started in surrey with Merriam & Muir at 6 A.M. Through old Placer County. Most interesting. Drove straight through 34 miles, stopping only to study sheep devastation along road. Within 6–8 miles of trees, & to the corner of branch road. Then through the Grove with Muir & Merriam and after supper a camp fire with them. Met Sherry & his son & found hotel admirable, & whole place enchanting. Did not see South Grove.

8/10 Big Trees to Murphy's & Sonora Left hotel about 7:30 & went on ahead to study effect of sheep. Some very interesting facts. When carriage caught up went on & we got lunch at Murphy's & dinner at Sonora. The dust something awful, especially a few miles before reaching Murphy's. Merriam & Muir told stories all the way. Two wonderful men to travel with.

8/11 Sonora–San Francisco Took 4 o'clock train & reached S.F. about 4. Dined with Muir (Merriam & I) at Muir's club, and after dinner tried to find Lowell White. Out of town. Warren Olney dined at our table, & we had a very satisfactory talk. (via Stockton & Niles) Met old J.W. Hutchings on the train and on the ferry introduced Muir & Merrian to Reinstein.

8/12 San Francisco–Redwood Canyon After finding Lowell White, we (Muir, Merriam & I) went up to Mill Valley, & were driven to the Redwood Canyon by one of White's men. Most delightful drive, & a beautiful place to see, but the redwoods not large. In P.M. relaxed and loafed. Newell turned up.

8/13 San Francisco To church with

Newell...At dinner long talk with Prichet who wants to set Hitchcock, his close personal friend, right in forest matters. I hope much from him.

8/14 San Francisco Called on William Mills again. Out. Also on Reinstein & Gleaves. I am to make plan for to spend $150,000 in forest work in California. Meeting of redwood men. Long discussion ending by subscriptions of $100 for Captain Nelson, followed by Dolbeer & others. $300 raised there. Voted to raise $1,000. Will give us free board & travel on train lines. A decided success.

8/15 Reno Took stage at Truckee. Good ride 14 miles to lake, & then capital steamer trip to Glenbrook whence stage to Carson, & train to Reno. Wonderful trip. Much devastation around this most beautiful lake. Possibility of reproduction not very good. In fact poor.

8/16 Odgen Most interesting ride around Salt Lake. Forest reserve should be made on Wasatch Range.

8/29 Washington Arrived at 6:42. Routine and annual report. Mr. Evans approved estimate for 1901 of $168,000. Mr. McGee wanted me to go to Berlin as delegate of National Geographic Society to International Geographers Congress. Secretary thought I had better stay here. I think so. Worked late over reports.

10/25 New York Saw Appleton & Gunns agent & submitted Primer.

11/5 Washington Dined with the Hagues. Mr. Hague thought I had better stick to the Division a while longer than attempt to get charge of the forest reserves.

11/6 Washington Failed to see the Secretary about consolidation of the forest work.

11/9 Washington Chiefly busy with routine & getting proposed amendment to consolidate forest work into shape.

11/10 Washington Talk with Walcott about consolidation. Showed him my amendment, of which he seemed to approve.

11/17 Washington Routine. Work on paper for Secretary to sign for The Forester. Pretty grouchy. Long ride on Jim, after which I felt better.

11/25 New Haven Met a number of prospective forest students in A.M.

11/29 Washington Newell to dinner. He told us about Rafter & advised me to take any chance (fair chance) to get hold of forest reserves without leaving Division of Forestry altogether.

1900

1/15 Washington To see Walcott about concentration...Exam for ranger approved by Procter & Seven. Talk with Jones about working plan, etc.

1/22 Washington Secretary Wilson told me Hitchcock was in favor of consolidation in Agriculture Department & McKinley also. Hermann said to be making trouble. Talk with Wadsworth, who is to see Hitchcock with Joe Cannon. Saw Senator Proctor about reprinting the Primer.

1/23 Washington Various small matters. Told Walcott & Hague the news of yesterday. Saw Wadsworth at the Capitol, who said Joe Cannon was against us, but he would arrange to see Hitchcock with him. Saw Secretary Wilson (after leaving word for Walcott as above) who said he & Hitchcock had agreed, after conference with the president, that Walcott & I should see the interested senators, & the matter would not be passed in the face of determined opposition. Told Walcott, who will see Canon & Hitchcock tomorrow.

1/24 Washington Talk with Proctor, who is in favor of consolidation in Agriculture Department. Tried to find Foster, but failed afternoon & evening. Short talk with Secretary who is very clear nothing will be attempted against opposition.

1/25 Washington Talk with Potter & Gosney about sheep in Arizona Forest Reserve. Then saw Senator Foster, who is probably against consolidation. Saw Wadsworth in P.M., who was to see Proctor & get him to see Foster.

1/27 Washington Wadsworth says Allison is ready to introduce consolidation clause in the Senate. Hale for it too.

1/30 Washington Talk with Senator Foster, who may favor consolidation scheme after all. Prepared platform for management of forest reserves which Secretary Wilson signed. Walcott proposed a plan, about which I took no action.

1/31 Washington Another talk with Senator Foster. No conclusion. Tried to find other senators & failed. Evening Elwood Mead & Coville on grazing in forest reserves.

2/1 Washington Talk with Clark, who is against transfer. P.M. saw Foster, who advised against any further agitation of transfer question, and Warren, who was for transfer. Foster had seen Clark, Shoup, & others, who were all against it. This kills it for this session.

2/2 Washington Saw Secretary & told him about transfer matter. He then advised working for a big appropriation & offered to send letter to committee. Was frustrated about defeat of transfer by a mere question of patronage (complicated by coming election.)

2/9 Washington Council of war with Harry, Sudworth, Toumey & Price tonight over plans for next year, especially about sheep and working plans in forest reserves.

2/10 Washington Sheep plans very much developed. Saw Wadsworth, who said he thought the Division perhaps get $150,000 for next year.

2/22 Washington Miss Bigelow came. I wrote letters, took a ride, had a very good talk with Mr. DeVries of California after dinner about the Calaveras Big Trees & other forest problems. He favors consolidation.

4/16 Washington Appeared before Senate Committee with Secretary Wilson. They decided to give Division of Forestry $80,000 for lump sum and to stick to it. So I suppose that is safe. Also learned today of $2,000 appropriation New York state for work plan of Division…Evening at dinner & after long talk with Holmes about Southern Appalachian National Park. Decided on working for appropriation for investigation.

4/17 Washington Arranged with Luebkert to be treasurer of A.F.A. Learned from Wyles we can have plenty of room in his building next year. Wrote letter for Secretary's signature to Committee on Agriculture & Forestry in reference to Appalachian Park. Ride with Harry.

1902

1/24 Washington Minnesota Forest Reserve mainly. Cass Lake delegation called, & reasserted entire satisfaction with forest reserve plan. Long discussion of estimated cost of forestry over lumbering with Ayers & Roth, & of proposed amendment to the Morris bill.

2/10 Washington Went to Senator Hansbrough's after dinner, & had long talk about irrigation. His position generally sound. Expressed himself definitely as in favor of transfer of forest reserves to Department of Agriculture.

2/25 Washington Busy day on the Philippine land & forest laws all day, nearly. Long talk with Allen after hours and with Price after dinner.

3/6 Washington Fairfield Osborn came in. Decided not to ask for his appointment as Superintendent Forest Reserves. Later with Osborn to see President. Talk about consolidation of science work & new building for National Museum. President said Mondell was non-committed about transfer of forest reserves.

F.H. Newell, chief engineer of the Reclamation Service, and Gifford Pinchot, chief forester, Forest Service, in the field in Wyoming. As friends, scientific colleagues, and political allies, Newell and Pinchot formed a tight linkage between federal forest and water policies. Forest Service.

President himself insisted of great importance. President getting in habit of calling me by first name.

3/7 Washington Saw Senator Clapp in evening about Minnesota forest fires. He is very anxious to have bill pass.

3/8 Washington Long talk at War Department with Messer Lacey, Cooper & Edwards & McGowan or McGown about legislation for the Philippine Islands. Then spoke to full Committee on Agriculture in defense of my estimates. Bill now gives bureau $282,360. Put in a word on Appalachian Forest Reserve.

5/29 Washington Office early. Student assis-

tants & other routine work. Saw Senator Platt of New York about printing Woodsman's Handbook…Saw T.R. about adding acres to Yellowstone Park Reserve (extended) to protect A.A. Anderson's water supply.

6/10 Boston Transfer bill beaten today by a speech of Joe Cannon.

6/12 Washington Back to the office. Everyone was rather grim about the loss of the transfer bill. Secretary Wilson said he wanted to know if I was [OK] & the lunch mess had a great time over it. Wilson advised letting our money all come back from the Land Office. Harry Graves came this morning. Evening discussing promotions etc. with Graves & Price.

Graves decided, I believe, to publish American Journal of Forestry at my urging.

6/13 Washington Lunched with T.R. & Garfield, & discussed forest situation and G.L.O.

6/14 Washington Told Sudworth he must reduce subject dealt with in his division. Hard talk, but came out well.

6/16 Washington Office from 7:45 to 6:25. Also saw President with Walcott to secure irrigation work for U.S.G.S. T.R. had already written to Hitchcock to that effect, & said so before we could say a word. We went back to praise Maxwell.

6/19 Washington Note from Moody & with him to see President. Waited 9:30 to 12:30. Then Moody protested against appointment of Dufur as supervisor in Mt. Hood region. I asked T.R. to encourage Maxwell to keep us in irrigation work.

6/20 Washington Decided to try for forest reserve in S.E., Indian Territory. Told Luebkert I could promote him only to $2,000, & Adams not at all. Both took it well.

7/2 Washington Routine. Saw Hitchcock about the Chippewas work. Met M. Schaeffer (?) great French geographer. Also Ross, state engineer of Idaho. Saw T.R. with Dwight Heard. Also got Santa Catalina reserve proclamation signed.

7/4 Washington Long talk with Wylie at the Cosmos Club...about the cooperation in place between our bureaus...Luebkert came for talk about correspondence. Walcott to dinner. Drive with him & von Schrenk. Long talk with the latter. Told him we must agree on what we are to publish, & what, Galloway.

7/5 Washington Reached office about 7:50. Arranged with Civil Service Commission [for] special board of examiners in Bureau of Forestry for student assistants, & got Secretary to request it. Arranged with Gannett that he

would not mind if I changed boundaries he proposed for forest reserves when T.R. sends them to me.

8/27 Washington Conferences with von Schrenk, Bean, & others. Told Professor Moore about the overauthorization of our appropriation, on purpose, & he said he would look out for us if the matter came up.

10/27 Manilla Down to Ahern's office early. Attended to mail. No word from home or the Bureau, but two cables which I do not understand...one from Price reading "If they disprove unchanged."

11/21 Manilla Landed about 4, and with Ahern home via Bureau of Forestry for mail. Everything going finely at home...Estimates approved unchanged by Secretary. Bureau running well.

1903

1/8 Washington Went straight from the station, where I arrived at 10:30 two hours late. With Price to the House Agriculture Committee & there talked for nearly two hours about the work of the Bureau, the need for more money, & the Philippines...Then to see the Secretary, who greeted me with "Well old fellow I'm glad to see you back." He was most kind. Then to the Bureau. Everything in fine shape. Delightful to get back. Had some good talk with the men, & came away before five. I do not see that anything except the transfer has suffered, & perhaps not that, because I have been away.

1/9 Washington Up in fine season. Stopped to see Beveridge on the way down, & had a good short talk. Took up the work of the office gladly. Consultations. Holmes came in about Appalachian Reserve. Made recommendation for Puerto Rico Reserve. Hiram Jones, Baker, & a lot of others came in. Saw Walcott at the Survey, & the Great Basin lunch mess. Then to lunch, with Mamee, at the White House.

Moody, Ware, General Wood, Wister, & others. A real good time. Then to the office till after six.

1/10 *Washington* Work on the Primer, & then to the office…With Walcott & committee of American Geographical Society & see Speaker with them about Appalachian bill, but failed. To see Wadsworth with Holmes & White of West Virginia about same bill. He was not hopeful, but endorsed conference with House leaders. Said I could not have whole estimate…Talk with R.P. Hayes about Appalachian Bill. He seems weak.

1/11 *Washington* A.A. Anderson and his sister Mrs. Caflin to lunch. Long talk about the Yellowstone Reserve. Anderson doing exceedingly well. Says Richards is in favor of the transfer of the forest reserves. Anderson advocated a separate division in Secretary's office at once, which was against the law last year, but OK now, Vandevanter says. Senator Mitchell at dinner. Talked most about Hawaii, but would not discuss sheep. I was not well impressed as to his candor & judgment. To White House. Met there Judge/Justice & Mrs. Holmes, & had excellent talk with T.R. Said he would ask Dalyett & Grosvenor to lunch, & there give me chance at them on Appalachian Bill. Instructed me to see Richards & tell him T.R. wants transfer this session.

1/12 *Washington* Office at 8:30, home at six. Holmes about Appalachian Reserve. Delegates from New Hampshire at 10. H. James 2nd, Dr. Merriman, Mr. Edmonds. Discussion till 11:30 to try & keep them from attacking Congress for a park in the White Mountains. Then saw Beveridge about forest matters in New Mexico. Allison about Appalachian Reserve. He promised to see the Speaker about it. Said Holmes plan to limit expense per acre would help very much. Saw Foster about proposed reserve in Skagit Valley & timber test. He favors

transfer now fully, he says. Took New Mexico delegation to see Secretary Wilson, who backed me up superbly. Long talk after with Commissioner Richards, who is fully in favor of the transfer, & in response to President's request is going to see what he can do to bring it about. Is for civil service reform all through & against patronage; & refused to help Mondel keep in his discredited men in Wyoming Reserve.

1/22 *Washington* Decided after consulting Secretary to see Secretary of the Interior & ask for return of our men. Morning spent in seeing men at Capitol. Henry C. Smith of Michigan repeated what he told me last Spring, & that Roth brought up subject of transfer in conversation, & made quite an argument against it.

1/27 *Washington* Talk with Price & Bruce about the Minnesota Forest Reserve, & to see Governor Richards w. Bruce to commend Warren (against complaints). Long talk with von Schrenk, who is doing finely.

1/30 *Washington* Office at nine. Corrected plan of forest investigation for Commission of National Academy & turned it in…Spent much time trying to see Senators Heitfeld & Simmons about appropriation for Bureau, Forestry & Agriculture bill. Failed.

2/12 *Washington* …With Becker arranged correction in report of [what] National Academy Commission does to exclude classification of public lands as mineral or agricultural.

2/16 *Washington* Routine, etc. Session with Vandevanter on rights of Department of Agriculture on forest experiment stations set aside by President, & saw about getting a clause on that subject in the Agriculture Bill. Also saw Secretary.

2/17 *New York* …dinner of New York farmers, where I spoke on Forestry for Farmers. Made a fair talk & was asked many questions.

2/18 New York …Dinner at Fairfield Osborn's. There to meet me (most proud) were, as Osborn said, the heads of scientific work in New York—Buinpus, Woodard, Collett, Thompson, Hornaday, etc. Also Madison Grant & Grant La Farge. On way home Madison explained that we ought to get together & agree on a general forest policy, which I declined on the ground that my policy was fixed. He objects to the cutting.

2/20 Washington Various routine. Chopping with Sampson & Garfield. At dinner Maxwell & Newell. Newell suggested plan for possibly getting reserves transferred this year by amendment to Committee to Agriculture Bill, which has already passed the House. Shall try it.

2/21 Washington To see Proctor, & got him to approve amendment. Then got T.R. to write & ask Warren to help Proctor get it on the bill. This on slip with amendment on it. Got Richards to write under it that he had no objection. Then took it to Proctor, Committee on Agriculture then sitting. He added it to another amendment on management of forest experiment stations, & the two were passed wholly without comment, because of very skillful handling by him. Committee also increased appropriation to estimate. Later saw Warren, who said amendment was not distasteful to him.

2/24 Washington Till about 2 busy with transfer amendment in Agriculture Bill, until it went out to the floor of the Senate. Hard luck.

3/2 Washington …To Capitol to see Scott of Kansas about proposed reserve in that state. He said he would get the petition I handed him signed.

3/9 Washington Good talk with Page Morris, who understands that Bureau of Forestry has done everything it could in Minnesota. Also with President & W.A. Richards about interview of Richards against forest reserve policy.

5/8 Cass Lake, Minnesota Talk with "Reverend Smith" & then with Bernard, who professed a desire to have everything sweet between himself and the bureau, & repudiated the obnoxious interviews.

6/17 Washington Most of day at home with Price on organization & promotion.

6/19 Washington Talks with Suter, Coville, von Schrenk, Price & Lott Bailey about Cornell Forest School, just abolished. Nothing to do about it. Talk with von Schrenk [about] his coming in to Bureau of Forestry, which, after a talk with Galloway, who took exactly my position, he decided to do fully, instead of merely being assigned to this work of ours by Galloway. This is a real step.

7/27 Grand Rapids …Roth & Professor Davis got on [train]. Talk about further work for Roth, who wanted to make general examination of northern Michigan rather than of the new forest reserve. Davis agreed. At Grand Rapids met Garfield for the first time. Also Wildey. Smith of the Agriculture College came also. Long conference, end of which was my strong opinion that Roth should make working plan for forest reserve at once, since he is the forest warden, & future reserves depend on use made of this one. Trouble likely between Agriculture College & its forest school & University & its forest school. To Garfield's for supper. Saw his interesting plantation. Pleasant talk after.

10/12 Cass Lake …Much work on train. Dictated report to Chief on Wyoming forest matters, etc.

10/13 Cass Lake In a launch to meet Bruce & Senator Oneil. Met them. Much talk about the reserve with Bruce. Back in P.M. Bernard, Hartley & Johnson announce the new town Richards to Bruce & me. Major Scott came up from the Agency & explained the serious Indian situation, caused by emissaries of the lumbermen. Joe

Leidig (or Lydig?) told me just where the trouble came from & how he knew. Shevlin & ??? through Allen & West. Later met Charles Weyerhaeuser. Thacker & Bell, who applied from working plan on what they own of the 500,000 acres of land on which they & their friends control the timber in Idaho. A busy day.

10/20 Washington All well at the office. Fixed up Minnesota rules with Price & Shaw. Saw the Chief. Lunch with Mrs. R., T.R., & Governor Chamberlain of Oregon, and explained forest reserve policy to him, to which he was but is no longer in opposition.

10/21 Washington Completed the Minnesota rules…Then reported to T.R. on summer's work, told him about Shevlin…

10/22 Washington …Long talk with Secretary Hitchcock. Told him all about Shevlin's doings in northern Minnesota. He said he would recommend transfer of reserve in his annual report…An intensely busy day. Delivered signed rules for Minnesota Forest Reserve logging to Secretary Hitchcock, who I hope will speedily approve. Important progress today.

10/23 Washington Office, etc. P.M. on forms in use & who used in Bureau.

12/11 Washington …Saw Richards. Sale of Chippewa pine most successful.

12/16 Washington …Then with Olmsted & Potter about reserves, then with Arnold Hague. Called on Mrs. Proctor, whence Ethel dropped me at Mondell's, who had got the transfer bill unanimously reported for the Committee on Public Lands today. A great thing.

1904

1/1 Washington …Consult with Newell, Bien, Bowers about lieu lands…Long talk with Richards, who approves my plan as to lieu lands.

1/2 Washington …2-hour talk with the Speaker about public lands and the transfer.

The latter he seems to oppose, but not finally. Then conference with Richards & Newell and tried with them in P.M. to see T.R. to make recommendation about railroad lands in forest reserves. Failed.

1/3 Proctor, Vermont …Wrote T.R. & J.W. Wadsworth about the transfer.

1/7 Chicago Worked & read. In Chicago saw Sterling, & dined with Boothe, Maxwell (host) and Newell. Could not see James, for I had to see Maxwell, who is getting very edgy, Newell says, because he is not recognized as much as he thinks right after what he has done for irrigation.

1/10 Portland Many conferences on train. Tim Kinney of Rock Springs, Jesse M. Smith of Utah, Hagenbarth, & many others (Collister etc.). A very interesting day on that account. Talk with Senator Warren.

1/11 Portland Many talks with many people. Getting started, Hagenbarth introduced countless [others]. Lunch with Maxwell as guests of Brainard Taylor then also P.M. Newell made his talk to woolgrowers about our work as commission members, and I, mine as to forest policy. Sentiment strong for reserves, and so far as I could [see] exhibited unanimously for policy I stated. Much favorable comment, none adverse. Evening talk with Governor Chamberlain & the land board, who all believed lieu provision the most serious evil in present laws. Governor & Dunbar for moderation of the 3 laws. Judge? Woods for desert law, & in general for very liberal policy. Board apparently anxious for closer relations with Interior Department, so as to get immediate information & be in touch. They have stopped sale of lands in forest reserves & favor strongly our policy.

1/12 Portland Newell taken sick with pains in back, & in bed. Moody came. He worked like a Trojan all through to give us help of all kinds (written up Jan. 18). Lunch with him.

Meeting delegates all day. Dinner with the Burrells, & in evening attended reception for delegates. Then long conference with Gosney about reserves.

1/13 Portland At 9 [Riscon?], of who I am not sure [about] an observation, then Judson of O.R.N. (useless), Governor Wells of Utah, Saunders of Denver (wide interests in cattle, & sheep, & especially in northern Arizona north of Cañon & said to be very wise), Isenbery (a kindly but not very vigorous man), Buckley (timber man strong against frauds, but pretty wild) & others. Lunch with Bob Platt. Fine time. At 2:30 conference till five with 29 representatives cattle & sheep men on control of range. 28 to 1 in favor of government control [over] summer range under wise management. A most important meeting. Jasteo presided.

5–6:30 conference with 18 cattle & sheep men users of Blue Mountains, as to method of settling quarrels. All favored government but one (Hanley).

6:30 dinner with Moody & McCormack. Talk & thought any repeal at present session unwise for political reasons, but believed these laws should be modified. 8:30 Isenberg & others about forest reserve matters. And more besides. A very hard day. Newell still sick.

1/14 Portland At nine met Bartrum, superintendent south part of Cascade Reserve, and talked. Then Cupp & others, & at ten Newhouse, who gave us most interesting talk (Newell & me) about public land matters in Oregon. Then others—at 12:30 went to lunch with Walter Burrell, editor Carroll of the Journal, & Capt. Voorhees, a cousin of Walters. At 2:30 to the convention. Then Newell spoke & then B.B. Brooks of Casper made a plea for state cession. Then long & most satisfactory talk with Jasteo & others (including Gosney about resolutions) and after dinner with him saw Clarke of the Bureau of Forestry & others about political situation in N.E. Oregon.

Political cartoon published in the Denver *Post*, October 17, 1908, reflecting western opposition to Pinchot's policies. Pinchot scrapbooks, Pinchot Collection, Library of Congress.

1/15 On train Pleasant ride through Oregon & past Shasta, which was superb. Further talk with Wautland, who explained N.P. system of leasing summer range, & other facts of its land policy, and M.K. Parsons, of Denver, who disagrees much with Wautland. Also with Charlton of Colorado…Feeling pretty weary after the meeting. Loafed a good deal.

1/16 Sacramento Arrive Sacramento about 5 A.M. Mr. Trye at the station to meet us. Then to Sut[t]er Club, where Governor Pardee (laid up at home) entertained us. Then a good talk with Melich at the State House, & later (at 11) a conference with the state officials. P.M. Newell & I spoke to Sacramento Valley Development Association on irrigation and forestry, & on public land inquiry, & then had conference with Governor Pardee, and a most satisfactory one. He is for withdrawal of all timberlands in California, so as to prevent further Timber & Stone fraudulent entries. Said that, after first howl, sentiment of state would be full for it in 2 months after action.

1/17 Reno Awake early, & saw the sunrise on the Sierras. Riverside Hotel. To church with Newell & Dahl. A capital sermon. After lunch drove out to Governor John Sparks' Alamo Ranch. Sparks is the best type of the freebooting cowman I have seen. He showed us his Herefords, & about his ranch. He has 2 buffalo. Sparks wants nothing done about the lands laws. Say the state should keep all the rights it has (meaning its citizens).

1/18 Reno Left Reno 8:45, got off at Salvia, & after visiting Reclamation Service camp (saw Swift McGregor) spent the day with Newell, Savage & Taylor looking over construction work of the Truckee Canal. Fearfully dusty, but a fine day just the same. Newell ought to be very joyful over the progress. Works very large. Weather cold, & views superb. Dinner in construction camp.

1/19 Ogden–Salt Lake Work on the train. Arrive Salt Lake about 4. Governor Wells, State Engineer Doremus, & Cal Howells came around, and after seeing Newell at U.S.G.S. office we agreed on meeting of State Land Board at 8. Present Wells & Byron Groo, secretary of BC [?], also Doremus, Newell, several others, including Reclamation Service man Ross among others. Doremus for local control, but for forest reserves meantime. Also governor, who ended by assuring me of his support. Groo opposed to reserves, illogical & contradictory. Final result that opposition comes only from State Land Board, who want to continue selling land in areas now reserved or withdrawn, a policy shown at meeting to be fatal to the welfare of the farmers. We can safely neglect his opposition. Called on Cal Nelson of S.F. Tribune & Mr. McKay of Herald. Real progress today, I think.

1/20 Salt Lake–Provo After breakfast to Bingham Junction to big meeting (about 250) about Reclamation Service's Utah Lake project. Good talk with Col. Holmes & Senator Bennion, who both favor government forest reserves. So did the meeting on show of hands, with only 4 adverse votes, and I fixed one of those later. Meeting unanimously for Utah Lake scheme. Returned to late lunch at Commercial Club, then met Governor Wells at tabernacle for a special organ recital for us. Effect simply superb. Then called on Editor [of] Deseret News, and [illeg.] Joseph Smith, head of the Morm[o]n Church. Short meeting with Arid Land Commission, & to Provo, where in evening a meeting of 150 was unanimously for government's forest reserve policy. Met countless people…A most interesting day.

1/21 On train …at work catching up. Also Primer II. Talk with Newell & Savage about latter coming into Reclamation Service, and later with Savage alone. Busy pretty much all day, but got little done. Arrive Denver at 11:40.

1/22 Denver Dictation, then visit with Newell, Savage, & Fellows to Governor Peabody, who wants more forest reserves right away. Also talk with Woodruff about exchange of state lands [illeg.] in forest reserves. There to examine operators meeting at Chamber of Commerce. They want the facts on the ground to govern, which is not the case now in granting patents. Then lunch of about 100, and long session in P.M. to hear discussion of land laws, forest reserves, etc. Fred Johnson & Clark Meeker the most sensible talkers. Few others…Supper on train. Governor Peabody's attitude most fortunate.

1/23 Cheyene All called on Governor Chatterton, who is a yellow dog, & then an all-day session in the Hall of the Representatives with men from every county in the state but 2, & they were heard from by messages. Land laws in A.M., all opposed to repeal forest reserves and irrigation. P.M. no serious kick. General feeling of irritation at government control of anything in Wyoming. Unanimous desire for [illeg.] to state. A very well run meeting (by governor), and every man who spoke (except Taliaferro, Hansen, & one or two others) had clear cut & defensible ideas. Ended at 6 P.M.…Clark declared against state session. A fine nervy thing to do. Evening conference with Chatterton, Tyran, Gilchrist, on reclamation projects in Wyoming. Chatterton lied & acted as he naturally would. A very tiresome day.

1/26 Washington …Got in after midnight.

1/28 Washington At eleven saw & had talk with Hemenway. Told him we could make Forest Service self supporting in three or four years if they give us export law & chance to charge for grazing. Saw Mondell & then he saw Hemenway & report his opposition withdrawn. That probably amounts to certainty bill will pass.

1/29 Washington …Conference with Secretary, Assistant Secretary Colonel Burch, & Whitney about taking King as auditor. Arranged that nothing happens for a month, that if King comes he comes as auditor not in charge of accounts, & that we are not to pay, at least this year.

1/30 Washington …Talk with Secretary Wilson about work when reserves come over. Gave outline of plan, which he approved

2/2 Washington Routine. Senator Clark of Wyoming spoke most appreciatively of the forest reserve sentiment work done in last 8 months. Talks with A.A. Anderson, Fairchild, Major Scott, etc. Mondell said he would try for special order for transfer bill. Price has investigation of work begun & not completed well in hand. Scott about selection by Minnesota of heavily timbered pine lands for swamp lands in Minnesota Forest Reserve.

2/3 Washington James came to breakfast with his son Frank. Talk about some Cherokee lumbering matters (bonds for railroad he was considering) & then session with Richards on lieu lands.

2/9 Washington Routine. Appeared before Senate Committee on Agriculture which added $50,000 to appropriation thus giving full estimates. Evening work at home, catching up with correspondence.

2/12 Washington Routine & catching up. Went to thank Senator Proctor for increased appropriation in Senate bill. Mondell said transfer bill now sure to pass the House… Evening Allan & Ripley re Colorado reserve. Walcott had told me in P.M. that Teller wanted to see me about Colorado Reserve.

2/13 Washington Long talk with Teller at the Riggs. He began fiercely, but ended by saying he was not opposed to forest reserves. I think he will not make much more trouble.

3/10 Washington Long conference with von

Schrenk, Price, & Sherrard. Arrange faculty procedure in New Haven central work & fixed terms of cooperation for his work. Long talk with Newell about terms of forest reserve exchange with railroads.

3/16 Washington …walked down town with Garfield. Talk with Bliss about Tahoe Reserve. To Capitol & saw A.J. Beveridge about Nelson's opposition to transfer, & he saw Nelson.

3/28 Washington …saw Newell & arranged with Blanchard for an article on forest reserves for Idaho papers. Office till 6:15, & then after dinner conference at White House of Committee on Organization of Science with T.R. & Allison, & Cannon. Bowles made an admirable statement of our case, & T.R. agreed with us fully. So did Allison and Cannon so far as the power for the president to make the transfers, but neither thought it could be done at this session, although Cannon suggested a way by which Allison might get it tacked on to a bill. We left finally with the idea in their minds that nothing would be done this year, in ours that it must. And it must. Pretty tired.

3/31 Washington Routine, etc. To see Lacey to get him to push immediate introduction transfer bill with Cannon. No success. Talk with Wadsworth on same lines. He will do all he can…Home in time to dress for banquet National Wholesale Lumber Dealers Association. Speakers Shaw, Cortelyou, Cannon, Heyburn, & G.P. Made sort of average talk, in part refuting Heyburn.

4/1 Washington Meeting with Richards & Newell at Cosmos Club. Finally decided to leave clause forbidding use of Commerce Clause in act opening agricultural lands in forest reserves, which Newell & I wanted, & Richards wanted out, to assist Hansbrough. Then meeting with T.R., & decision to report 3 bills on Monday at 9:45 to him for transmission. Then home, where

Mrs. Hobson had told people of some pleasant things Taft said to her about me.

4/6 Washington …Richards about transfer. T.B. Walker, who is against retroactive laws affecting forest reserves…T.R. about Heyburn.

4/8 Washington Long conference with G.G. Hartley, who wants us to give up about forty thousand acres of the Minnesota Forest Reserve. Had to turn him down. Conference with men from the Biltmore School, who want Dr. Schenck to give better preparation for the government work. 3 P.M. Kittredge had a hearing before Senate Committee on Public Lands. He made a long talk, basing opposition to transfer on mineral interests, followed. Committee voted to postpone whole matter till next December. Nelson, Kearns, Gamble, Fulton, Detrich, Berry, Gibson, McEnery for Hansbrough, Dubois, Newlands, Bard, against. That settles it for this session.

6/6 Washington To the office early, & then to see T.R., who wanted to show me some correspondence with Heyburn of Idaho. He is certainly a most unsatisfactory person.

6/7 Washington Catching up. Started to get our salaries…on a new & better basis.

9/14 Washington At home nearly all day catching up, & a little on the second part of the Primer. Then to office. Long talk in evening with Garfield & Smith about labor & capital, & the administration of the General Land Office. Newell suggested today a club or biweekly meeting of chiefs to discuss problems of administration.

9/16 Washington Routine. Arranged with Richards for Big Horn Reserve examination by Bargett & Koch. Walk with Dol & Jim Garfield…Busy day. Good talk with Secretary Wilson.

9/29 Washington Routine. Long talk with von Schrenk about use of coop funds.

9/30 Washington With Galloway & Wood

decided von Schrenk [not] being present, he should give up being chief of products, & that all cooperative money should be depleted first in Washington. Rather a strenuous session.

10/5 Washington To see the President about appropriations & the Secretary later. I hope the Bureau will not suffer…Long talk with George & Dol in evening, mainly about successor to von Schrenk as chief of Products. Am uncertain, but inclined toward Chittenden.

11/5 Washington Long talk with Hatt[?], in which he agreed with my position as to Dr. von Schrenk. Saw T.R. & lunched at home… Dinner en famille at the White House, & a long talk about election & other matters. T.R. agreed to classify the Forest Service immediately after election…

11/9 Washington With Jim Garfield to see the Chief…Busy catching up, & with organizing Office of Forest Products…Many telegrams sent & received. Everyone seems to be jubilant, & no wonder. The electoral votes stand 343 to 133. An amazing vote of confidence, in honest frankness.

11/2 Washington Long talk with Ahern & then rather stormy interview with von Schrenk in which I was obliged to speak plainly.

11/19 Houston Arrived about 6:30. Von Schrenk & Frank Thompkins met me. Want to go to Somerville with them. Train time change. Went to see plant of southern pine for pickling ties & timbers. P.M. to theater. Then talk with von Schrenk about organization of Products. Not very satisfactory. I may have to let him go.

12/2 Washington The transfer bill passed the House.

12/13 Washington …to see Mondell about the passage of the transfer bill.

12/14 Washington …Mead getting office in Atlantic Building into shape. At office till after six.

12/21 Washington …Agreed with Hall…on

reorganization plan for Products…At White House Allison said science reorganization bill could not pass this session, but he would introduce it at beginning of next Congress.

1905

4/25 Washington Routine. Consultation with Dubois about Heyburn's attack on forest reserves in Idaho. Dubois will make a statement. Conference with Price & Sherrard about forest maps and organization of work on the reserves. P.M. talk with Hall & Dr. Deans, who agreed to take charge of our chemical work at $1,500 a year.

4/26 Washington A hard day of grinding routine etc. Planning the new map system with Gannett.

5/1 Washington Dictating at home, & then office routine. Appointment of technical assistants & inspectors to forest reserves. J.A. Holmes came in after dinner & described his plan for an advisory council of presidents of associations interested in his testing work. He suggested I should adopt it, which I shall be only too glad to do.

5/18 New York 2nd breakfast at Yale Club with Dol & long talk about publicity. We decided we must "make the necessity for forest preservation a household commonplace throughout the U.S."

5/23 Washington …Dol & I talked much about our new plan to force adoption of forestry throughout U.S. by force of public opinion.

5/24 Washington Reuss of AT&T Company down for the day. Long talk about von Schrenk, whom he wants back & is to see. Consultation with Moody & others about the right to charge for products of reserves & about arrests.

6/2 Washington …Heard that Russell had prepared letter for signature of Attorney Gen-

Political cartoon in the Denver *Post*, August 11, 1909, reflecting western opposition to the national forests. Pinchot Scrapbooks, Pinchot Collection, Library of Congress.

eral to say the Secretary of Agriculture can charge for use of forest reserves.

6/3 Washington Much conference with Holmes' advisory Commission on Testing. Gave them a lunch (16 in all) & Bureau of Forestry came in formally as a part of the general plan. Conference with Secretary about continuing special fiscal agent. He agreed, but said see Evans. Also talk with him & Galloway about von Schrenk, in which Secretary agreed with me altogether.

7/5 Washington …Getting red tape out of Section of Forest Reserves.

10/16 Washington …Evening a long talk with Grubb of Colorado on fishing first, & then on public sentiment in Colorado as to the charge for grazing. He advised cutting it out altogether.

11/3 Washington Mail, conference with Wollman, Hammond, & Marbury, representing Houston Oil Company, who want a man to carry out the working plan. Another with Potter about grazing, and with Cutter about Forestry & Irrigation etc. Secretary Wilson later said he would be satisfied to have all agriculture publications sold if all other departments were treated that way.

11/16 Washington …Lunch with Potter. We decided not to abandon grazing fee, & to make no public decision on paying questions till after the meeting on December 1. Long talk with Coville, who wants to have prepared book on useful plants of Panama. Secretary's report before dinner & after. Also mail after. Dol Smith at dinner…I have been foolish not to get Secretary's material done sooner.

11/27 Washington Intensely busy getting ready to leave. Told Senator Warren in strict confidence that I would not put Anderson back on the Yellowstone. He promised to keep it private. A man named Trowbridge, I saw twice about rights of way for Edison Power Company in southern California. Agreed to certain principles, but refused to consider his bill till I return. I'd not read it.

1906

2/28 Washington George Woodruff & I had a conference with Smoot about his reply to Heyburn. Arranged with Wadsworth that I would agree to omit the $15,000 from the Idaho battle bill in the Senate. We agreed to give me a hearing on Lacey's game bill.

3/1 Washington New organization in effect today—3 districts & all chiefs of offices signing their own forest reserve mail. Conference with Burkett on grazing bill & with Carter on agricultural entry in forest reserve bill.

3/24 Washington Before Senate Committee on Public Lands at 10:30. Hansbrough, Nelson, Carter, Clark, Smoot, Flint, & later Fulton & Newlands. Got all the changes I wanted, but these included provision for estimates from Forest Reserve Fund after 1908 (June 30). Had seen Allison at nine this morning, & he approved my plan. Bill included 10% of receipts to the states for the counties. Lunch with John Reynolds, & all afternoon perfecting the bill at the Committee till nearly seven.

3/25 Washington …Work with Woodruff on Timber & Stone repeal clauses approved with Hansbrough.

3/29 Washington …After lunch to office & to see Secretary who agreed for me to sign contracts if McCabe said it was legal, & McCabe did.

10/23 Washington F.S. work again. Not very much to do.

11/9 Washington …Had long conference with Woodruff and Peck, general counsel for CM&STP. He suggested a 500 foot strip cleared by the railroad to guard against fire.

11/10 Washington Routine catching up. Refused sale on Cascade Reserve. 1.2 million board feet at $1.00. Said I would not consider less than $2.

1907

1/28 Washington Found everything in good shape in the office. Price & Woodruff have handled the work beautifully.

4/1 Washington Finally got the new organization into Branches fairly settled.

11/21 Washington …Told Garfield and Shipp of my new scheme to assemble all parts of the conservation problem in the Department of Agriculture, perhaps under the name of Department of Natural Resources.

11/24 Washington …Lunch with Jordan (of N.Y.), Armsby, etc. Carroll D. Wright meeting on Committee on Organization of Agricultural Research. I suggested joint advisory board for Department, & Agricultural Colleges & Stations …States rights very strong in subcommittee report of Armsby & Jordan.

12/2 Washington Went partly over Hall's admirable report on southern Appalachian and White Mountains.

12/5 Washington Routine. Suggested to McGee and Newell idea of a Conservation League to be composed of R&H Cong., Irrigation Congress, Mining Congress, etc., etc.

12/16 Washington …To Department to attend meeting of chiefs to discuss proposed Hall of Records. G℘

Yale Forest School

"The best on earth"

The Yale University Forest School accepted its first students in the fall semester of 1900. The school was funded by a $150,000 endowment gift from the Pinchot family, an amount that would shortly be doubled. Henry S. Graves, assistant chief of the U.S. Division of Forestry under Gifford Pinchot, was its dean.

The Yale Forest School initially had as competitors only the school at Cornell University, where Bernhard E. Fernow was dean, and Carl A. Schenck's one-year program at the Biltmore Forest School. The Cornell and Biltmore schools had been founded two years earlier, and schools in Michigan, Pennsylvania, California, Washington, and other states would appear by 1910. But Yale led and set the standard for the others to attain. The Yale forestry faculty were among the most prestigious, and their textbooks were adopted nationwide. When Lyle F. Watts, a University of Michigan graduate, became chief of the Forest Service in 1943, he was the first not to have a Yale degree.

Pinchot graduated from Yale in 1889 and remained a Yale booster, and a fan of the football team, for the remainder of his life. Thus, it is a bit of a surprise to see diary entries for 1894, 1895, and 1896 about establishing a forestry school in New York City at Columbia University. The entry for April 23, 1896, breaks the New York train of thought, as we read, "Talk with Professor Marsh as to forest department at Yale," which Pinchot would head. We see no more of Columbia.

The academic world was simpler then, and a family decision reported in January 1900 to endow the Yale School resulted in a degree-granting program in the fall. Included in the package was a forest school camp at Grey Towers; the entries reporting on the Grey Towers summer camp show well the Pinchot family's delight in the school.

Shortly, Pinchot would attempt to raise money to endow a companion school of irrigation at Yale. Having both schools made a lot of sense, given the strong political and scientific linkages between forests and water. After all, Congress had authorized creation of the national forest system primarily to protect western watersheds. The

Forest Service Organic Act passed in 1897 and the Reclamation Act only five years later in 1902, after clearing the same congressional committees. Scientists in the U.S. Geological Survey—John Wesley Powell, WJ McGee, Frederick Newell, and Arnold Hague—plus Bernhard Fernow in the Division of Forestry had been instrumental in informing Congress about the tight relationship between forests and water. Newell would become chief engineer for the Reclamation Service, which initially was a branch of the Geological Survey. The Forest Service Organic Act was actually an appropriations measure for the Geological Survey, and Pinchot was personally close to Newell, Hague, and McGee. Nevertheless, Pinchot could find little interest in establishing a complementary irrigation program at Yale.

Pinchot would lecture at Yale from time to time, usually about his own experiences in creating forest reserves and developing his agency. We can imagine that the students were much impressed by these first-hand accounts. We can also imagine Pinchot's crusading tone, given his report that Yale President Arthur Hadley "approved entirely of my making political talks here."

Pinchot's interest in Yale went beyond that of the Forest School, and he routinely talked with university officials about conditions and funding. Whenever he could, and he generally did, he returned to New Haven for his class reunion, and the later entries include a count of how many of the class of 1889 "were left." Yale was important to Pinchot, and Pinchot was important to Yale.

1894
12/4 New York To see Johnson & Morton about Forest School for New York State.

1895
1/14 New York A hurried day. Saw President Low in A.M. about forest school.
1/15 New York All day, practically, on paper for N.Y. farmers & scheme for a forest school.
1/17 New York Forest School scheme.
1/18 New York Forest School schedule.

1896
1/22 New York Evening talks at Century with Stiles and Britton, who broached forest school scheme.

3/3 New York …Professor Britton at 3:30, about forest school, of which he wants me to be director if it is founded.
3/6 New York …4:30 meeting with President Low, William D. Dodge, & Professor Benson regarding a forest school.
3/9 New York …Britton to dinner. We made scheme for Forest Department in Columbia, using practically mine of last winter.
3/12 New York …Britton came in about the Columbia matter.
4/23 New York Talk with Professor Marsh as to forest department at Yale. He said Farman, Brush, Dwight, & he were strongly in favor of one, & approved of me for the place.

1900

1/27 Washington This evening a capital talk with Father about the Yale forest school. He is for having it start next fall. Believes strongly in it as a fine thing for the family to do.

1/29 Washington Father left at eleven, after deciding finally in favor of the Yale Forest School, with Grey Towers in the plan.

2/3 New York–New Haven–New York Decided in family conference to give $150,000, and use of forest, etc. at Grey Towers for 21 years, to Yale for forest school. Harry & I submitted plan to Hadley, Ray Palmer, and Brewer. Fully approved to use Marsh house for the school. Most satisfactory talk. Governing board to consist of Hadley, Brewer, Graves, Sudworth, and me.

2/4 New York Saw Harry Stimson about deed of gift & grant…

1902

6/8 New Haven To the Forest School after breakfast with George Seymour, where Toumey showed us the improvements. The whole building is now used for instruction. Then to Chafee (late) and after lunch to see Hadley with whom I arranged for Harry to have two thousand straight from the corporation, I agreeing to put $40,000 additional endowment March 1st, 1903, or return the money. He told me & George of John Hays Hammond's advisory professorship, and we discussed a school of irrigation. I was instructed to see Newell about it.

6/18 New Haven …Took 6:20 train, & stopped to talk with Hadley, who is very enthusiastic over the irrigation school plan, & the general government training idea.

6/25 New Haven Got to New Haven about eleven, and got something to eat with Lewis Haslam. By so doing missed seeing the 8 forest school men getting their degrees—first graduates of the institution.

8/27 Washington …Bean said he intended Yale Forest School should get bulk of St. Louis forest exhibits for a museum, & had been working to that before I even knew it.

9/9 Paris Long talk with Walsh driving about Paris on his business! I set forth the irrigation school plan, but he said he could not take it up now, having too many other things on hand. Said he annually gave away more than a quarter of million. He said he might take it up later, but I am not very hopeful.

1903

2/12 Washington Long talk with Graves & [George] Seymour. Arranged for West Point work, and talked abut my proposed lectures at New Haven. George against my giving them.

2/21 Washington …Yale dinner in evening. Before it arranged with Hadley not to take professorship, but to give two lectures.

3/14 New Haven …Lectured at 3 on forest policy, after lunch at 337 Humphrey Street. Dr. Munger present & spoke pleasantly of the talk afterward. Then talk with Hadley, who thinks well of my taking [a] place as a professor in the forest school. He agreed to try to raise $50,000 to add to the same amount Mamee & I are to give. A very pleasant talk. Supper with all the forest students at their arrival [and] dinner at the Country Club.

7/23 Grey Towers …A great pleasure to get to Grey Towers. Professor Brewer there. Drive in P.M. on to Forest School camp. Had quiet evening.

7/24 Grey Towers Hear Professor Brewer on forest physiography at 9, & then to village and camp with Father. Lectured on forest policy at four, took dinner with boys at camp at six, played baseball with them before & after dinner, & gave them a talk on professional training &

attitude afterward. Professor Brewer there for dinner & lecture. Then they all escorted us back to Grey Towers.

7/25 Grey Towers Hear Professor Brewer again. Down town again with Father. Long talk with Father, Mamee, Professor Brewer, and Stuyvesant at & after lunch about various government matters…Father said that of all things he would most like to be busy about the summer school of forestry in his old age. He seems immensely pleased.

1904

2/14 Washington …Dr. Gilman favored forest museum plan strongly, & advised me to see Carnegie about giving the money.

6/1 New York Breakfast with Father. Errands. Then went over plans for Forest School building at Milford with him & Joe Hunt.

10/3 Grey Towers To the village on foot with Mamee & Amos. Business about the new forest hall.

10/24 New Haven Out to see Proctor at Fordham in P.M. Dinner with Amos & Gertrude. Seymour met me at station in New Haven. Stayed with them.

10/25 New Haven Preparing lectures & talking with Seymour…Gave lecture on the West, introductory to course on forest reserves. Hadley told me he approved entirely of my making political talks here.

10/26 New Haven Lectures at 10:15 & at 5.

10/27 New Haven Lecture at 8 A.M. Discussed catalogue with Graves. Various errands, etc. Lew Welch gave me a dinner at the Graduates Club…Long talk with Sam & John Schwab about the condition of the university.

10/28 New Haven Lecture at 8. Then long talk with Anson about the university. He finally agreed that we were being passed by our competitors. We are to have more discussions.

10/29 New Haven Lecture at 8. Talk with

Lew Welch about getting the Hillhouse place for the forest school.

10/30 Highhold …Mabel, Harry, & I rode over [to] Walter Jennings' place for lunch, jumping many fences on the way. Pleasant time there. Got back for supper, & had talks about the condition of Yale & about Harry's work, especially in policy matters. This was a superb day in weather, ridings, & people.

11/1 New Haven …Lectured at 5, & with Toumey (am staying with him) to dine with the Schwabs. Pleasant evening.

11/2 New Haven Talk with Welsh about state of things. Prepare & lecture on California reserves at 10:15. Lunch with Anson Stokes, with Greying, Keller, & Huntson. Decided that Sloties will see Hadley at once about getting the nine cabinet officers to describe their work at Yale this winter, & also about getting the best Washington men in scientific lines connected regularly with Yale as lecturers & advisers. Both of these things I took up with Hadley one or two years ago with no result.

11/4 New Haven Getting ready to leave. Gregory explained how then in a double experiment at Yale in Geology & other things. I had long talk…about Hillhouse property, raising money for Yale, & general condition of the university—very serious. Also a talk before that with Dr. Munger, who is much disturbed.

11/5 Washington …Talks with H.S.G. about the Yale Forest School, which is the best on earth.

1905

4/26 Washington Evening Newell & I dined with Newlands & tried to interest him in raising fund for a School of Irrigation at Yale. Not much success, but am to see him again. Good talk with Newell walking home.

5/18 New York …Evening, Otto Barnard's dinner to discuss Yale financial situation. 22

men. Stokes, Howland, Pinchot, B. Townsend …& others spoke. I spoke poorly. Stokes announced Alfred Vanderbilt's $1,250,000, but not by name & the lumbermen's $100,000.

5/19 New Haven Long & final conference with Daggett Scudder, & Hillhouse. Contract of sale to be signed tomorrow morning. Hillhouse has certainly showed a very ungenerous spirit toward Yale from the very first to the very last.

6/2 Washington…In P.M. saw Secretary Wilson & told him of our educational plans, Yale School Professor of Lumbering & Hillhouse place, etc.

11/7 New York …had a long talk with Archer & Mrs. Huntington & spent the night. Mrs. H. seemed more interested [in a school of irrigation], but said she could not fund a school now.

1906

10/21 Washington Long talk with Graves all this morning, in which I agreed with his plan to take the seniors into the shortleaf lumber woods in the Spring, arranged he should take complete supervision of all sample plot work, and arranged we should publish together a book on treatment of American forests as soon as possible.

1907

11/15 New Haven To Yale Forest School. Gave two lectures. A wonderful evening in the T with Fisher, Gill, & Dol Smith. One of the best talks we ever had. Mainly about religion. Lasted till 2 A.M. & after.

11/16 New Haven Gave a lecture in the morning, & to see Yale-Princeton game with Sam Fisher & Charley Gill. First half Yale 0,

Yale Forest School summer camp at Grey Towers, 1909. Pinchot is in the center of the front row. Grey Towers Collection.

Princeton 10. Second half Yale 12, Princeton 10. The finest uphill game I ever saw played.

1911

1/24 New Haven …Lectured to senior class Yale Forest School at 2. Not much of a lecture. Then long walk with Seymour and Toumey, after seeing Phelps, who owns only virgin forest left in Connecticut.

1/25 New Haven Lecturing & preparing lectures.

1/27 New Haven Finished lectures. Did a good deal better this year than for some time.

1/28 New Haven–New York Took 8 A.M. train to New York…Lunched with Mrs. Jesup, who promised me card of introduction to Mrs. Sage, and said she would speak to Mrs. Kennedy (all about Yale Forest School).

6/12 Washington Saw Toumey & Graves about completing endowment for Yale Forest School. Protested strongly against taking less than $100,000 from Carnegie.

8/11 Bar Harbor Lunched with George Door, after seeing Mrs. Kennedy about Yale Forest School. Not much luck.

8/19 Grey Towers …After lunch examining chestnut blight, which is less severe than I feared, and to a reception at the Chapmans. Spoke at camp fire later.

1912

1/11 New Haven Finished lectures Yale Forest School—last on forester's point of view.

3/23 Washington Lunch Graves, Toumey, Price & Greeley on proposed school forest for Yale Forest School. I am for small area (2,000 to 3,000 acres) at Milford.

1913

1/6 New Haven …At 4:30 lecture in North Sheffield to forest students. Both Hadley & Anson came. Hadley introduced me. "No recent graduate of whom they were more proud. No work started by any recent graduate of which etc. as conservation." Also invited me to dinner.

1/7 New Haven Lecture (2) Carried my bags over to the Forest School. Then with Toumey to see George Paruely Day, who wanted my book on conservation for Yale University Press series. Did not say he could have it, but that I would consult him about the matter when the book was done.

2/18 Washington Talk with Harry about Toumey's stampede at Yale of our decreasing attendance, & lack of vision about it.

2/22 New Haven Forest School commencement. Spoke on attitude toward life & work of a forester…Also told the grade crossing fable. Graves also made talk. Lunch with Toumey & others to discuss means of keeping Forest School a national institution. Main thing is to do national work.

1940

2/23 New Haven 40 anniversary Forest School. Graves spoke in the morning, G.P. in P.M.

1941

7/2 Milford …separating material for Yale Forest School library. Wrote to Record yesterday suggesting that material collected by Phil Wells on water power, coal, etc., should be kept separate as a memorial to him.

7/16 Milford …Bill [Hinkel] took a truck load of books, pamphlets, and duplicates to Yale. GP

FORESTRY IN THE PHILIPPINES
"Taft is splendid"

The conclusion of the Spanish-American War placed the United States in an unfamiliar and uncomfortable situation, that of being an imperialistic nation with overseas possessions. The acquisition of the Philippines from Spain squeaked through a Senate that had cast a tie vote on treaty ratification, a tie broken by the vice-president. By this narrowest of margins, the United States joined England and all the European nations as a colonial power. When that war's most famous hero became president in 1901, it is not surprising that Theodore Roosevelt would be much interested in the distant Pacific possession.

In 1902 George Ahern, whom Pinchot had known from earlier visits to Montana, was in the Philippines and bolstering its bureau of forestry. This effort was part of a long-range U.S. plan to develop infrastructure that would allow eventual independence. With Ahern's invitation to visit in hand, Pinchot talked with Roosevelt, who not only encouraged the trip but also provided letters of introduction. The forester would be the president's emissary.

William Howard Taft was the appointed governor of the islands, and Pinchot and he would begin their initially friendly relationship at that time. Although Pinchot's trip added only modestly to the story of conservation, it is included here because it illuminates that portion of his autobiography, and also because it offers yet another illustration of his broad role in the Roosevelt administration.

Pinchot's route included Russia via the trans-Siberian railway, through Manchuria, Japan, and then to the Philippines. He continued eastward and returned to the United States through San Franciso and then by train to Washington. Thus, he traveled around the world at age thirty-seven. Some segments were rather arduous, even primitive, but he was young and enthusiastic, and his daily entries are generally upbeat. Today, when travelers fume about thirty-minute delays and complain about unattractive meals, it is instructive to gain perspective and to understand that we are very well off indeed. Of course, Pinchot traveled with his personal secretary, Mark Winchester, and could afford the best of whatever was available along the way, so what we read about his 1902 venture does not fully represent general travel conditions at the time.

When Pinchot returned to Washington, D.C., in January 1903, he found that he was a sort of celebrity, being asked to describe the Philippine situation to a range of audiences, including congressional committees and the president. In 1935, as he dictated his 1902 diary as part of the larger preparation for writing *Breaking New Ground*, he substantially embellished the earlier account; such a revision of history is not apparent in dictated drafts of other years. Obviously he was remembering his adventure as he read and dictated, and he fleshed out some of the events. The version that follows fairly sticks to the original.

One topic that was typically embellished in the 1935 version was the status of the military in the Philippines. Pinchot often would add a full paragraph of description about the American soldiers (some would become famous later in their careers), and in one entry he added that he had sent some captured "bandit guns" to T.R.—just the sort of things the president would relish.

Box 640 of the Pinchot collection at the Library of Congress holds Philippine materials. In it are a 175-page typescript on Philippine forests by "Sherman" and a 30-page draft by Henry Graves dated 1904, "Confidential Report on the Condition of the Philippine Forest Service." There is also a draft of a general plan by the National Academy of Sciences Philippine committee that included Pinchot. The opening statement tells us, "The United States has undertaken to develop an Anglo-Saxon civilization among a non-Aryan tropical race, the first serious attempt of the kind in the history of the world." We also see his notes for two lectures on the Philippines that he gave at Yale.

During 1902 and later, Pinchot and Ahern became close friends. Ahern is remembered today mainly for his contributions to the forestry of the Philippines, but he also wrote two protoenvironmentalist books, *Deforested America: Statement of the Present Forest Condition in the United States* (1929), and *Forest Bankruptcy in America: Each State's Own Story* (1933).

1902

8/25 Washington Routine. Decided on Trans. Siberian route. Saw Kennan & others in preparation.

9/1 S.S. Lucania Clear & smooth. Perfect weather. Getting acquainted. Got a good deal of work done on my annual report, & disposed of some periodicals.

Russian forester, 1902, photographed by Pinchot en route to the Philippines. Grey Towers Collection.

9/15 Petersburg To the [illeg.] for mail. A letter from Mamee. Reading up about Russia and reducing permitted baggage. To the Ministry of Agriculture (Ministstvo Gemledich, or thereabouts) where I met first Mr. Tromitsky, [illeg.] of the minister, then the assistant chief Forestry Division, Mr. Uien; the chief, Mr. Nikitin, and was turned over by him to Mr. Rauner, one of the vice-Inspectors, who has been in America & thinks he speaks English. All the Forestry Division publications are to be sent to me in Washington. Then with Rauner to the Imperial Forest Institute, where the director, Mr. Kern, was very polite. Drive takes nearly an hour each way. Very cold. Evening, letters etc. & reading.

9/16 Petersburg At work on material for the president's message nearly all day. A few moments in the Alexander Museum. Late P.M. with Rauner to the largest lumber yards in Petersburg, those of Gromoff & Co. Very primitive.

9/17 Petersburg–Licina–Petersburg Left Petersburg about 9...There was, however, a

German overseer for a banker named Black. He drove me the 16 versts [approximately 10.5 miles] in about three hours and half, and at the castle I found the assistants to Forstmeister Kravalinski, who was himself away. Telegram had been delayed. One spoke a little French, the other a little German, & I managed to get more or less about the forest. Stuffed animals in the Imperial hunting castle, where we dined most simply.

9/18 Petersburg–Moscow Read through the long trip through the deadly uninteresting flat country, mostly covered with young timber, chiefly birch & Scotch pine.

9/19 Moscow Ran into Dick Welling as I came down stairs. Just in from Port Arthur. Then drove to Petrovoski–Ra–Zumsovski, & found there Nesteroff, who has a superb red beard. Nesteroff showed me the school forest, which was a delight, and then we drove about Moscow…Spent night unwashed in a second class carriage.

9/20 Moscow–Hrapovitsky Breakfast after hours…Spent the day first going in the forest …another night in a second class carriage.

9/21 Moscow …Nesteroff has a wonderful fund of information about Russian forests, but talks English poorly…Having a fine time.

9/22 Riash–Voronege–Liski Down through a wonderful fertile agricultural country spotted with woods, but inhabited by paupers…a pleasant day.

9/23 Talovarah–Stone Steppe–Tal.– Khrenovoia Reached Talovarah very early, got tchai, & then drove 8 versts across the steppe to Stone Steppe forest house. Like the West. Black earth, no waste soil. Saw flock of 8 bustards on the way. Breakfast at Stone Steppe forest house & then the day spent in seeing plantations.

9/24 Khrenovoia A shave at last. Tea, bread, butter, & eggs for breakfast…through the village

to the forester's house, & then a long drive in the forest…

9/26 Samara, Abdonhins–Ufa We were waked just before dawn, & saw the Volga, a mighty stream in the feeble light…great increase of grazing area…more prosperous.

9/27 Ural Mts. Glalonst Steppes Woke up in the Urals—a fine open country of large hills, with a low mountain ridge on the divide. Splendidly long sweeping lines of forest clad ridges—birch, pine, spruce, & larch…local gems for sale. I ought to have bought more.

9/28 Petropavlovsk—Sunday A cold wet, windy day. Steppe with birches, then latter dreary marshes. Hot bath at Petropavlovsk, which for some mysterious reason took 3½ hours to find. I was glad for the delay, for I used it to finish my will & mail it to father together with check…Read some of Norman's book— ate too much candy.

9/29 Tatarskaia–Obi At work all morning and part of P.M. on the Primer. Marks of fire a good deal today.

10/2 Polovina–Irkutsk A forest region in the morning, running into open farming country in the P.M. Rode in the engine nearly all the afternoon…

10/3 Irkutak–Lake Baikal–Misovaia …best dining car I ever saw, but slow service. The Russians along played & sang charmingly after dinner.

10/4 Petrovski–Zavod–Bada Mountains and forests, both rather small. A semi-arid or sub humid country.

10/6 Manchuria We reached Manchuria about noon.

10/7 Manchuria–Khailer Our car is a very rough second class, but we manage to be fairly comfortable. We have lots of grub…we wash dishes in turn.

10/8 Boukhaton–Djalantoune Up very early…trains wretched…I was orderly for dinner.

10/9 Scaakhadga–Anda–Sungari Through a vast plain all day, a few faltering pines…flea bitten & wretched, we did not get to sleep till about 2 A.M., after waiting no less than 1½ hours for a glass of tea.

10/10 Harbin Up early, feeling like a boiled owl. We dressed & went to look through a Chinese market.

10/11 Donan–Koundiunline We are heartily glad to be rid of Blackall…The car we are in is Second Class but better than the other. There is, however, no lock to the water closet, and the seats are very bad to sleep on. We live on sardines, canned beef, bread…We are all feeling pretty ragged.

10/12 Monkden–Ioviane All day through a most enchanting country…As we reached Port Arthur it became increasingly difficult to keep people out of the car, and in the middle of the night I let it fill up. Hard rain. Not much sleep. George and I had a long laugh over the situation in the middle of the night…

10/14 Chefoo–SS Shengking Up about 6:30. Rainy. Had a good wash…deeply appreciated baths. Clothes off for the first time in twelve days.

10/15 SS.Shengking A good deal of talk this day with Mr. John Peig Bland, secretary of the Marine Council of Shanghai, regarding Russia and our consular service in China…also did a little work on Philippine forestry.

10/16 Shanghai Off the mouth of the Yangtsze early…A most interesting talk with Bishop Graves about our consular service.

10/17 Shanghai Bishop Graves sent me in the letters he had promised, and I called on Frank P. Ball (Yale 90)…agreed to send us each a 70 lb. box of fine black tea, and gave us a small one.

10/18 Shanghai In the morning I bought our tickets. In the afternoon George Seymour, Winchester, and I took a guide and went to see the native (walled) city. Streets 6–8 feet wide, filth smells, and crowding. I marvel any human beings can live in it. What it must be like in the summer I can only guess.

10/19 Shanghai–SS Loongmoon Up in good season…On way to steamer bought brass figure…which dates from about 1500, and is by a famous brass foundry of the Ming Dynasty.

10/20 S.S. Loongmoon Beautiful weather. Work catching up, & on Ahern's special report.

10/21 S.S. Loongmoon Another beautiful day, with some sea from the N.W. monsoon behind us. Work on Ahern's special report all day, & after dinner on Siberian notes…Talk in evening with Hwang. He said his government might want a forester. Could I get him one. I advised report first. He said it would take 2 years. Said they could probably pay $400 to $750 a month [illeg.] & all expenses, and would give every facility. Said there was great lumber trade in South China. Does not mind Christians but objects to missionaries. Did publish a paper but it was suppressed.

10/22 Hongkong Whole place full of fine buildings, placed up there at immense expense. The finest view over the harbor and town I almost ever had. A marvelous place.

10/23 Hongkong–SS Loongmoon Up early and to the market. Then to Happy Valley in rickshaws. The cemetery is a perfect dream of beauty, full of flowers and butterflies under the trees…

10/24 Loongmoon …Some work on Philippine reports. Fine black cat. Deck load of cooleys. Hose played on us on deck for bath. Good grub. Some motion. Very warm.

10/26 Mariales–Manila (Malacanan) Smooth sea at daybreak & Luzon in sight. Passed Subic Bay, stopped at Mariales, and found Ahern in a launch near the city. Customs. Up the Passage to Malacanan where Governor Taft met us at the landing of the palace. Met

Moses, Ide…Then with Ahern called on Philippine family. Saw Mrs. Ahern, & to [illeg.], a wonderful scene. Talk with Greene, president Chamber of Commerce, especially on price of timber (5% tariff all right)…Taft is splendid…Ahern has trip finely laid out. Taft will give me his own yacht (gunboat), the General Alava.

10/27…to sawmill of Philippine Lumber & Development Co.…Then to Malacacan. There Judge Taft showed me Roosevelt's cable offering position on the Supreme Court, & his refusal just simply superb. At 8:30 dinner given by Ahern at Army & Navy Club. Present Judge Taft & about a dozen others. A fine time. Taft's speech.

10/28 Manila Breakfast with Mrs. Taft & General Bell. Then to office and to visit various sawmills with Ahern. In rotten condition, & making rotten lumber. Also saw rafts & timbers being brought in by train.

10/29 Manila Breakfast with Judge Taft, who talked at length about the trouble between Ahern & Worcester, & said that if I could not straighten it out it might have a very serious ending for Ahern's work. He had already given me the papers. Then to the office, and a long talk there with Brent & Wilson.

10/30 Palnan–Calausan trail …travelled with frequent rests through most interesting tropical forest…camped out…Filipinos built us a shelter, thatched it partly with a palm like nipa, and made a bed of poles about 18 inches off the ground. Nothing on the poles. Roof leaked …jovial time.

10/31 Calausan trail–Palnan Some time after midnight it stopped raining…

11/1 Dioso River Under weigh early & to the mouth of the Diaso River about due north of Palnan. Landed there, and spent nearly all day careful going through the forest. Although we made but a short distance, heard monkeys & gecko lizards, but saw none. Wild pigs here. Then came back to the Alava & started for [province of] Camarines Sur. This day I took Ahern's book with me, and read up about the trees as I came to them. Found a good deal of meolane & some Calantas. Found wood cutters huts on the shore, & immense quantities of worm casts in the woods. A useful day because we went slow. Ahern & George Seymour did not make the hike, nor Dorsey.

11/2 Dalupan–Banihiam Landed at Dalupan about ten, & found young Green. Went to the company quarters (Philippine Lumber & Development Co.) & saw superb molave door panels & 3 toucan heads. Decided to go to Banaluan (Gatusan) to see John Orr superintendent of this station. Landed about 1:30 P.M., & did not find Orr. Then crossed the point took [illeg.] to Bauo, & into the superb molave forest from there.

11/3 Banihiam–Buries Ltd., Mesbate–Ticao …met by Presidente & principal men of the town, including municipal police and some old [illeg.] scouts, one of whom went into the woods with some of us. Wonderful cocoas palms, between small steep eroded hills …wonderfully beautiful scenery all day.

11/4 Gandara River–Calbayoc …Got in trouble crossing bar on Gandara River. Philippino boatman would not show us passage.

11/5 Leyte–Cebu Landed at town of Silar in Cebu after several hours spent looking over timber from General Alava.

11/6 Cebu–Straits between Negros & Panay–Iloilo Got off early and passed many islands on the way to Iloilo…Landed at Iloilo in the afternoon. With Ahern to find his forest ranger _____, and through all the books in the office. Everything in perfect order. Evidently a good man. Also bought some jusi cloth.

11/7 Iloilo–Southern Negros Left Iloilo early…We got some coconuts, and then struck into the woods on a trail through a wonderfully rich forest. The trail ended at a church of bamboos, and we came back. Saw some monkeys on the trail.

11/8 Santa Maria–Zamboanga Ran into Santa Maria early and went ashore at the mill of the Philippine Lumber & Development Co. [illeg.] & there into the woods. Most serious destruction. The hottest walk yet. Many landslides. Much timber immersed along shore. Old Spanish fort…Left at eleven, & then down along the wonderful coast to Zamboanga. Steep ruts, wonderful forests…& saw Datto Mandi, Ahern's forester, his assistant, & one of the inspectors (a Filipino). Mandi can only just write his name, but his name is useful. Office in poor condition.

11/10 Mataling Falls–Camp Vickers–Mataling Falls Started about 7:30. My packs slipped off & caught & my horse bucked till it

came off. The left bridle rein broke at the lip, but I stayed with him all right…At Vickers met Capt. John J. Pershing in command. He gave me suit of Moro rawhide armor. Met Datto Mandi.

11/11 Matching Falls–Malabang Left Matching Falls camp about 7:30…took many pictures [along trail]…I sent back my copy of Trees of the Philippines to Capt. Pershing. Feeling pretty tired & sleepy.

11/16 Sandakan–at sea On shore at six to see the market, which was purely Chinese. Then to get breakfast at the hotel, and after getting some things for Ahern, who has developed severe stomach trouble since last night, to buy the orangutan George saw yesterday. Found him, but had to give 25 pesos.

11/17 At sea In sight of Balabac early… Fooling with the orangutan in the morning, putting a bell on him which he took off at

Philippine sawmill, photographed by Pinchot in 1902. Forest Service.

once. A most interesting beast. We have also ten parrots. Rather rough weather, Ahern not so well. His dysentery is not getting better. I loafed all day, & read The Forest Lovers, the first play book or article since I left home. Was a little uncertain of myself in the rough water, & so read. George looked after Ahern this night, & I slept in the wardroom, as he had my bed.

11/18 Malanpaya Bay (Paukal) Off the coast of Paragua early...Much bamboo... Ahern better...Good talk with Seymour about the forest situation before dinner.

11/19 Malenpaya Bay (aground) ...I put in the time partly on Philippine forest law (proposed) & partly wasted it.

11/20 Malanpaya Bay–at sea Up anchor early...Most wonderful coast I ever saw.

11/21 At sea–Manila ...After dinner George & I went to see Judge Taft, and had a very pleasant talk with him, Mrs. Taft & Capt Noble...Mrs. Taft accepted the orangutan and Judge Taft gave me the Alava for the northern trip & to Japan. If Ahern were only well everything would be most flourishing. Certainly it has been a wonderful trip in every way, but that, and most comfortable considering. Also I believe very useful.

11/22 Manila After feeding E. Sandakan Dooley [the orangutan], George & I took him to Malacanan, where he was not very tractable. He got away from his rope, & built him a nest in a tree top and at dark had not been permanently caught. To the office, where I wasted some time with reporters, and wrote home after lunch. Busy nearly whole afternoon over a letter on forest policy to Judge Taft which I dictated in the morning. Very pleasant here. The rest is delightful. Ahern continues to improve steadily. I am more & more thankful over the good news from home. Very tired at night. Dinner quietly with Mrs. Ahern & George.

11/23 Manila Loafed in the early morning, and to church with Mrs. Ahern. Bishop Brent preached an excellent sermon. Siesta after lunch, and then to the Palace to call, after a talk with Brent, who came in the afternoon. Sandakan still up in the tree, even higher than before...work on letter to Judge Taft until eleven thirty.

The service in the morning, & the quiet day, were both a real satisfaction.

11/24 Manila Work on my letter of recommendations to Taft. Winchester worked hard at it & got it all done about 2:30. I took it to the governor, who called in Worcester, and read it to us both. At the end he said without comment that anything that would suit the two of us would suit him. Then the other members of the commission came in, & I had to leave. But first I had a short satisfactory talk with Worcester about Ahern, and accepted his invitation to dine on Wednesday night. Also arranged for a conference with Worcester, Ahern, Niederlein on Friday morning.

In the evening Bishop Brent came in, seeming very tired indeed, and then we (Ahern, Seymore, & I) had a long & most interesting talk with Filipe Calderon, perhaps the leading Filipino lawyer...I was pleased to have my letter off my hands. A strenuous life.

11/26 Manila With Bishop Brent to the Settlement House, a fine big place. Then to Worcester's office, where I met Niederlein & then Ahern. Ahern's letter of apology sent in ahead. Then Ahern & I went in. At first I thought Worcester was going to talk to Ahern very hard. But he moderated, made a straightforward manly statement of the attacks on him, & said with absolutely clearness he did not now & never had had any interest, direct or indirect [except] the security for a loan of 250 pesos for which he thought a mortgage had been given, & the rented house he lived in. Then a long talk about St. Louis. Niederlein's ideas rather small and old fashioned. Worcester impressed me very well, and still more so during a long talk at his house this evening, where I met Drs. Freer and Sherman. We reached a complete agreement on all points in my recommendations except for a forest entomologist. Worcester wants work done under government labs. I agree, but he is not sure about getting a man.

11/27 Manila, Thanksgiving Day With Ahern to call on some Filipinos…& leave some parrots. Then to Bureau of Forestry. Talk about licenses. Then Thanksgiving service…Brent preached. All stood in silence during Star Spangled Banner…Then conference with Taft at palace. He gave me messages for Root, & described situation of islands & measures needed at length. Agreed full with forest program, and promised entomologist. Said of law "Let me know what you want & we'll pass it." Said of measures, "Tell me whatever you want, and I'll see that Ahern carries it out." Situation most hopeful. Then to see Aguinaldo with Ahern, Seymour & Calderon. Not impressed.

12/3 San Vicente–at sea Weighed at daylight…I had to leave the table at dinner in a smooth sea (I think it was this night) & promptly lost what I had eaten.

12/4 Off south coast of Formosa–Buadores Channel Sighted the coast of Formosa early…At work & watching the coast all day. Ranger school plans with Ahern.

12/5 At sea coast of Formosa–Tamsui Well out at breakfast from the Formosa coast …to a Japanese hotel, where we had a dinner of fish, chicken etc., all very good, eaten with chopsticks. The two maids of all work were most friendly in a perfectly unconscious way, and insisted on helping us to undress for the night. But I escaped that.

12/9 At sea More or less under the weather, but came to all meals. At dinner George exploded on the subject of my calling him professor, saying he would not come to my house nor should I to his unless I quit. I was greatly surprised and a good deal hurt.

12/10 At sea Packing etc. Before breakfast a long talk with George about my calling him professor. It seems he was deeply hurt, & I never knew it. I am keenly sorry for the discomfort he has had. We made it up. It was very stupid of me, and excessively sensitive of him. Seasickness nearly gone. At work again with Ahern. High seas continues. The Jap continues dead to the world.

12/11 At sea–Nagasaki Clear fine cold day…to the coast of Nippon…Pine plantations common…worked till about midnight on cables etc.

12/11 Nagasaki Up at 6:30, & ashore at 7:30…Ahern & I worked on our recommended actions till dinner.

12/12 Nagasaki Engaged passage on American Maru. Ahern and I working on our recommendations. Young Watanabe, our Japanese passenger, still seasick.

12/13 Moji–Shimonoseki–Kioto Up in the dark…Did a good deal of work during the day with Ahern, and saw much interesting forest, including planted pine, & planted against erosion as have granite sand hills…Very good dining car ridiculously cheap.

12/14 Kioto In spite of the day [Sunday], Ahern & I went straight at our work after breakfast, & stuck at it till lunch.

12/15 Tokio In the morning we decided to go to Tokio…Ahern & I worked from arrival at say 11:15 to 1, & after lunch I took an hour for shopping, & Ahern more. Then work till nearly dinner time, & then another short jaunt…I went to bed early. Very tired, but the report made progress.

12/16 Tokio–Yokohama Out for an hour at once after breakfast…Then to Yokohama to grand hotel & at work right along after getting money & seeing about redemption of tickets …Agent would not guarantee but that they would demand 10%, so I kept tickets for redemption in Washington…After dinner at it again, & at eleven whole thing finally & fully complete.

12/17 Yokohama–at sea Up at sunrise to try & see Fuji, but there was too much haze…I let Ahern get away without the signed copy of our letters to Worcester or the copy for Taft, like an idiot that I am. However, he has his copy, & I will mail the others from Honolulu…Ahern went off in fine spirits. A good man. Very much tired out.

12/18 At sea–second day begins at noon Fairly smooth. Loafed till after lunch, reading Bunyan's Holy War & Thackeray's Burlesques. After lunch wrote up diary for 2 to 3 [illeg.]…Read Rodway an hour after dinner. Also some Bunyan (Grace Abounding) in P.M. This is a fine boat, with much vibration.

12/19 America Maru, 3d day Established these hours for work last night.

Rise 7. Bkfst 8:30. Work 9:30–12:30
Lunch 1:00 Work 2:00–4:00
Dinner & Reading 8:30–9:30

In bed 10 o'clock. Total work 7½ hours. This day: Law & Regs. morning & after +40 mins

Old Diary 5–6:30
Evening 8:30–9:30 Guiana Fuest.
Total this day 8 hours 10 minutes.

I hope for some work on the Primer before we land, if the weather holds good.

12/20 America Maru Heavy wind from south…Got nearly my full stint of work done, but with some difficulty, it being so rough. George's stateroom & mine very very wet, leaking through the windows and along the deck, & especially through the door in the passage between them.

12/21 America Maru Slept little last night on account of the gale…had [Sunday] service in my cabin alone but for my Dearest. Sat about & read the rest of the day, which was wet & uncomfortable…Read most of Worcester's book on the Philippines, which is poor.

12/22 America Maru A quiet night… Worked hard all day, doing my full number of hours, but feeling more or less weary. At night finished Worcester's book, & then like a fool read Thackeray till eleven.

12/23 America Maru This day at seven P.M. we crossed the dateline, so that it was Tuesday till that hour, & then Monday evening. Feeling very much used up all day. I don't know why. Did some work in the morning, but none afterward…Began to read Margaret Ogilvy.

Much better this morning. More or less work all through the day. Sea smoother & a good deal of sun. Finished Margaret Ogilvy. A most beautiful book, before outrage to make public the family life it describes.

12/24 America Maru Did my full task today up to dinner time, and then, this being Christmas eve, I knocked off. Got a good deal done on the regulations especially…Read too late tonight (10:30).

12/25 America Maru Christmas Day. George came in before I was dressed with a beautiful vase and A Merry Christmas. I gave him a paper [illeg.] of tortoise shell, & Winchester a couple of bronze crabs. It seems a great pity to be away from home today. I have been thinking of them a great deal…Decided today to write a full account of the Philippines forest from experience & all available sources as my report.

1903

1/8 Washington Went straight from the

station, where I arrived at 10:30 two hours late. With Price to the House Agriculture Committee & there talked for nearly two hours about the work of the Bureau, the need for more money, & the Philippines.

1/11 Washington ...Talk with Whelelous Reid at Mrs. Coweles: he was full of questions about the Philippine Islands especially Mindanau.

1/22 Washington ...Put off meeting tonight, having had no time to prepare my proposed talk on Philippine forests.

1/30 Washington Office at nine. Corrected plan of forest investigation for committee of National Academy & turned it in...Consultation & lunch with Professor Brewer & Merriam. To committee, National Academy proposed to have forestry unrepresented except by botany on proposed Philippine Survey Board. I protested vigorously, but appear without effect.

3/19 Washington At nine meeting of the Board of Philippine Surveys. Lasted till 11. Was made chair of subcommittee to formulate plan of organization, etc.

5/20 Washington ...Evening meeting of subcommittee to prepare plan for Board Philippine Survey (Coville, Tittleman) at 1615 [Rhode Island Avenue].

6/7 Washington ... P.M. Garfield went over the proposed Philippine Island forest laws & suggested some excellent changes.

7/25 Grey Towers Hear Professer Brewer again. Downtown again with Father. Long talk with Father, Mamee, Professor Brewer, and Stuyesant at & after lunch about various government matters, especially Board Philippine Surveys, Taft's approval of government plan for which had just come from T.R.

1904

1/30 Washington Lunch at White House, T.R. & Mrs. Roosevelt, Mrs. Holmes, Miss French, Taft, & I. Most delightful. After, talk with Taft about work of Board Philippine Surveys. He said he cared nothing for professional jealousies, and recognized that the Philippine Bureau could not do it, but was anxious Philippine government should not be put in position of asking for this work. If that can be arranged, go ahead with the surveys. Fine news.

10/6 Washington ...Lunch with Ahern & discussed Philippine Forest Act, which is excellent.ᏩᎵ

GOVERNMENT ORGANIZATION AND EFFICIENCY
"Perfecting scheme for reform of government business methods"

In early 1903 Gifford Pinchot talked with Charles Walcott, director of the U.S. Geological Survey. The two had a substantial history of working together on forest and water issues, and they agreed that the government's technical work ought to be redistributed among the several agencies. They easily persuaded President Roosevelt to appoint a Committee on the Organization of Government Scientific Work and to name Walcott chairman. Others on the committee were William Crozier, in charge of Army Ordnance; Francis T. Bowles, the Navy's chief of construction; James Garfield, head of the Bureau of Corporations and a close friend of Pinchot's; and of course Pinchot himself, whom Walcott appointed as secretary.

During approximately thirty meetings, many at Pinchot's home, the committee came up with two general recommendations, neither of which would be adopted either by Congress or via an executive order. The first recommendation concerned scientific research itself: that the government should limit itself to studies of utilitarian nature and leave so-called basic research to private laboratories. This clearly did not happen. The second recommendation proposed that by executive order the Geological Survey, Office of Indian Affairs, and the General Land Office be transferred from the Department of the Interior to Agriculture. Jurisdiction over the national parks—no single agency yet managed them—would be under Agriculture as well. We can see in the diaries that Senator William Allison and Representative Joseph Cannon—towering figures in Congress—discussed transfer strategy with Roosevelt, Pinchot, and others. They predicted that despite the president's authority, Congress would balk. They were correct: the 1905 transfer of the forest reserves from Interior to Agriculture was the only fragment of the larger reorganization package to be realized.

Pinchot's next effort at improving government began in 1905, following Roosevelt's election in his own right. The Chief, as Pinchot sometimes referred to Roosevelt, was again easily persuaded to appoint a committee, this time the Committee on Department

Methods. The charge was to study current procedures and report back with recommendations on ways to improve efficiency. The committee was named for Charles H. Keep, assistant secretary of the Treasury. Other members were Frank H. Hitchcock, first assistant postmaster general; Lawrence O. Murray, assistant secretary of Commerce and Labor; and (no surprise) Jim Garfield, soon to be secretary of the Interior; plus Pinchot and his associate chief, Overton Price.

In *Breaking New Ground*, Pinchot wrote that "the Keep Committee made no less than sixteen investigations and reports in the twenty-one months of its active life." His diary provides information on day-to-day activities. The end product was a more cost-efficient government, and the Forest Service was singled out as the most efficient of all the agencies. Even if a subsequent independent study had not confirmed the agency's management quality, it is a matter of record that Pinchot himself was a superb bureaucrat, in the best and finest sense of the word. He knew how an agency should be organized and how to get the most out of his employees. There is even a scholarly treatise by Harold T. Pinkett, one of Pinchot's biographers, that describes his management innovations. Files and related recordkeeping systems and the structuring of a meaningful operating budget were only two Forest Service management methods that were adopted governmentwide. It is fair to say that Pinchot's management abilities, which included hiring men of the caliber of Herbert "Dol" Smith, Overton Price, Philip Wells, and George Woodruff, advanced the conservation cause well beyond where it would have been based solely on its merits.

1903

2/24 Washington …To custom house. Long talk with Walcott about a committee of five to suggest reorganization of government work, to be appointed by President. Walcott was not very enthusiastic over the idea.

3/8 Washington …Gave Pres. final draft of paper for Committee of Five on scientific work, & he said he would appoint it.

3/19 Washington …11 to 1 meeting of Committee on Organization [of] Government Scientific work. Was made secretary. Long & good first meeting.

5/21 Washington …Meeting of Committee on Organization at 10. Long & fruitful discussion.

6/8 Washington …Meeting Committee Organization, U.S.G.S. 9–11:45.

6/17 Washington …Eve meeting of Garfield, Bowles, & myself on plan for Committee on Organization work, 8:15–11 P.M.

7/27 Grand Rapids Dictation—minutes of Committee on Organization on train…

10/21 Washington …after seeing T.R. & having a long talk w. Pres., [saw] Butler who, after seeing Garfield also, came entirely to our view as to the disposition of the Bureau [of] Education.

10/24 Washington Hard work today. Routine, etc., etc. Garfield & I agreed with Walcott better to make no report of Committee Organization Science work till President gets power from Congress to make transfers.

1904

3/28 Washington Office early. Committee Organization Scientific Work 9–12:30…after dinner conference at White House of Committee Organization with T.R. & Allison & Cannon. Bowles made an admirable statement of our case, & T.R. agreed with us fully. So did Allison & Cannon so far as the power for the President to make the transfers, but neither thought it could be done at this session, although Cannon suggested a way by which Allison might get it tacked on to a bill. We left finally with the idea in their minds that nothing would be done this year, in ours that it must. And it must. Pretty tired.

1905

5/23 Washington Breakfast with Dol & to office with Garfield. Various routine. Long talk with Jim at lunch & after perfecting scheme for reform of government business methods. Short talk with Chief to make appointment for full discussion. Talk with Newell on same subject, & Dol.

5/24 Washington …Talk with T.R. (Garfield & I) at 10 P.M. at which we submitted & discussed our plan for general improvement in the government service. He recognized the great necessity, but was not sure of the means.

5/25 Washington Long consultation with Garfield about reorganization of government business, during which we formulated some principles. At 12:30 meeting with T.R., Cortelyou, Metcalf, Jim, & I on reorganization. Read the principles. No objection made. Decided Murray, Hitchcock (of P.O.) & Keep should take matter up. President offered to put Jim & me on. We declined…Eve long conference with Murray & Jim. Murray agreed with

us throughout, & said he would try to carry out the work as we wanted it done. Very satisfactory talk.

6/2 Washington Garfield & I had a conference with T.R. & told him we wanted to be members of the Committee on Organization of Government Business, & he said he would put us on. In our presence he dictated the letter, using the material (principles, etc.) we had prepared.

6/4 Washington …Long talk [with Newell] about the Committee on Business Methods. He made some capital suggestions.

7/3 Washington …A long day at the G.P.O. investigation. We got a good deal, Garfield being in the chair.

7/5 Washington …Evening long talk with Jim about Committee on Business Methods. We are far from satisfied with progress, or with the zeal of the 3 Assistant Secretaries. Prepared some questions to send to the Department.

7/6 Washington A long & very wearisome day at the Government Printing Office investigation & not much result.

7/11 New York …went & saw Hal, of the AT&T & got his promise to spend a week in Wash. next fall going over government business methods.

9/26 Chicago Long talk with Ted about the public printer…

10/2 Washington …Then Jim came in & we [T.R. and G.P.] discussed the appointment of a Public Printer. Richett's report on possible improvement was turned over to us to examine.

10/13 Washington At dinner in the evening Secretary Wilson, Hays, Galloway, Wiley, Whiting, Howard, to meet Keep, Murray, & Garfield…

10/16 Washington … Introduced Leavenworth, Yale '97, to the President. Then submitted draft of letter to the K.K. (Keep Committee) directing us to investigate Interior Department…Lunch with the Keep Committee, and afterward to see Richards & tell him about the examination of the G.L.O. we are to undertake.

11/2 Washington …A quiet easy evening in my study, discussing the public printers with Dol. Keep's proposed report is not good, & I won't sign it. It is very incomplete.

11/3 Washington …Garfield, Murray, & I decided we ought to take up business side of Government Printing Office & also hold daily meetings of KKK [sic].

11/14 Washington Office routine. K.K. (Keep Com.) at 11. Heney (F.J.) gave us a capital talk on the land frauds, saying among other things that 90 percent of the frauds could be traced to bad administration. P.M. I arranged with Walcott & Newell for 6 of their best men to investigate local land offices, Indian agencies, & Suveyors General's office.

1906

3/29 Washington At home catching up & at [KK] report on census…Talk with Walcott, to whom I told what the President said about not knowing much of his scientific work. Walcott will give me a list.

10/19 Washington Completed first draft of Keep Committee report on the Interior Department today, & went over it with Murray & Keep at eleven.

10/20 Washington On the report all day. Went over it with Davis, Fitch, & Bien. T.R. sent for me this afternoon to find out how it was getting on. He said he had seen for a good while that he must get rid of Richards & thanked me for suggesting Malcolm Moody as his successor. Report in evening also. 19 pages of final copy done.

10/21 Washington …Morris Bien came to help me with the report in afternoon. Also Hill. Evening called at White House. Very pleasant talk with Mrs. R. Then more work on report.

10/22 Washington Completed report on Interior Department and in P.M. went over it with Keep & Murray. Then beat T.R. three sets of tennis and sat by while he read the report. Wanted one paragraph left out that I had arranged for that, and then said he had not the change of a word to suggest. Said it was just what he wanted.

10/23 Washington Report signed and handed in. GP

THEODORE ROOSEVELT

" 'Drenched! You've been out with the President' "

What we look back on and call the Conservation Movement is linked directly to the seemingly unlikely relationship between two men, Theodore Roosevelt and Gifford Pinchot. In 1901 Vice-President Roosevelt became president upon William McKinley's assassination, and Pinchot was chief of a minor bureau in the Department of Agriculture. In part because of their personal relationship, Pinchot's political stature rocketed, and by the end of Roosevelt's presidential tenure in 1909, no one would see the Forest Service as a "minor" bureau.

The two were cut from the same cloth and were relatively young at the time of their first national prominence; Roosevelt was born in 1858 and Pinchot in 1865. Both had inherited wealth, both were athletic, both held strong values, and both saw themselves as having a destiny. Roosevelt and Pinchot liked each other as people and admired the other for his achievements. The diary entries that follow report on their broader interactions; those related specifically to the Forest Service and conservation are included in other chapters.

They became acquainted while Roosevelt was governor of New York and Pinchot advised him about forestry matters at the state level. Pinchot concludes his diary entry for November 11, 1899, "Boxed and wrestled with T.R. before dinner." This sort of manly gusto would become the trademark of their ever-closer relationship, as their frequent tennis matches, vigorous hikes and horseback rides, and just plain chopping wood and picnicking at Sagamore Hill, the president's Long Island home, provided opportunities to discuss world matters on a presidential scale, and for the forester to offer advice that the president sought. In a town that measures influence in units of access, as does Washington, D.C., Gifford Pinchot and the Forest Service acquired a temporary level of influence that has not been achieved by any other agency, or its chief, since.

They were both avid hunters. Like the state dining room in the Roosevelt White House, Pinchot's den in his Washington, D.C., home was lined with mounted heads of moose, deer, and elk, plus trophies of his saltwater fishing. Their candor is even more arresting; in a series of diary entries we learn that Pinchot recommended that he be appointed as first assistant secretary of the Interior, for six months, so that he could remedy that department's ills. Roosevelt seemed to agree, even wishing he could appoint him Interior secretary. In all, an incredible series of conversations.

Pinchot's diaries for 1908 and 1909 are missing—perhaps he never compiled them—so we do not have his impressions of Roosevelt's final years as president. Roosevelt crops up again, frequently, during the 1911 and 1912 presidential campaign. Pinchot was very active in support of the Progressive Party candidate and made many speeches in his behalf. The final Roosevelt entries were made in 1913, as the former president is writing his autobiography and asks Pinchot's assistance. By now their famous relationship has been strained, in part because of Roosevelt's impatience with the radical politics espoused by Gifford's younger brother Amos. Nonetheless, Pinchot agreed to draft a chapter on conservation during Roosevelt's presidency. Pinchot's mother was indignant over an early draft that to her failed to give Gifford adequate credit for conservation. The published version is very generous: "among the many, many public officials who under my administration rendered literally invaluable service to the people of the United States, he, on the whole, stood first." What bureau chief could hope for more?

1899

2/5 Albany Stayed overnight with Roosevelt, who approved entirely with plan to legislate Forestry Commission out & put one man in charge.

11/27 Albany …Talks with Governor Roosevelt & Burns. General decision to acquire facts about the mismanagement of the Commissioner of Fisheries, Forests, & Game & then decide about single commissioner or appointment of good men under the present system. Also to agitate Burns to present system with good men. Dinner with the Parsonses. Boxed & wrestled with T.R. before dinner.

1902

2/16 Washington …To walk with T.R., Tainsford, & Lodge in afternoon. Climbed the cliff below the zoo in a new place. Fine walk.

2/26 Washington …Ride in P.M. Met President & rode with him. Fine gallop.

5/25 Washington Evening to call at White House. Pleasant time. T.R. showed pictures of him jumping his horse.

5/30 Washington To White House at 3:45. Drove with T.R. & Leonard Wood to Chain Bridge & walked down Virginia side.

5/31 Washington Routine. To see T.R. with Garfield about a trip to Difficult Run, and at four to ride with them & Wood. Capital ride.

7/3 Washington …saw Secretary and then with Walcott & Foster to see T.R. Told him about the boy [Amos's son]. Also introduced Foster to have him tell about Kent, Roosevelt's applicant of Chief Justice of Arizona Territory. Roosevelt, on my urging some of us thought Foster could carry Arizona for the Republican cause, expressed the greatest interest. That he would be immensely delighted if any could guarantee or could even give him a reasonable hope of getting two Republican senators from Arizona when it became a state. Had thought presidential election best time to try for it.

1903

1/9 Washington …to lunch, with Mamee, at the White House. Moody, Ware, General Wood, Wister, & others. A real good time …T.R. said a lot about a letter I wrote him about the conduct of our troops [in the Philippines], etc. Had it printed in the Star…

2/15 Washington …After dinner to White House. Saw Sargent's unfinished portrait of the President. Very fine indeed in general effect. Face too supercilious or displeased.

6/7 Washington …Evening to the White House. Mrs. T.R., Mr. Otis Proctor, & the chief, who said I was the one man who had helped him in the western speeches, & that he had read the material I sent him right along, whenever the crowd was quiet enough so that he could work out a continuous line of thought. He thought well of putting the speeches all together & elaborating them, & said he wished I would ask help for them. We went & looked at all the presents of the trip, which were more interesting.

6/19 Washington …Tennis with T.R. & Garfield…

7/1 Sagamore Hill Shot with Proctor. Made 81 at 50 yards with .22 S & W pistol…Long talk after ladies had gone up about the war. Rough Riders lost 25 percent of men & 40 percent of officers in battle in Santiago campaign. Telegram from A.J. Beveridge, which T.R. answered by an invitation to lunch tomorrow. President stated his views about Russia & Russian & U.S. policy in Manchuria. Mosquitos bad.

7/2 Sagamore Hill Talk with Mrs. T.R.

after breakfast, & then work on T.R.'s western speeches. After lunch, at which President arranged with Hambley that Secretary Moody, Garfield, & I should go & address Harvard students next winter on the public service, played tennis. T.R. & I beat Captain Preston of the Sylph & Lt. Manner 14-12, a long set. Then some chopping just before dinner, and after a fine sail on the Sylph.

7/3 Sagamore Hill With T.R. & Mrs. T.R. rowed to a picnic ground at mouth of Huntington Harbor. 16 children & about 25 in all. Fine time. Also rowed back 1 hour 45 minutes hard. Most interesting talk. T.R. spoke of element of luck (which I believe, & told him, is Providence) in his career in the most modest way, & he agreed when I said I thought the most important result of his work would be an entire change, which it should & I believe will make, in the attitude of people toward government service. Spoke of Wood's & Taft's next work, and I told T.R. what Beveridge said of him also the final reason at the bottom of his decisions being the question of right over wrong. Much interesting & confidential talks.

10/21 Washington …[T.R.] told me he favored my material for his speeches more exactly than that of anyone else.

10/23 Washington …Dinner at White House & to "Nancy Brown" with Mrs. R., Ethel, Mrs. Otis Proctor. Very funny indeed.

1904

1/27 Washington …to see T.R. about 8:30. Pleasant talk with him. He was much pleased with result of the western trip.

1/30 Washington Lunch at White House, T.R. & Mrs. R., Mrs. Holmes, Miss Grench, Taft, & I. Most delightful.

2/12 Washington Long talk with T.R. in P.M., & fine intimate talk of men & things. Was greatly pleased when he said I did not show at

Political cartoon published in the Denver *Post*, January 24, 1909, suggesting Pinchot's undue influence on President Roosevelt. Pinchot scrapbooks, Pinchot Collection, Library of Congress.

all the lack of political training in dealing with men.

2/14 Washington …Saw T.R. in evening. He arranged with Johnson that I should write article on irrigation and forestry, and later agreed to give me a letter to Carnegie [funding for Yale forestry museum], although he had always refused such letters hitherto.

3/16 Washington …Wrestling with the Japs at White House…Told T.R. some of what Carnegie said.

6/5 Washington …Evening good call at White House. T.R. was specially cordial, & showed me his record at Santiago as per official reports.

6/6 Washington At 5:30 tennis T.R. & Garfield against Smith & I. We beat them again in sets, in spite of my bad playing, but again we came out exactly even in games. Played five sets. Very hot indeed.

9/23 Washington With Garfield to see T.R.…Pleasant talk…discussion about Collier's letter to T.R. Collier is to my mind a bad egg. The letter seems to be intended for a threat …To see T.R. again in evening about Collier & land matters with Jim. Told chief our plan of reoganization with G.L.O. & how conditions are in the West.

9/25 Washington …in evening to White

House to see T.R. Taft & Mrs. Taft there. When they left we three had a talk till nearly midnight. Very interesting & important.

9/28 Washington …Then tennis with T.R., Garfield, & Oliver. We beat the latter two.

9/30 Washington Lunch at White House. Taft, James Br[y]ce & Mrs. Br[y]ce, Garfield, & I, & O'Brian of N.H. Very interesting time…later Murray & I beat T.R. & Garfield 3 sets.

10/7 Washington …Played tennis with T.R. & Ted against Murray & me. They beat us.

10/8 Washington With Ahern to see T.R., who will look up the medal of honor matter. Jim Reynolds came in. P.M. walk with T.R., Ted & Hale for over three hours…T.R. said he hoped I would pound the stump in Indiana, & of course I will.

10/19 Washington Further talk with Amos. Then with him to tell T.R. and more pleasant talk. I am intensely sorry for his going to New York, but it seems best. Routine. Tennis at the White House.

10/20 Washington Getting ready to leave. Took George Woodruff to see T.R. & later lunched with George at White House.

11/5 Washington Dinner en famille at the White House, & a long talk about election & other matters.

11/8 Washington Amos & I voted about 10 o'clock…went to White House. Everything lovely. Enormous majority probably 325 votes all total. Nice talk with T.R. who was immensely pleased & very friendly. Signed big photo for me.

11/9 Washington With Jim Garfield to see the Chief.

11/10 Washington Long talk with Jim Garfield about social matters at the White House. I am much dissatisfied.

1/11 Washington After talk with Jim decided not to speak to T.R. about it just now. Lunch at

White House to meet John Maley, Secretaries Wilson & Hitchcock…

11/14 Las Vegas Today completed message to the Irrigation Congress which T.R. asked me to prepare & present in his name, saying he would stand for whatever I said.

11/22 Washington Arrive early. A very busy day getting ready to leave. Saw T.R. & gave him his message to the Irrigation Congress. Saw Secretary & generally rushed around. Packed at night & took midnight train with Jim.

12/13 Washington …To White House with Jim…Lunch at White House. Seth Low Spenser of the South Railway, Jim, & T.R.

12/21 Washington With Anson Stokes to see T.R. about Dodge lectures of Cabinet. T.R. said he would see Cabinet about it himself.

1905

5/23 Washington Tennis with T.R.

6/4 Washington …Dinner at the Garfields', & after a good call at White House. Am to go down in August or September to Oyster Bay.

7/6 Washington Today remind T.R. about speaking about forestry at the U.E.A. Convention tomorrow.

10/2 Washington To see T.R. Very pleasant talk. Discussed situation in Colorado…and in Oregon. T.R. asked me to wire Scott and Chamberlain about Wolverton's candidacy. I explained what I know about Fulton, & showed him wire received today from Henry on that subject…Tennis with T.R. in P.M. I beat him 5-6, 6-2, 6-0, 6-3, I believe it was. He told me about the hard time Ted is having at Harvard because of newspaper stories. Dinner at White House. Mrs. R. Taft, Root, Mrs. Cowles, the Richardsons…& G.P. Most interesting talk about the peace treaty, etc.

10/11 Washington Various work. In the afternoon late came a telephone message from

T.R. to go for a walk. So I went as I was from the office, & found Bacon there. Jim was sent for, but was out. Bacon also in street clothes, rather good ones, too. It had been raining hard. We went down by the Potomac, & soon got wet to our knees. Then, at dark, we came to the canal that runs up west of the monument. T.R. suggested that we swim it, & he & I gave all our valuables to Bacon. But he would not be left behind, so we put our wallets, etc. in our hats on our heads & swam across. It was not a cold evening. The tide was up, & then we walked back to the White House with much merriment. Bacon & I had our umbrellas along, & swam with them in our left hands. When I got home I touched Mamee's hand with my sleeve, & she said "Drenched! You've been out with the President." T.R. said on the way home that, if it were possible, he would cheerfully serve as Secretary of State or War or Navy under Taft or Root.

10/13 Washington At dinner in the evening Secretary Wilson, Hayes, Galloway, Wiley, Whiting, Howard, to meet Keep, Murray, & Garfield. Like a fool, I told the story of last Wednesday [10/11], at Secretary Wilson's suggestion. The evening was real success. Secretary Wilson made an admirable talk about the Department, & I think everyone had a good time.

10/14 Washington Tennis at the White House.

10/16 Washington To see T.R. first thing …Met Taft on the way down, and had a long talk with him about affairs in Ohio…

11/2 Washington …Fine tennis at White House. T.R. & Herbert Knox Smith against Garfield & me (we won) followed by tea & a pleasant talk.

11/4 Washington …I believe we played tennis at the White House & took the night train.

11/10 Washington Routine. Tennis at White House. Newberg, Jusserand, & I.

11/11 Washington Routine. Walk with T.R., Garfield, Newberg. The latter had to drop out because he was too stout to stand the pace. I was very sorry for him. We were walking down Rock Creek from the Military Road.

11/27 Washington …T.R. and I lost 2 out of 3 to Jusserand & Garfield at tennis.

1906

10/21 Washington …Evening called at White House. Very pleasant talk with Mrs. R.

10/22 Washington …beat T.R. three sets of tennis…I told him I had considered suggesting that he put me in for six months to clean up the G.L.O. as Commissioner, with distinct understanding I should return to the Forest Service. He obviously liked the idea. Said also: "Fond as I am of Jim [Garfield], if you came from a western state I would put you in as Secretary of the Interior. But I cannot put a N.Y. man there." Then we discussed Woodruff for Assistant Attorney General Interior Department, T.R. liked the idea very much. Altogether a capital talk.

10/23 Washington …Medicine ball with George Woodruff who is considering whether he would accept, as I am about temporary charge of G.L.O. J.B. Reynolds favors it strongly. Evening to White House to meet members of the People's Lobby. T.R., Taft & Root, Reynolds, Needham, Alexander Allen, Sullivan, Colby & about 7 others. T.R. made admirable talk. Said we would surely get in trouble with Japs if we were not courteous & did not keep up our navy. Said Japs have about completed two ships equal to best of ours.

10/24 Washington Various routine. Tennis at White House in P.M. I thought I should hear something as to why a N.Y. man (Strauss) had been put in the Cabinet after I had repeatedly been given that reason why I could not, although according to T.R. the best man he knew for Secretary of the Interior. I shall ask him why at the right time. Cortelyou, without financial experience, goes to Treasury. Metcalf, an admitted failure as an administrative officer, goes to the vital Navy. Meyer, who looks like an ass, goes to Post Office. It looks like playing with the Cabinet. Garfield, the best possible man for Commerce & Labor, is to go to Interior.

10/25 Washington Routine all day. I suggested yesterday after tennis Woodruff for Assistant Attorney General Interior Department, & that I might take G.L.O. for 6 months only. T.R. seemed to like both ideas. So I talked

them over with George. I think it is a better plan that I should go over if at all as First Assistant Secretary. It would have to be stated very definitely that I was there only for a few months for a specific purpose, and that I was going back to the Forest Service.

10/26 Washington …Evening Garfield's to dinner. Jim thinks with me about the 3rd N.Y. appointment to the Cabinet. So does Helen. Jim & I agreed he is to ask T.R. for me as First Assistant Secretary for 6 months and Woodruff as Assistant Attorney General. George is to decide in the morning if he will take it if it is offered. Jim & I agree fully about the recent Cabinet changes.

10/27 Washington Routine etc. After the

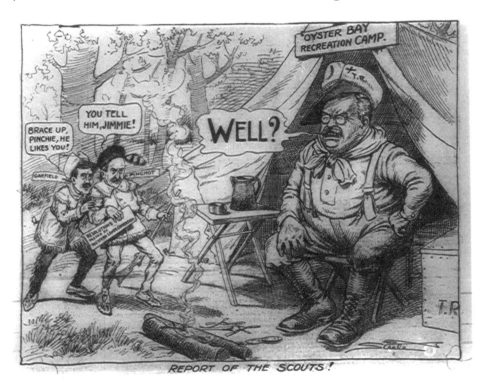

Political cartoon published in the Denver *Post*, June 28, 1907, showing President Roosevelt as a stern task master. Pinchot scrapbooks, Pinchot Collection, Library of Congress.

day's work at six I went to meet T.R. & Jim, and Jim set the Department of the Interior plan before the Chief, who agreed fully. So I am to help Jim for a time as First Assistant Secretary, and George as Assistant Attorney General. T.R. said he could not promise that all this, including Garfield as Secretary would happen, but there was only one chance in a thousand that it would not. So it was arranged.

10/29 Washington Various routine, and trying matters. Got a long letter describing the N.Y. situation from Sherrill. Thinks it very dark for Hughes. I read it to the Chief, who thought it was an "admirable letter." Medicine ball with Woodruff…Dol came in evening, much delighted over news about George.

11/5 Washington …[T.R.] took me aside & told me Hitchcock will resign (to take effect March 4) immediately. T.R. was much delighted for there will be no friction. Five sets of tennis in P.M. Afterward long talk with T.R. & Garfield. T.R. said, among other things, that if I had been from a Rocky Mountain state he would have put me in as Secretary of the Interior long ago. That of Jim & I, who had borne with him the burden & heat of the day, it was a matter of chance, or locality, which went into the Cabinet. Said also Strauss went in as a Jew, & his locality indifferent.

11/11 Washington …Talk with Walcott. He is anxious I should take no work that would endanger my continuing in forest work for political reasons. I told him the First Assistant Secretary plan. Also that I thought Hayes ought not be Director of U.S.G.S.

1907

1/28 Washington …Walk with President and Garfield in P.M. T.R. said that somebody asked him at Gridiron dinner how "Jimmy" Garfield was going to do as Secretary of the Interior. T.R. replied there were four men

"whose brains he had picked, whose writings had most often appeared over his signature, who were part of the syndicate, & who had constructed most of the policies of his administration—Taft, Root, Garfield, and Pinchot."

11/9 Washington With Judge Richards to see T.R., who agreed to include Mining Bureau in his message. P.M. Jusserand and I beat T.R. & Garfield 3 sets to 2. Pretty good tennis. Jim to dinner & then to White House to go over part of message with T.R.…In conversation about Sargent's attack on me to T.R., T.R. said to me "I have never known a more disinterested public servant than you are, or a more efficient one—there couldn't be."

11/11 Washington …Lunch at White House. First real meeting Tennis Cabinet—to present silver cup with our signature on it to Robert Bacon for saving a man from drowning. Present Mr. & Mrs. Bacon, Mr. & Mrs. Meyer, Mr. & Mrs. Conley, Madame & Monsier Jusserand (Vice President of Tennis Club), Garfield, Murray, Mr. & Mrs. Winthrop. T.R. made presentation speech & did it beautifully. Bacon was much affected. Answered capitally. We had the merriest time yet at the White House. Then Jap. heavyweight wrestlers.

11/23 Washington Walk & medicine ball with T.R., Garfield & Jusserand. The muddiest tramp yet.

11/24 Washington Dinner with the Garfields. Then pleasant call on Mrs. Roosevelt, & long & very confidential talk with T.R. He thinks with me that no crisis except the Civil War is as serious as the present in determining great policies.

11/29 Washington …Saw Plum of the Sage Foundation who said he thought rural organization the most important problem at present. Walk with Garfield. Saw Chief &

introduced Dr. Roberston at 6:15. T.R. said rural organization not surpassed in importance. I had made progress with Wilson on that line. Mamee & Father to White House to dinner.

12/2 Washington Tennis at White House. Jusserand & I against T.R. & H.K. Smith. Tie in sets.

12/7 Washington …Dinner at White House. Small family. T.R. gave me new double eagle, I of course to pay cost. Specially struck for him.

1910

4/11 Porto Maurizio, Italy One of the best & most satisfactory talks with T.R. I ever had. Lasted nearly all day, and till about 10:30 P.M.

1913

2/4 New York …To see T.R. at his phoned request. He asked me to prepare for him statement about our seven years' work in conservation, which he said was 4/5 my (G.P.) work. Said he would begin that chapter in his autobiography saying conservation was the one great continuing policy of his administration.

3/6 Washington Got started on account of T.R.'s work in conservation during his administration with Price.

3/13 Philadelphia T.R. most cordial. Invited me to spend night at Oyster Bay to discuss conservation material I am preparing for his autobiography.

4/7 Washington Mail & wrote on conservation chapter of his autobiography for T.R.

4/8 Washington All day on mail & T.R. autobiography till meeting with Progressives…

4/11 Washington Mail & on material for T.R. on conservation during his seven years. Overton helped me a lot with it all through.

4/12 Washington All day with Overton on work for T.R. till 3.

4/13 Washington All day with accomplishments of conservation in his administration for T.R.

4/14 Washington Working on conservation material for T.R.

4/15 Oyster Bay …Reached Oyster about 8. Found the Lees of London there. Pleasant evening. T.R. went over the 10,000 words, or part of it, I brought him, & said he was much pleased. Said he would send me all his conservation chapters & have chance to go over them, correct them, & send them on to Jim.

5/28 Marquette …T.R. said no other man in his administration had so many different kinds of business with him, & said I was to quote him on that.

6/13 Milford …evening read Mamee T.R.'s article on conservation in his administration. She was very indignant at his scant mention of me. So was I, a little, especially in view of his declarations that he would give me much credit & several times repeated.

6/24 New York After lunch T.R. took me aside & said he had intended to treat me as he did himself (in his autobiography) by merely reciting facts, but now he had decided to say <u>what</u> I had done & what I was. Never mentioned Mamee. He had previously told me both in N.Y. & on way to Marquette that he would give me full credit for what I had done during his administration.

7/2 Newport …Talk with T.R. in morning. He repeated he had intended to treat me as himself in his memoirs, but was deeply obliged to Mamee for calling attention to the matter, and would now say in detail, "what you did & what you are." A very confidential talk. He is doing his best to be nice. Ǥ

SECRETARY BALLINGER

"The opinions seem to be sweepingly our way"

Of all the experiences and challenges in Gifford Pinchot's long life, the most significant to him was his conflict with Richard A. Ballinger, secretary of the Interior during President Willam Taft's administration. Or so it would seem, as judged by his diaries and autobiography. Not only is a full third of *Breaking New Ground* devoted to Ballinger, but his diary entries for the time he was writing the book show that he spent more time and sought more expert advice on that subject than on any other, as he literally relived the earlier period.

Scholars have been fascinated as well. There are two full monographic studies and many chapters in other books that treat in detail just what happened and why the Ballinger controversy was significant to history. At the time, it was a scandal of national importance, and newspapers from coast to coast featured daily stories both before Pinchot's termination and for the months of the ensuing congressional investigation, held by the Joint Committee to Investigate the Interior Department and the Forestry Service. The voluminous official hearings themselves were published in thirteen volumes. It is fair to say that the conflict so weakened President Taft that he was denied a second term. It is also likely that Roosevelt decided to run once again for president as the "Bull Moose" candidate to salvage his programs that Taft seemed to be dismantling. Further, because of this Republican split, Woodrow Wilson was elected president, the first Democrat since the Civil War, except for Grover Cleveland's two terms. And a discredited Forest Service under Chief Henry S. Graves would face tough times in Congress. This is, then, a huge topic, portrayed here only in its narrowest context—that is, how Pinchot recorded it in his diaries.

Unfortunately, Pinchot's diaries for 1908 and 1909 are missing, and the 1910 volume contains only eleven entries related to the Ballinger conflict during the first four months of the year, when the controversy was at its peak. What follows mainly is an account of an Alaskan trip in 1911, at his own expense, as he walked the contested land to see for himself, and as he accompanied Secretary of the Interior Walter Fisher, who wanted more specific information on the Alaska situation. Not all that much of a historical record, but it does show just how important it was to Pinchot to gather even more evidence for the court of public opinion that he had indeed been "right" all along.

Perhaps the story begins in late 1906, when President Theodore Roosevelt created a reserve of coal-bearing lands in Alaska, an action important enough to Pinchot that he noted it in his diary. It was not much of a headline grabber during an administration that was at the same time creating vast acreages of national forests, wildlife refuges, and national monuments. As with many such withdrawals—which suspended homestead and related laws—the deed was seen as more or less temporary, until Congress came up with a fairer way to distribute the valuable land than allowing it to go in 160-acre parcels to those who "claimed" them. So the withdrawn coal lands sat, until newly elected Taft asked Ballinger to be his secretary of the Interior.

James A. Garfield was secretary of the Interior during President Roosevelt's second term. Pinchot's diaries report that Roosevelt had considered the forester for the post, but the nod went instead to Garfield because Pinchot was a New York resident, a geographical fact of life that westerners in Congress would challenge. But Pinchot harbored no grudge against Garfield; the two were close friends and worked comfortably together on a range of issues. Despite the many diary entries about Garfield's actions, there is nothing in the 1907 diary to suggest that Pinchot was concerned when the secretary picked Ballinger, recently mayor of Seattle, to be commissioner of the General Land Office. And no entries describe his dispute with Ballinger when the commissioner proposed that the coal lands be sold rather than leased—a view that was not all that popular in the Roosevelt administration. So, the diaries do not help us to understand the beginnings of the controversy. Ballinger left the General Land Office in 1908 and returned to Seattle.

During its territorial days, Alaska held special interest to the state of Washington, and especially to Seattle, the gateway to Alaska. It might be for this reason that Ballinger had a special interest in Alaska, but more probably it was that he held traditional, conservative, Republican views instead of the "Progressive" Republican ideas espoused by Roosevelt and Pinchot. President Taft certainly held conservative views, and he was legalistic to an extent his predecessor had not been; in fact, Taft would ultimately be appointed to the U.S. Supreme Court. He also appointed five corporation lawyers ("trust" lawyers, Pinchot would allege) to his cabinet, and one of them was Ballinger. The Taft administration would obey the law, and if a law was "defective," the solution was to get Congress to make things right.

One of Ballinger's first secretarial decisions was to eliminate Pinchot's unique access to Department of the Interior agencies, mainly the General Land Office but also the Bureau of Indian Affairs. Information now had to be channeled from Pinchot to the secretary of Agriculture to the secretary of the Interior and only then to the agency— a big change, and insulting to the forester. Pinchot was especially irked over losing a management program for Indian lands along the lines he had worked out earlier with the General Land Office while the forest reserves had been under Interior jurisdiction. Then there was the matter of water power sites on the national forests. To prevent these sites from going freely to private power concerns, Pinchot claimed them as building sites for ranger stations, but the secretary of the Interior had jurisdiction, and Ballinger denied the forester his "unlawful" tactic. Thus, when Ballinger approved resumption of the processing of Alaskan coal claims, it was yet another rejection of the Roosevelt-Pinchot view of the world, where "right" comes first and the law catches up as best it can.

What had begun as an angry debate over water turned uglier over coal. The thirty-three Cunningham coal claims in Alaska were unofficially named for Clarence Cunningham, who had located them. During subsequent review of the claims, there were complaints of fraud that pointed to the Cunningham group and its arrangement with the Morgan-Guggenheim Syndicate. Ballinger had served as attorney to Cunningham following his stint as commissioner of the General Land Office and had clear-listed the claims while still in public office. Taft saw no evidence of wrongdoing, but Pinchot did.

Pinchot had received information from Louis Glavis of the

Political cartoon published in *New York Times*, August 11, 1909, portraying Secretary of the Interior Ballinger as an enemy of Roosevelt's conservation policies. Pinchot scrapbooks, Library of Congress.

General Land Office that the Cunningham claims were fraudulent. When Taft was informed via Pinchot of the Glavis accusations, he forwarded them to Ballinger, who fired Glavis for insubordination. There was no turning back; when their disagreement had been limited to water, Pinchot declined public comment about Ballinger. Now he spoke out, even after Taft asked that he let the matter rest. It was only a matter of time for the president to fulfill widespread newspaper speculation, and he removed Pinchot from office on January 7, 1910. He also removed Overton Price, Pinchot's second in command, and Alexander Shaw, a member of his legal staff. Henry Graves, Pinchot's good friend and the dean of the Yale Forest School, was named chief.

The diary entries that follow begin with Pinchot's 1906 note of Roosevelt's coal land withdrawal. Then we skip to 1910 to see fragments of the Ballinger conflict. The main story begins in 1911, as Pinchot continues to assess the situation and plan for a trip to Alaska to visit the infamous Cunningham claims, and to meet and learn from and perhaps influence Alaskan politicians and newspapermen.

1906

11/5 Washington …to White House with Hayes and Walcott to recommend withdrawal of coal lands in Alaska. T.R. approved.

1910

1/1 Washington Went to reception at White House. Taft spoke to me pleasantly, wished me a Happy New Year, and I him.

1/14 New York Finished & sent to Shipp in Wash. by Smith of Amos's office my poor statement.

1/17 Washington All the morning preparing speech to the Civic Federation at suggestion of Bass, seconded by Pack, Price, & Shipp. Made talk in P.M. Seemed to succeed.

1/30 Washington Jim Garfield & George Woodruff here. Went over dates and various questions all day. Brandeis, Cotton, & Glavis to dinner. With Price, Slocum & Arnold, and Amos here too, it made quite a formidable Bar.

1/31 Washington …Signing mail. G.P.'s mail in very bad shape. We have about two thousand letters of congratulations [for taking on Ballinger] to answer.

2/1 Washington …Glavis on again at 2 P.M. Donald A. McKenzie's statement of why Garfield was not retained. Root jumped in hard, but accomplished nothing. Garfield was cross-examined all afternoon & lost not a point except initiation of entry.

2/3 Washington …P.M. at work with Nat Smythe on preparing for going on stand…

2/16 Washington All morning with Nat Smythe reviewing my testimony regarding coal claims. Also till about 4 P.M. Dictated nearly the whole story.

3/7 Washington …Took my confidential files back from Joint Investigating Committee Room.

4/11 Porto Maurizio, Italy One of the best & most satisfactory talks with T.R. I ever had. Lasted nearly all day, and till about 10:30 P.M.

4/18 Paris …Good talk w. Mrs. T.R. & Ethel. Also the Jusserands. Most interesting report from home. Taft losing ground steadily.

1911

6/26 New York …Announcement that the Cunningham claims are cancelled. Howard of the U.P. came up & he, Amos, and I got out a statement. Shipp & Welliver called up from Wash. The opinions seem to be sweepingly our way. So that job is done.

7/28 Washington On Alaska article nearly all day. Went with Amos to see Walter Fisher, and warned him that documents had been denied to exist in Ballinger investigation & afterward produced. Also that evidence had been manufactured, as in Wickersham brief. He must not let himself get caught up in case same game was repeated. He asked me to come to consult about coming Denver convention. My statement seems to have gone finely. Nearly all N.Y. & other papers carry it in full. Brandeis

asked Amos to assist him as assistant counsel to the Graham Committee. Fine, if the Committee approves.

7/29 Washington Most of morning over Alaska coal leasing bill with Brooks (USGS) and then with Robinson. Amos & Brandeis told me Graham had agreed to ask Amos to be assistant counsel to his committee…Alaska article in evening.

7/30 Washington Finished first draft article for Sat. Eve. Post, "What shall we do with the coal in Alaska" before supper, & got it off tonight.

8/18 New York Amos & I talk with T.R. He wanted to see me about Alaska & other matters.

8/20 Grey Towers Puzzling over whether or not I ought to drop making a second swordfish trip & go to Alaska. Amos & Price both thinking

Political cartoon published in the Denver *News Times* on August 15, 1909, as Pinchot's conflict with Secretary of the Interior Ballinger was heating up. Pinchot scrapbooks, Pinchot Collection, Library of Congress.

well of it, & I too, tho' not willingly, decided to go. Took afternoon train to N.Y. & went in. I don't think I ever hated to leave any place (of late years) as much as I did Grey Towers this time.

8/21 Washington Went first to see Bob. He thought I ought surely to go to Alaska. Then to see Tom about it. He thought so too in spite of the Kansas City Congress. Then to see Poindexter, who decided to go. Gibson for my going, & in fact everyone. WJ McGee strongly, & Dol. So I will.

8/26 Chicago Came in a morning train and had a long talk with Colver, mainly about Alaska…

8/27 Des Moines Arrive in the morning and found Uncle Henry Wallace not well, but able to be around. Fine talk with him. He agreed it was right I should go to Alaska even though I had to miss the Kansas City Conservation Congress. Read him & his son Harry my Sat. Eve. Post article on Taft. Both said I ought to print it. Uncle Henry was emphatic.

8/31 Seattle …Hotel Washington. Poindexter came in about same time.

9/4 Ketchikan, Alaska—at sea Reached Ketchikan about 1:30 A.M. Was waked up to see a lame correspondent of the Outlook just going South on the Alameda. Also met Rush, a kicker against Forest Service, and others. At daylight to see marvellous run of humpback salmon up a small stream…

9/5 SS Northwestern Long talks A.M. & P.M. with Levy (Agr. Dept) who gave Poindexter and me recast etc.…Afterward he & I agreed to work together next winter. He is [one] who suggested long ago that F.S. should take charge of Indian timber lands.

9/6 Cordova Reached Cordova…No committee to meet us…Decided to go to Seward at once.

9/7 Valdez …Talk with president, Cordova Chamber of Commerce. A small child would talk more reasonable. A strong Guggenheim supporter, organizer of the Cordova coal party.

9/19 Copper River Delta …Met Winkler …& Nathan at the Guggenheim's camp. Arrive Katalla; first man I met, McLeod, said he was my supporter…

9/21 Pile Driver Point—McDonald's Claim …Slept in the sawmill with Dalton & Roswell. Saw a lot of coal this day.

9/26 Katalla Still raining hard…After telephoning Poindexter and Hawkins about getting away on Bertha with the Swan, dictated notes to Stahlnecker & walked over the Martin Point with Lathrop. Helped F.S. boys (Weigel, Hunt, Johnson, Perkins; and Ned Darlee of Katalla) to try to float launch…

9/27 Katalla Still waiting. This A.M. Dalton & I started early for Martin Islands with Johnson (Geo L.) forest ranger to help get the r[u]stlers off the beach, but heard on the way that the Bertha was due any moment, so came back. Long interview with Kennedy, giving his views on the Bering Coal field…

9/28 Katalla The Bertha arrived and we went out to her in the first grey of the dawn in the corsair…

9/29 Cordova–Chitina Took train to Chitina …Reached Chitina about 9 P.M. Met Poindexter & Hawkins. Went around the town, called on editor of newspaper and had good talk with Miles.

9/30 Chitina–Cordova Up early to take train at 7:30…Got in about 4:30. Dietrich met us & told of his & Thislect's arrangement for the meeting the chamber of commerce wouldn't call. Dr. Chase presided, & the meeting was the largest ever held in Cordova. Poindexter especially made a fine talk—anti-monopoly. There were probably 400 people—the hall jammed. It went well.

10/6 Valdez Spent the day seeing people.

Political cartoon published in the Denver *News* on April 17, 1909, suggesting that President Taft would relax conservation policies inherited from President Roosevelt. Pinchot scrapbooks, Pinchot Collection, Library of Congress.

Good talk with Judge Cushman...Am getting to feel the Alaska Road Commission needs a thorough exam.

10/7 Valdez More interviews. Am getting awful tired of waiting for steamers...Friend of Elmore Brown came & told me had been opposed, but had changed his mind. I think I did pretty well in Valdez, as to changing public opinion.

10/8 SS Admiral Sampson Reached Cordova early A.M. Saw the Daltons, Prendergast, and others. Prendergast said he had just heard on good authority that the Syndicate people were tired of Steele and had decided to bounce

him & put Mrs. McAvoy in charge of the Cordova Alaskan...

10/12 Juneau Spent most of the morning at the Land Office with Walker (Registrar) & also Millen (Recorder) on the Ryan claims. Got their status, which is anomalous & may show collusion with the Registrar & Secretary, probably Mullen...After lunch (best Salmon (King) I ever tasted) to Treadwell & Miles...Met by Kinzie & Heywoody. Went down in mine. Went aboard cutter Rush. Met Judge Gunnisan. Supper with the Cobbs. Meeting largest ever in Juneau. Well received. Explained what Conservation really is. Bought $50 of Indian things from Winters and Pond. They are to send them to Wash. with my other things. Met Michell of the Pedwater Mine. Woke up Gabriel, a nice young fellow. Ryan surveyor, & a job with information about claims.

10/13 Juneau–SS Humboldt Sailed about 8:30 A.M. Leaving Juneau with a most kindly feeling for the town and all Alaska…

10/14 SS Humboldt Through Wrangel narrows in the dark. Stop at Wrangel. Most interesting town I have seen yet in Alaska. Old & full of Indian totems. Another sawmill & fine lot of logs…Dictated a lot of stuff to Stahlnecker & went through a lot of papers. Good talk with Miles. Find we agree on pretty much the whole Alaskan question.

10/28 New York After breakfast straight to Amos' office. Worked a little on Alaska Report…

11/12 Washington Working on Alaska article. Just begin. Not much progress…Dr. Precher & Woodruff at dinner. Fisher told George this P.M. he wants me to get behind his Alaska policy. I was behind it long before he ever saw Alaska. He has simply taken on ours.

11/13 Washington Brandeis came after breakfast, & Amos before. Then M.K. Rogers. Conference at which Rogers told about Katalla & Conliotter. Then long conference at Gibson's office. Amos, Brandeis, Gibson, Colver, & I, writing letter to Graham Committee ending investigation. I insisted it should declare reversal

of policy by Administration & adoption by it of ours, & mention had action of B.T.[?] as to Conliotter.

11/16 Washington Completed first draft of Alaska article by working tonight. Overton selected pictures…

1912

1/27 Washington …Judge Wickersham came & said he would stand by me on the leasing proposition. Wanted me to take up the bill for an Alaskan legislature.

3/24 Washington …rest of morning with Price & Holmes on letters [regarding] Alaska Bill, which has good points, but is obviously intended as an Administration substitute for Robinson Bill. We told him he could not substitute it.

1913

4/3 New York–Oyster Bay Went to Ethel Roosevelt's wedding. Stayed with Jim & Helen most of the day. Lots of friends there, a nice wedding & a good time. On way back William Loeb told me the Guggenheims, under his audit of their affairs, want no more coal land in Alaska in fee, but prefer to lease—had offered to lease already, and were willing to sell their RR to the Gov't & then lease it, extend it under government guarantee & in general do just what the government wants them to do. GP

THE NATIONAL CONSERVATION ASSOCIATION
"Public control or no control of lumbering"

"Conservation is a moral issue." Thus wrote Gifford Pinchot in his letter to prospective members of the National Conservation Association after he was elected its president in 1910. The association grew out of the 1908 Conference of Governors, at which Theodore Roosevelt had called conservation a patriotic duty. Patriotism, morality, conservation; the organizational goals were not humble.

The National Conservation Association was formed on July 29, 1909, and Charles W. Eliot, president of Harvard University, was elected president. Soon after Pinchot was removed from office as chief of the Forest Service in January 1910, Eliot stepped down and nominated him to be his successor. Pinchot provided for much of NCA's financial needs, but he also recruited members whose dues would provide income; annual dues began at $2 per year.

"The National Conservation Association is fighting for the prompt and orderly development of our natural resources, for the welfare of ourselves and our children, and for the rights of the plain people." Since the organization had no official connections, "It is free to speak the truth." This sort of high-minded language peppers NCA's promotional literature, language not all that uncommon for advocacy groups. Continuation of Roosevelt's conservation targets, apparently so disrupted by President Taft, was an important goal: protect the public's interest, expand the national forest system, retain mineral rights on public lands, sell water rather than give it to users, and so on down the list. All efforts were characterized as a "battle" or "fight" that led either to "victory" or to "defeat." The moral ground of conservationists would be seized a half-century later by environmentalists, whose brochures would ring much the same.

NCA was just what Pinchot needed to continue his conservation battles at the national level, and his diaries for 1910 through 1914 report on its activities, generally lobbying for and against bills in Congress. Overton Price, Pinchot's associate chief, whom Taft had also fired, and Harry Slattery would manage the organization on a day-to-day basis. Price committed suicide in 1914, and Slattery sustained the program until 1917. Slattery appears again in the diaries for the late 1930s, when he is advising Pinchot from his vantage point in the Department of the Interior. Philip Wells, former Forest Service law officer, also wound up at NCA.

Although it is not always clear whether Pinchot is reporting about NCA or about his personal doings, there are several themes to follow. First, NCA itself: its quest for funding, publication of its magazine *American Conservation*, and Overton Price's deteriorating mental state. Too, we can follow the water power story. The possibility of monopoly control of water power had long been debated and had been a key issue of the conflict with Ballinger, and we know now that the conflict resulted in the 1920 Federal Water Power Act, which generally pleased the conservationists. Also, there is a bit on grazing, and a tantalizing glimpse of the infamous Hetch Hetchy controversy, the damming of the "other" valley in Yosemite National Park that still rankles modern-day environmentalists. Pinchot advocated, successfully, that a Bureau of Mines be established as part of his larger effort to increase federal involvement in natural resources management. Finally, there was states' rights, the at-times strident philosophical debate on the proper role of the federal government in resource management. That controversy has continued to the present day, albeit under different names, as when during the presidency of Ronald Reagan it was called the Sagebrush Rebellion.

Overton Price merits a paragraph of his own. Diary entries confirm what we have read elsewhere about Pinchot's very high opinion of the man. In his foreword to Price's 1911 *The Land We Live In: The Book of Conservation*, Pinchot wrote, "I believe it would be found that he had more to do with the success of the [Forest] Service than I had." In the dedication of his own *Training of a Forester*, which was published in several editions beginning in 1914, he wrote, "To Overton W. Price: Friend and Fellow Worker. To whom is due, more than to any other man, the high efficiency of the United States Forest Service." Price killed himself in Washington on July 11, 1914, but Pinchot made no mention of his death in the diary.

When Woodrow Wilson became president, he named Franklin K. Lane as his secretary of the Interior. Pinchot initially approved, but as so often happened, he and Lane eventually had a falling out. But he worked hard to be effective with the Wilson administration, even hosting at his mother's suggestion the entire cabinet, as a means to be certain they knew who he was. More specifically, we can see conflicts over grazing on the national forests and Pinchot's significant decision to "force" the lumber industry to "practice" forestry. While he had been chief, he made every effort to work cooperatively with the private sector, but out of office he became much more aggressive. History remembers him for his latter pose. And we can see a good example of Pinchot working the media—in this case the *Saturday Evening Post*—as he sought to bolster public opinion. Those who think of Pinchot only as a forester will be surprised to read just how thoroughly he considered heading an agricultural organization to aid farmers.

The National Conservation Association fizzled out in 1923, no doubt because Pinchot had been elected governor of Pennsylvania and was turning his attention away from conservation matters. The Pinchot papers held by the Library of Congress include fifty-four boxes of NCA records, extending to 1923. However, the diary itself ends in 1914, so we read only part of the story here.

1910

1/30 Washington …Phil Wells finally decided, with Graves & me, to leave the Forest Service & come to the N.C.A. Harry agreed it was wise.

1/31 Washington …with Pepper and Newell all the morning on power withdrawals. Very satisfactory. At the Willard. Also Phil Wells. Lunch with Pepper, Wells, & Bass. Considered whether I should go & see Taft on the conservation bills. No decision. Afternoon Davis (A.P.) came in. Excellent talk with him & Pepper.

2/16 Washington …Regis Post came into N.C.A to raise money @ $100 per month & expenses. Talk with Melendy. Told him to organize Chicago Conservation Committee soon as possible, & keep N.C.A. clear. [B]ig meeting [is] Taft's to address.

3/7 Washington …At conference with Price & Shipp approved general organization for N.C.A.

1911

2/9 Washington Preparing for talk tonight with Price & Graves. Got Judd Welliver to see Wells about water power steals. He will make them public in the Times. "American Conservation" nearly ready to appear.

2/16 Washington With Holmes devising amendments for Nelson leasing bill. Talk with McGee about his item in Agriculture bill. Writing speech for People's Forum. Learned that sheep men are trying to get rates reduced in national forests and that Crane's new power bill is bad…hour's talk with Graves about above. Then with Shipp going over speech, which he likes.

2/17 Washington Saw Bristow in A.M. Madison was there too. We wrote out proposed amendment to Agriculture bill directing Secretary of Agriculture to charge sheep men what the range is worth, for Bristow to introduce. Later in the day, Graves told me he had decided to report adversely on Crane bill, & not try to suggest amendments. This was right. The Crane bill was procured by the powermen in spite of their agreement with Graves.

3/3 Washington Got to Forest Service about 10:30. Looked up Record, & found Heyburn Amendment (to exclude every 160 acres with less than 4 thousand board feet of timber) had been adopted. Potter said that it had not, although he was there at the time. Sent for Shipp & Price. Dol came in. We four prepared statement for the press, Price arranged for me to address Lumber Dealers then in session, and I did so at 12:30. By 2 strong resolution backing

Forest Service had been unanimously adopted and went at once to President by delegation, with letter asking him to veto Agriculture bill if the amendment went through. It was effective, and great fun. Like old times. Also we wired all over West, and protests began reaching Warren (acting chairman Agriculture Committee) at once. Heyburn amendment went out in conference this P.M. Also Carter's amendment favoring fake miners. But Dixon failed to press his advantage, & we got no increase in Senate. He was sick.

3/7 New York Work on train on editorials for March American Conservation. Finished two.

3/23 Naples …Quiet evening. Copied & mailed edit on waterflow.

3/25 Rome …Letters from Shipp, telling how Fisher sent for him & Wells.

4/16 Rome …I returned Price's article on lumber situation with a lot of corrections. He was too hard on H.K.'s report.

5/25 Washington At work catching up with mail, etc. Talk with Price & Shipp. N.C.A. magazine late in appearing.

5/28 Washington…Read 3 chapters Price's book. Admirable.

5/29 Washington Talk with Graves. Plan to tell all about attacks on conservation now being planned in my speech at Conservation Congress. Also to force lumbermen to go into forestry in fact. Letters etc. Talk with Price about some things & money for Forest Service & grazing fees…Reading manuscript Price's book. It is A1.

5/31 Washington …Harry Stimson for medicine ball & dinner. Then Overton & I went to see Graves, who had sprained his ankle. We decided to start forcing the lumbermen to practice forestry, for the time has come.

6/8 Milford …Working on odds & ends, especially foreword for Price's book, & editorial on George Otis Smith's holding up Appalachian purchases for American Conservation.

6/9 Grey Towers …Finished foreword to Price's book & mailed it. Nearly finished editorial on George Otis & Appalachians for June American Conservation.

6/10 Grey Towers …Completed & mailed editorial after showing it to Bill Kent, who approved if facts were O.K. Wire George Bird Grinnell & others I must resign if Audubon Society doesn't rescind acceptance of $25,000 a year from arms people…

6/12 Washington …to N.C.A. Conference with Glendenning. Tom, Overton, & I decided we must have $7,400 for K.C. meeting Conservation Congress.

6/16 New York …meeting to decide about Audubon Association taking $25,000 from Winchester & other arms people. George B. Grinnell voted to keep it, all the others against. I spoke against.

6/26 New York …Working on editorial on water power for American Conservation.

6/27 New York Met Harry Graves for breakfast at the Belmont. He wanted me not to attack Administration so I could be called into conferences next winter by Fisher and Stimson. Told him why I could not hold off.

7/21 New York Good talk with Woodrow Wilson at the Collingwood. Said he had always been clear that national government should hold its own things such as forest & water power, & not cede them to the states. Will come to Conservation & Public Land Congresses if he can…Miss Julie Jones came at 3:30. Arranged to go to Alabama, if possible with Hobson & make addresses on conservation.

7/29 …Talk with Price about Adirondack work. Signed letter to N.C.A. directors advocating dropping magazine…Talk with Price about his relation to N.C.A. He is depressed & must have a long rest.

7/31 Washington …Another talk with Overton, who is afraid there may be no work in N.C.A. that would justify his keeping on. He is badly overworked.

8/1 New York Started at 6:30 on editorial for August American Conservation giving readers why this will be last number. Dictated it in Amos's office. Met Ikkes (?) of Chicago. Then to Outlook. While waiting for T.R. read editorial of issue August 5. It certifies to Taft's good intention in a wholly false & needless way. I told T.R. so vigorously. He took me in to editorial counsel & I explained I objected & why. Told him I could not peacefully look forward to 4 extra years of fighting for conservation, & thing to do is to beat Taft from nomination.

Said any other Republican that could be nominated would be OK on conservation & T.R. agreed.

11/16 Washington …[Price] will stay with N.C.A. if I don't have to carry it financially. Will put all he earns outside into it & proceeds of The Land We Live In. Also had reduced his salary to $3,500. He is one of the finest, most high minded men I ever knew.

11/24 Washington At work at home all day with Price on Adirondack report. Got first draft done & went over it with Graves after dinner. He is for waiting 10 to 20 years before cutting on state lands. Told me about Fisher wanting to take Forest Service away from Agriculture Department, and probably control grazing also

Conference in Battle Creek, Michigan, January 1911, "To consider how the human race may be improved." Nutritionist John Harvey Kellogg is at center. Pinchot Collection, Library of Congress.

on public range. Also to control water power development in national forests. Gave material to N.Y. American about water power monopoly. *11/25 Washington* Conference with Coville about Fisher's probable desire to have charge of grazing on public domain. Saw Galloway & suggested dinner on December 1 to agree on a plan. He did not want to come to such a dinner, but suggest…Graves should call a meeting. As soon as I left, I found out later, he went straight to Wilson & told all about it & apparently garbled the story, too, & Wilson told Graves he wanted no such meeting. With Price finished Adirondack report.

11/29 Washington Mail & at N.C.A. Grazing & water power bills. Talk with H.K. & got his draft of water power bill.

11/30 Washington Morning on mail & grazing bill with Price. Got a pretty fair draft. Walk with Billy Kent in P.M.

12/1 Washington Grazing bill in A.M. Bill Kent not well satisfied with it…Water power bill in afternoon and evening.

12/2 Washington Kent & Coville about grazing bill. H.K. Smith about water power bill…With Price took 12:30 to New York. Got plans for N.C.A. straightened out on way, or rather simply OK what Price advised.

12/3 New York After lunch wrote & before dinner mailed to Price amendments to Robinson bill for Bob [LaFollette]. Fairly good job, I think. Long talk with Moore about water power. Very useful as showing what I have to meet tomorrow. He agrees with me, mainly. Also talk with Burke (?) attorney for Conservation Commission on land laws.

12/26 Washington …With Price went over report of N.C.A.

12/28 Washington Pretty much all day on 1. Meeting Board Directors N.C.A. White, Farquahr, Amos, Price, & I. 2. Speech for Ohio. Amos helped me a lot.

1912

1/5 Washington Forest Service at nine preparing a statement on Raker's water power grab bill. Then to meeting Advisory Board proposed Conservation Exposition. Then to see Raker & tried to get him to withdraw bill temporarily. He wouldn't. Got Lenroot, Graham, Copley, Sweet, & Billy Kent interested against it. Mann objected, it went to Union calendar. Goodman & Ellis at N.C.A.

1/11 New York Took 9:35 train with Slattery. Talk about office organization on train. He had excellent ideas. Lunch at Century. P.M. on mail—especially letter to Dan Beard about my Adirondack report.

1/13 Washington Took 10:08 train with Slattery…Price reported fine results from Raker bill circular.

1/15 Washington Mail. Trying to see congressmen about Raker bill, etc. Poor luck. Lunch with Dol & Price.

1/16 Washington Mail. Saw Lever about A.K. Fisher's work & the Raker bill. Graham about grazing & water power bills. Talk with Billy Kent. Could not get his attention.

1/18 Washington …At N.C.A. most of day. Ride in P.M.

2/2 Washington …N.C.A. Senator Gibson & Chubback came in. Talk with Price about letter to Bob. Talk with him & Graves about Smoot bill, Forest Service appropriation, & Adirondack situation. P.M. & evening on letter to Bob Gibson & Woodruff & Mamee went over it in evening. R.S. Baker said he was sure Bob would soon attack T.R. I believe so too, & that he will then get after the rest of us. All in evening strong for a radical stand.

2/4 Washington Mail. Conference with J.A. Holmes & Johnson about Conservation Committee of International Chemical Congress. Price about N.C.A…dictated statement on Adirondack situation & answered letters.

2/9 New York …Baden Powell Boy Scouts Dinner, at which I presided. About seven hundred men & women at Hotel Astor. I did only fairly well, I think. Still it was a lively & good humored dinner, & all seemed to have a good time. Dan Beard made the best speech.

2/15 Washington Mail & catching up. Raker bill fight going finely. So also fight to prevent cut in fire prevention funds of Forest Service. Saw Morse & told him I didn't think his statement will do much harm…Executive meeting S.A.F. After good talk with Graves. We decided N.C.A. should make statement about Forest Service cut.

2/18 Washington Price, Holmes, Johnson, McGee to confer on chemical congress next fall—conservation section.

2/20 Albany To Conservation Committee first. No one, practically, at hearing till after or just before lunch. About 6 Camp Fire men came up. Only reached Section 88 (control of logging on private lands) just before adjournment in P.M. Lumbermen evidently a good deal interested. Good attendance. Evening gave illustrated talk on Adirondack problem in Assembly chamber. A good many standing up. Did fairly well.

2/21 Albany Met Dr. Culver, a progressive Democrat. Hearing continued. Got pretty mean at times. Meigs, Jones of Emporium Lumber Company, Parker of Sklyn Cooperage company were very main speakers on their side. Kellar, Parker's lawyer, asked me questions, but got little satisfaction. Lunch with Moore & others. Hearing again in P.M. We have clear cut issue of public control or no control of lumbering. Prof.[?] Section 88 will be cut out of bill, but we have a plan.

2/23 Washington …Lunch with Price at Cosmos. Our conservation work going finely. He has a fine plan to make agitation for getting Forest Service funds cut down by House Agriculture Committee replaced in Senate.

Agreed to write article on control Adirondack lumbering for Outlook if they will take it.

2/24 Washington …Saw Pickett, who agreed to take up getting hearings on grazing bill. Told him about hotels on rim of Crater Lake…Graves getting very much like a T.R. man.

2/28 Washington Meeting advisory board national conservation exposition.

2/29 Washington …Met Joseph Vels at N.C.A. Am to arrange for him to see T.R….

3/2 Kaukakee Today up late. Finished & mailed article for Outlook on effort to restrict private logging in Adirondacks.

3/11 Washington Talk with Adams (assistant secretary of the interior) about getting H.K.'s water power report made public in time to kill Raker bill next Wednesday. Adams flabby. H.K. very much otherwise.

3/13 Washington Forest Service increase for roads & trails for $270,000 to $500,000 was carried Monday (I think) by 74 to 70 & lost on Tuesday after several readings of bill by party vote after caucus. Lost because Graves' testimony was so weak. A shame. Raker bill killed this P.M. 128 to 10! Great credit due Price & Slattery.

3/23 Washington Mail, etc. At headquarters. Talk with Gibson about article…P.M. with Graves. Saw Underwood & got his strong approval of grazing bill & less strong approval of water power bill.

4/29 Washington Disposed of nearly all my mail & some back papers. Price back, & had a good talk with him…Lunch with Price & Harry, bracing Harry up to fight hard on the grazing bill. Good talk.

4/30 Washington Mail. Seeing Newlands & others. Left word at Borah's office I would publish statement on 3 year Homestead act, approving 4 conditionally. He wanted me to wait. Stopped to thank Chamberlain & Grove for getting back amount of estimates reduced by House in Forest Service appropriation. Talked with Fisher about 3 year statement. Getting N.C.A. matters in order. McGee to dinner.

7/27 Washington Saw Slattery first after breakfast. He explained situation. Then Billy Kent, who suggested statement by N.C.A. After conference with Rainey on Omnibus Dam bill with Frankfurter in P.M. & evening got up statement showing it should provide for compensation to government & right to fix rates if necessary. Finished about midnight. Supper with Newell.

7/28 Washington Working at signing letters to congressmen on Omnibus Dam bill. Lunch at the Graves' with Billy Kent.

11/7 Washington Mail first. Then to N.C.A. after lunch. Overton feeling very much better. The work in fine shape. Walter Page came in at 4:30 to get advice about Secretary of Agriculture for Wilson. I recommended C.S. Barrett, Joe Teal, & Clarence Poe.

11/8 Washington Mail, etc. Talk with Price about plans to fight states rights in coming session. N.C.A. will be busier than ever.

11/9 Washington …letter to Brandeis, Crane, Page, & Hapgood to get their help against dismembering national forests by securing statement from Wilson. Hanson & Price had a talk on government organization.

12/1 Washington …called up Dixon, & showed him draft of bills to be introduced at once. He agreed to introduce them with a speech.

12/2 Washington Short dictations, then at N.C.A. with Price going over plans & getting bills for Dixon corrected and rewritten. Lunch with Price & Graves. Good talk. Also Dol Smith…Mark Sullivan after lunch to get material for articles on Coosa Dam steal & states rights & attack on national forests. Is to make

this the big issue of Colliers. More mail. Newell came in.

12/3 Washington Called up Dixon about the bills. He wanted to postpone them all till after the Chicago meeting. I went up & saw him & he agreed to introduce them, most of them, Wednesday. Most of the day with Price on conservation plans & annual report to directors.

12/5 Washington …to N.C.A. for meeting of directors. Also present Farquhar, Bass, & Teal. Good meeting.

12/16 Washington …walk with Norman Hapgood & Will Kent. Norman confident Wilson will be for conservation & also for North American or Pan American Conference at Knoxville, of which I told him. Also of world conference on inventory of natural resources.

12/26 Washington Mail. Arranged with Bill Kent to write letter to Bryan about Ferris & the chairmanship Public Lands Committee. He gave me to read his letter to McAdoo. P.M.… Billy came in & then started for Northern California. He is much worried over threat to contest his seat, & attack on conservation.

1913

1/2 Washington …Fight on Forest Service & Phil Wells about nine on water power…Called on Harry Stimson—a good talk about his great success in getting Stout & Webster to agree to compensation to put in Connecticut River bill.

1/5 Washington …8.30 saw Senator Gow(?) to protest against Norris as Secretary of the Interior (possibly). Said he doubted whether any western man should be appointed. Told him I would help Wilson if I could to help the country. Good talk.

1/8 Washington Found all well. Mail…Told Lowry Stewart at N.C.A. no work for him there, but I would see what I could do to help on return to Washington. A.F.A annual meeting. Saw a lot of men. At lunch Fisher spoke about his new permit to the Great Falls Power Company in Montana (Amalgamated) but gave no credit to Forest Service. I followed & showed Forest Service came first in unofficial way. Made speech about attempt to cede national forests to states.

1/10 Washington Found Herbert King here. He said, after examination, Charley Walcott's condition very serious. Graves came in. Arranged to meet attack on agricultural land policy of Forest Service.

1/11 Washington …Lunch with Harry Graves, E.T. Allen, Capt. Adams at Cosmos Club. Long talk with Walter Fisher after. He wanted power to issue water power permits in national forests. I objected. (Smoot bill was the occasion.) Phil Wells came & told me about it early this A.M. Then I told Walter I would be glad to see him stay as Secretary of the Interior.

1/12 Washington Up late. Working on mail, and preparing statement on bills introduced etc. in time of turning resources over to the states. Slattery gave me a wretchedly incorrect summary of bills.

1/13 Newport …under auspices of Progressive League, I spoke on conservation. About 550. Pretty fair talk, but not A1. They seemed pleased.

1/16 Syracuse Went over proposed speeches on train. Arrive about 11. Spoke first to meeting N.Y. state Forestry Association, and to forest students. Substitute Yale lecture on personal attitude. Then big lunch Syracuse Chamber of Commerce. About 250. Some 100 could not get in, I was told by Woodworth who presided. Spoke on conservation & present attack on Forest Service. Did fairly…Hugh Baker impressed me very much. Strong anti states rights resolution almost passed. Many lumbermen present. I suspect their effort to control forestry association.

1/17 Washington …Lunch with Graves at Cosmos, to get material for answering editorial in Saturday Evening Post. Prosser came in at 5:30 in interest of the Page vocational education bill. Slattery with more letters about states rights fight to sign. A lot incorrect, as usual…Charley wired me to send material on states rights to his friend Vernon of Reston at Princeton to get it thus to Wilson. I did.

1/18 Washington …Beveridge for a walk. Says Clapp is very downcast. Dol with material to answer unfounded editorial on Forest Service timber sales policy in Saturday Evening Post.

1/19 Philadelphia …Walk with Needhaus & Lorimers about L's place. Pleasant dinner. Lorimer said when I left, "send me material about the conservation situation in Washington and I'll do my part." He meant from time to time…Took 3 P.M. train to Washington. Dinner with Mamee & Polly at Wills'. Antonette Frizzell there. Told us Newlands told her he was for Teal for secretary of the interior. At 9 got to Newlands' house (he told Mamee he must see me). Newlands asked Newell & me many questions about Teal. Said he would recommend him to Wilson, whom he sees tomorrow. Said Norris & Haroby had no show. I came back much delighted & told Mamee.

1/20 Washington Mail, etc. Walk with Beveridge, who pressed me to go to St. Paul with him. Can't possibly. Got Graves & Greeley started on return editorial for Saturday Evening Post.

1/21 Washington Mail, etc. Greeley came up with a revised flier draft for Saturday Evening Post. Price back from British Columbia to my great satisfaction. A man named Knowles of Pittsburgh Flood Commission came in to talk on water matters. Price had a very successful time in B.C. Lunch with Price at home. To N.C.A. after. Slattery is getting unbearably sloppy in his clerical work. Walk with Newell.

1/22 Washington Mail, etc. Finished and

mailed to Lorimer suggested editorial for Saturday Evening Post in defense of timber sale policy of Forest Service. Went over with Bill Kent conservation situation before his visit to Wilson tomorrow. Worked at night on editorial. Talk with Henry Stimson at his breakfast at National Hotel. Got his passive assent to Farmers Union endorsing him for Secretary of Agriculture. Duebeonth took it up.

1/23 Washington Mail, etc. Lunch with Frankfurter and Josiah Newcombe on Brandyce bill (Connecticut River power development by Stone & Webster). As result he was persuaded our publicity plan was right. Stirred up Duckworth & Davis about Barrett. They were using mails, not wires as they should.

1/24 Washington Getting pretty near to top on mail. $14.00 worth of stamps used in my office since January 1, not counting mail sent out from N.C.A. Bill Kent told me Wilson said to him in public. His clear duty was to support national against states rights view in natural resource matters, & that Wilson agreed fully & cordially with him (Kent) as to conservation. Wilson agreed with Kent that if Fisher had been Secretary of the Interior from first Taft would now be president elect. That disposes of fear of trouble in conservation with Wilson. Newlands told me Wilson was questioning wisdom of appointing any man from West because of local influence upon him. This quoted from Wilson. Lorimer wired he could take article on Forest Service. Frankfurter & Josiah Newcombe came in P.M. to see my statement for N.C.A. on Brandyce bill, & Newcombe called up Boston to arrange for statement by Stone & Webster.

1/25 Washington All day, nearly, on article for Saturday Evening Post. Got material from Forest Service. Discussed outline with Price. Saw Barrett & Duckworth in P.M. & had walk with former. If he is offered Secretary of Agriculture he says he wants my help. I said I couldn't enter Department, but would help all I could. Scheme to write every newspaper editor in U.S. for conservation is working out. An excellent plan. My scheme, I'm proud to say. Justice & Mrs. Lamar, Dr. & Mrs. Woodward, & Bob & Mrs. Chapman, & Slattery to dinner. Reception. Very tired. A hard week. Duckworth & Davis working hard for Barrett for Secretary of Agriculture.

1/26 Washington Horace Plunkett came. Wants me to quit active connection with politics and take up reconstruction of agriculture in U.S. Thinking hard about it. Barrett (Farmers Union) at lunch. Made unexpectedly poor impression—yielding to pressure and not leading his men. All day on article for Saturday Evening Post. Very tired & making slow headway. Walk with Graves. I suggested possibility of his retiring to New Haven & Price taking Forest Service. Wants Price back in larger government field. So do I. He is too good for his present work…Quiet dinner at home. F.H. Newell came in after. Also strong I should take up agriculture work. He had seen Horace.

1/27 Washington Saturday Evening Post article. With Horace after lunch to see Olmsted at Department of Agriculture to get some facts about condition of farms & soil in U.S., preparatory to his speech…Very tired. Stomach bad. Have been eating too much trash.

1/28 Washington Finished up Saturday Evening Post article. Got it checked by Greeley & Price & approved, and sent it off about 5:45.

1/29 Washington Got Graves's OK on two year statement of delay in claims (Saturday Evening Post article). Various odd jobs. Long talk with Newlands about Brandyce bill (water power). He did not promise what his action would be. Contemplates retirement. Talk with Price & Slattery about prospective attacks on Forest Service.

1/30 Washington …Mr. Bryce told me I ought to get out of all other work & stick to conservation for a year or two or three years on account of serious attacks he saw coming.

2/2 New York Up very late. Amos & I lunched with Charley Crane at Century Club…After lunch Charley told me Wilson will send for me, & that he is sound on conservation.

2/3 New York …Lunch with Alec Proctor at Century. Meeting Legislative Reference Committee. At my suggestion we decided at last to make a general plan. At Heney's we took up water power legislation & decided to take a strong position. Also on other conservation matters…They all…want me to head an agriculture organization society in U.S. I said I would consider it.

2/4 New York Met Horace & McCarthy with Amos at Prichett's office…Pritchett said he thought he could get half a million for Agricultural Society.

2/5 Washington Mail mainly. Conservation matters with Price. At his suggestion we decided to make the director of the N.C.A. responsible for financing its work…Signing 3d sheets letter on states rights & Forest Service to editor. Shall go to every edition of a daily paper, a bi or tri weekly, & best weekly in each town of any size.

2/7 Washington …Signed about 500 letters to editors in evening. I find my regular rate will run about 300 per hour under perfect conditions & without strain. Good time at the club with Price, Graves, Greeley, & Adams.

2/8 Philadelphia …Meeting Legislative Reference Committee…at Dean Lewis's office. Present Miss Kellor, Heney, H.K. Smith, Weyl, Lewis. General plans for special & most regular sessions of Congress. Decided to push water power & Alaska legislation at once, decided to issue statement at once on Coosa River & Connecticut River dam bills. I wrote it & Weyl made some changes in style.

2/18 Washington …Agreed with Overton to make systematic effort to spread water power facts between sessions of Congress this year. Also to make special effort to push idea that conservation does not delay development. Spoke at Nurses Club this P.M. on conservation. Took up cost of living & present fight in Congress. Connecticut River bill passed in bad form yesterday. Newlands double crossed us again.

2/19 Washington …Letters to editors getting good response. Planning next on water power with special matter to each state.

2/25 Washington Saw Poindexter for Dr. Merriman about seal islands appropriation in Alaska. Newlands & Pittman for Ellis about appropriation for conservation exposition.

2/26 Washington …Saw Chamberlain of Oregon & arranged he should present letters from settlers favoring national forest if there was a fight in Senate.

2/27 Washington Mail. Am really catching up…Work afternoon & evening. Agriculture bill passed Senate today without a fight on Forest Service. This is the very first time since the fighting began. Talk with Newell about Agriculture Organizations Association. He approves. My article "Uncle Sam's Woodlot" in Saturday Evening Post out today.

3/1 Washington Mail & catching up. Getting into really decent shape again as to back work, or nearly so…Much speculation about Cabinet. Stories of Norris of Montana for Secretary of the Interior thick again. I don't believe them. Neither does Charley Crane. Chamberlain of Oregon called up, much exercised about this.

3/2 Washington Will Ellis to see Governor Jess Cleary of Kentucky about getting Sheeley of Kentucky to favor National Conservation Exposition appropriation.

3/5 Washington …Called to Congressman Franklin K. Lane. He was out. It seems to be an excellent Cabinet. Houston says Needham this evening, is a dandy. Sam McClure much worried about his future.

3/8 Washington …Went to see Lane. Very pleasant talk. Said he was greatly delighted with Wilson. I spoke well of Wells, the only man who knew whole conservation situation, & told Lane I was not going to offer advice, but I was at his service.

3/18 Washington All morning meeting Board of Directors N.C.A. Finance committee provided for and 6 new directors.

3/21 Washington Got little done in A.M. …Price came in. Much discouraged & inclined to quit N.C.A. I am awfully sorry he is tired out again.

4/2 Washington …Long talk with Price, he's very much & very seriously depressed. I am afraid. Harry & I both think he will have to leave the association.

4/3 Washington Catching up. Long talk with Mrs. Price about Overton, & then with Dol Smith & later Harry Graves. Something must be done. Slattery got me some material & Harry & I read papers to a big meeting S.A.F. in evening, on states rights. He took what the states have not done to show they are capable of handling the resources, and I [gave] facts showing how serious the movement was before we beat it as to national forests. Talk with Overton & Harry after the meeting.

4/7 Washington …Talk with Overton, who got a lot of good for his nervous depression from Dr. Harden. The evening I saw Dr. Harden, who says Overton's trouble is all nervous and can be cured. Meeting with District Foresters at two, on working plan preparation.

4/9 Washington …All day on mail and reception for Lane & Houston. Overton getting gloomy again.

4/13 Washington …meeting with Lane, Bill Kent, & Lenroot at Lane's office this P.M. First long talk about F.H. Newell. Lane took the position that F.H. could not be a good executive because he offended certain people, & that he must be relieved for that reason. I said he ought first to talk with F.H., then announce definitely he would not stand for repudiation of debts to Reclamation Fund, and then go west & see the work & the people. I did not at all like his attitude. Then we talked about a conservation program for next session. He is against states rights, evidently, but vague & inconclusive. We talked in all about an hour & a half to get half an hour's business done. Work again in evening. As I told Lenroot & Kent, I must go after Lane publicly if he fires Newell. I told him how it would encourage the grafters.

4/15 Washington Saw Mrs. Vrooman, who was very much disturbed because the anti-conservation women threatened to oppose my speaking to D.A.R. Spoke, & no trouble. Did rather poorly.

4/26 Washington Overton is certainly no better. Work on "Forestry as a Profession" and letter to Lawrence Abbott in "Do Forests influence streamflow." Evening big reception for Secretaries Lane & Houston. About 800 came. Seemed to be a great success. Secretaries Garrison, Bueleson, & Redfield came also. A lot of Justices, etc. It was a great idea of Mamee's, holding this reception.

4/27 Washington Walk with Dol Smith & fine talk about cooperation.

5/19 Washington …Overton saw Houston today, who arranged with him to come back into the Forest Service, if Wilson agrees. It is just the right solution. I am delighted.

5/20 Washington Mail, etc. Saw F.H. & congratulated him on result of hearings before secretary of the Interior.

6/4 Washington Mail. N.C.A. coupons. Made deposit of coupons in Mundy Trust Company.

6/25 Washington Up early. Bill Kent came & took me to meeting Public Lands Committee on Hetch Hetchy. Lane & Houston testified, & then I came. Opposition reduced mainly to "nature-lovers." Scott Ferris doing best to be cordial. Raker also. Taylor of Colorado made us attack. Slattery says House is safe on conservation, as shown by recent attack on Forest Service. Vic Murdock says Republicans were much peeved by Humphrey's attack on Forest Service.

7/3 Newport Conference on Conservation. Mrs. Edith Ellicott Smith, Lewis Frizzert, P.P. Wells, and H.K. Smith. A good meeting, with about 110 present. Leroy wanted us to hold that in his big tent.

7/29 Eldorado, Arkansas …Reading Hetch Hetchy hearings, part II.

8/18 Washington All day on mail, etc. Long talk with Graves, who is stampeded, I think, about getting agricultural land out of the national forests too fast. Told him his plan would ruin half the state forests of Europe & am sure it could.

1914

1/8 Washington Coville came in on grazing bill—then Price & Graves ditto…Met Mrs. Pryor & Price at Conservation Association & she told her story. I have seldom heard a more convincing statement. She has evidently been treated unjustly. The Forest Service is in real danger because she has told Senator Williams & will tell others. Graves does not seem to get the point.

1/9 Washington Senator Williams came in. Very determined. But Graves had already been there & told me he would set Mrs. Pryor right.

2/24 Washington …Spent day on mail, etc. Tried to see Wilson about water power policy, but he was too busy with Mexico & the canal tolls. Slattery reported on conservation matters. Said Garrison was not telling truth when he said he approved Roanoke Dam bill as matter of routine.

5/6 New York …Finished & mailed letter to Scott Ferris against proposed transfer national forest water power control to Interior Department. GP

Part II
1936 –1946

GIFFORD PINCHOT THE ELDER STATESMAN
"The Old Guard loses, the conservation idea wins"

When we last saw Gifford Pinchot in his diaries, it was 1915. Then, he was much involved with the National Conservation Association and beginning his marriage to Cornelia Bryce. Now it is 1936, when the diaries resume, and he has failed at bids for the U.S. Senate but succeeded twice at being elected governor of Pennsylvania. He also served as commissioner of forests for the state of Pennsylvania and sailed the south seas with his son Gifford Bryce Pinchot, who was born in 1915.

When his second term as governor ended in 1935, Pinchot was looking for things to do. We can see in his diaries, and especially in the much larger context of his papers at the Library of Congress, that he collected and organized family history. He sorted photographs and dictated his mother's diaries and parts of his own, as well as much early correspondence. A member of his staff waded through many cartons of newspaper clippings dating from the 1890s and assembled enough scrapbooks, arranged roughly by chronology and topic, to eventually require twenty-six reels of microfilm to record them all. The writing of his autobiography, *Breaking New Ground*, was a part of this historical effort.

His associates had changed after twenty years, except for Harry Slattery from the National Conservation Association, who was now a high official in the Department of the Interior, and Herbert "Dol" Smith, former Forest Service editor and soon to be major contributor to *Breaking New Ground*.

A new face, as it were, was that of President Franklin D. Roosevelt, who had been governor of New York when Pinchot governed Pennsylvania. They knew each other and had a basically friendly relationship; Pinchot often refers to "Franklin." Just as Roosevelt was a moderate, if innovative, Democrat, Pinchot was a progressive Republican: they really were not all that far apart politically. FDR stayed the course while Pinchot edged left and in effect became a Democrat himself by 1940.

Their wives are an important part of this story. In 1915 Cornelia, or Leila, and Pinchot had gone to Europe to help with relief for refugees from a war that had yet to reach the United States. Since then, she had campaigned vigorously for him as governor, run for Congress three times herself (when Pinchot dictated his 1910 diary, the stenographer typed it on the backs of leftover "[Cornelia Bryce] Pinchot for Congress" letterhead), and was a significant figure in women's suffrage. Now in the diaries she is C.B. and sometimes C.B.P. She and Eleanor Roosevelt had known each other since dancing school in 1912, and we can see them working together during World War II.

Gifford Bryce Pinchot is in college and deciding to enter medical school, and he and Sarah "Sally" Richards marry. "Giff" and Sally are frequent visitors at Grey Towers, and Gifford is always delighted to see them, their dogs Nietsche and George Rat, and eventually their children.

Politics is still important. Pinchot very actively campaigned for Alfred Landon, governor of Kansas, who was Republican candidate for president in 1936. Briefly, Pinchot considered the possibility of being his vice-presidential running mate, but nothing came of it. Perhaps it was just as well; Roosevelt trounced Landon, producing one of the most lopsided Electoral College tallies in history. Landon was the last Republican presidential nominee who had Pinchot's support; he could not stomach Wendell Wilkie in 1940 or Thomas Dewey in 1944. To him, both were "Old Guard plutocrats."

In 1937 Pinchot cautiously agreed to run for a third term as Pennsylvania governor. His reluctance stemmed mainly from the disarray in the state's Republican party. However, he failed to attain the nomination, losing heavily in the primary. His 1938 diary is fragmentary, recording political news only for January of that year.

We have seen in the earlier diaries that Pinchot supported what we now call civil rights and affirmative action. In the last decade of his life he became more outspoken. During his failed gubernatorial campaign, he pledged to the people of Pennsylvania that he would "give women equal consideration with men and equal pay for equal work." He issued a campaign flier on April 5, 1938, with the headline, "Race Pride Demands that Negroes Support Pinchot." The text began, "Gifford Pinchot is opposed to all forms of segregation and proscription." Later, he and Cornelia hosted officials from Tuskegee Institute, became involved with the National Negro Congress and the United Negro College Fund, and worked to help singer Paul Robeson gain entry to auditoriums that had been closed to black performers.

A great many Pennsylvanians were not favorably impressed by his liberal views, however; his open support of labor leader John L. Lewis received critical editorial treatment in Philadelphia and Pittsburgh newspapers. He was also harshly attacked for having signed into law during his second term a bill that legalized the playing of baseball and football on Sunday afternoons. With this stroke of his pen, Pinchot "was responsible for the start in breaking down the Sabbath observance laws," according to an anti-Pinchot magazine called *The Right of Way*, published in Harrisburg. Other hostile articles were titled "More than a million spent by Pinchot to gain public office"; "Ickes tells inside story of Pinchot's attempt to sell out G.O.P."; and "A vote for Pinchot—A vote for Lewis."

In late summer of 1937, Pinchot toured the West as part of his preparation for writing *Breaking New Ground*. In Pinchot fashion, he shipped his Buick touring car by rail to Missoula, and with his long-time chauffeur Bill Hinkel at the wheel, he and Dol Smith and Harry Graves—the three old conservation warhorses—examined landscapes and especially national forests and national parks on a 5,200-mile trip. Snapshots by Graves show Pinchot in a very rumpled business suit with necktie. At times we see him without a coat, but never without the tie.

Pinchot thought that the national parks had been taken over by concessionaires and saw that Timberline Lodge on the Willamette National Forest in Oregon might presage an invasion into Forest Service domain. However, he very much approved of the highly visible signs posted by the National Park Service, and he grumbled to his diary that the Forest Service could take a page from its rival's book on that matter. Once, just once, he tantalizes us with "If I were [chief] Forester," as he sees what to him is too much logging activity on the national forests. Apparently he wrote these diary entries while jouncing along in the car, as his usually clear penmanship—using a pencil instead of a pen—bobs and weaves across the pages.

Pinchot suffered three heart attacks in 1939 that made him a near-invalid for many months, during which he dictated his diary to a nurse. But he gradually recovered, picking up the many threads of his life, although obviously at a slower pace. Two other Forest Service leaders suffered heart attacks that year—both fatal: wilderness advocate Bob Marshall and Chief Ferdinand Silcox. There are eleven Marshall entries in the 1937 diary, and one in 1939, that tell us of their friendly relationship.

We see less of Silcox, but there is a story here. When Silcox died, Associate Chief Earle H. Clapp was named acting chief until Silcox's successor could be selected. Pinchot immediately appealed to President Roosevelt that he be allowed involvement, and shortly thereafter proposed Earle Clapp for chief. But there would be no replacement until 1943, as a president angered by Forest Service impertinence in openly opposing his government reorganization proposals let the agency stew without a formal leader for four years. One thing that this sorry episode clearly shows is that from time to time, raw political acts have surrounded the selection of Forest Service chiefs—a fact of life inconsistent with agency folklore, which has insisted that its chiefs are selected on the basis of merit only.

As World War II began its sweep across Europe and Asia, Pinchot followed along in detail, listening faithfully to radio newscasts and studying the newspaper, and recording events in his diary. He wanted to help, but being both elderly and in questionable health, he apparently was not to be among the many "dollar-a-year" men who brought skills and influence to the war effort. C.B., however, was very much involved, and Pinchot assisted her on her several assignments, some of which included working with Eleanor Roosevelt.

Pinchot did manage involvement: he sat on a commission to bolster civilian morale, developed fishing tackle to be used by military personnel who found themselves in lifeboats, demonstrated that juice from raw fish could substitute for fresh water, and personally campaigned for the Ball Resolution, stemming from the Senate Foreign Relations Committee, which supported creation of the United Nations to maintain postwar peace. He sent 1,781 letters to newspaper editors, in standard Pinchot fashion, to gain public approval.

As we can read in another chapter, soon after the "atom" bombs were dropped on Japan, the Pinchots hosted "atomists"—distinguished scientists—to help develop policies for civilian control of this incredible force. Gifford even wrote a white paper on the subject for President Truman's consideration. Knowing the man in the diaries, we should not be surprised that he did find ways to help after all.

Grey Towers and Milford remained his home, despite the other addresses he used over the years. When the Library of Congress wanted to accession his vast collection of papers, staff came to Grey Towers to cart it to Washington, D.C. The materials had been stored in what were called the Bait Box and Letter Box, two of the estate's outbuildings. When the great man (to most he was "governor," and not "chief") was invited to speak to the Milford High School commencement, he spent parts of several days preparing: no top-of-the-head speech for him, no matter the audience. At war's end, he and C.B. went down to the "village" and rode on the fire truck in the victory parade. He died on October 4, 1946, two months after his eighty-first birthday.

1936

1/6 New York [Theodore] Roosevelt Pilgrimage about 26. Mrs. T.R. still in hospital.

1/19 Washington Ogden & Mrs. Mills to tea. He thought Franklin licked already. I told him he was all wrong.

1/28 Washington Very satisfactory talk with Harold Ickes. Nothing special.

2/2 Washington Jim Garfield to breakfast. He regards stable dollar at least value of all reforms. (Is back with conservation in the old sense.) C.B. & I called on Louis Brandeis in P.M. He looked preoccupied, as if by coming T.V.A. decision.

2/7 Washington …Mutiny on the Bounty the best movie I ever saw.

3/16 Driving …Saw about 75–100 W.P.A. workers along a road in Luzerne Co. [Pennsylvania] with 10 flagmen to protect them & nearly all the men were well back from the road.

4/5 Milford Giff arrived with Sally last night. Announced his engagement to his Mother. Saw them not so excited this morning. "Sally, come here & kiss your new Dad."

5/28 Topeka …Like Landon decidedly. I think he is on the level…confidence in himself. We talked from 7 to after 12. He said he wanted me to take a "major part" in his campaign, and asked me to draw planks on labor, about which he knows little, utilities, & conservation. Advised him to campaign every state.

6/2 Milford …It is getting clear that my chance for V.P. is practically nil. It may be just as well.

6/11 Milford …John Fine & Dick Jones over phone both said my chance for V.P. was gone (if ever had any).

6/26 Milford …Leila & I read Democratic platform. A most efficient & convincing document if you don't know the facts. Taken by itself it is admirable. Short, too.

7/7 Milford …Back [from New York] for late supper after seeing Giff & Sally…Giff seemed much older. They are both taking the same course needed for Giff's degree.

7/11 Milford …Back to dinner at 8:45. 21 at table around the Finger Bowl. New lighting most effective. It was a fairylike place.

7/15 Milford To see Wesley Bowers' assistant about ears buzzing. Hearing excellent. Nothing to do. To see Weeks about eyes! Stye on inside of right lid. Getting better.

7/19 Milford Sitting in A.M. Silvette [artist] not very well. Picture fine, I think…Nurseryman Moon came to see about our A. concolor, & showed me how to prune the yews on the terrace.

7/22 Milford Sitting all day. Silvette finally got the head right. A fine job.

7/24 Milford …dinner under lights of Finger Bowl. Sally & Giff standing 1 & 2 on their difficult Physics work. Splendid! They came about 8.

7/26 Milford …Twenty six at lunch. More sitting in A.M. Picture finally finished, after Silvette had "pushed back" the background. I think it is a knockout.

8/2 Milford …The Amoses left for Southampton to spend a month. We shall miss them immensely. The hen that raised the pheasants, or one of them, is laying eggs in the living room fireplace.

8/5 Milford …C.B. is reading to me a great deal. Tonight Douglas Murray's Joan of Arc. That hen laid the fifth egg in the fireplace.

8/7 Milford Smith Riley, Dol writes, is dead. Another of the old men (FS) gone. That song sparrow comes every morning at breakfast & takes bread from the bread loaf half a dozen times. She must be raising a second brood.

8/11 Milford …Many telegrams of congratulations. 71 years today.

8/16 Miford …Read Hide in the Dark,

about the best detective story there is. To bed about 1.

8/18 Milford …Dictated long speech on conservation for Landon. Tennis but not much. Feeling a little dim.

8/26 Milford …Giff & Sally went to N.Y. leaving the two Dane pups on our hands. Some job. Feeling rotten. Took castor oil. Landon's speech at Buffalo on government finance. Very much better. He said something anyhow.

9/2 Milford Teeth troubling. Went to Dr. Trangott in Sanlin's office at 10. He put cement filling on a lower right molar, which Vaugh said will probably have to come out…Talk with Amos, who thinks Landon's only chance is to be bold & convince people L. is big enough for the job.

9/18 Milford Mail etc. Listened to Landon's speech to the young Republicans. Mostly wind & when he said anything it was wrong. He used not a word of the speech I sent him.

10/11 On train Working on Rapid City & Battle Creek speeches. Saw American Falls. Whole country vastly improved & developed since I saw it last.

10/19 Milford Spoke [from Scranton] over nationwide hook up, 7 P.M. for East, 11 P.M. for West…for Landon.

11/4 Milford Dictated big mail…Amos believes good times coming if F.D.R. goes after increased production. Said the Republican National Committee wanted to print ten million copies of his letter to Ickes…This is at least a temporary change of direction for America. The Old Guard loses, the conservation idea wins. Corrupt politics wins also, and corrupt politics loses too. Big money loses most of all.

11/5 Milford F.D.R. wins by ten million. I take it as a tremendous defeat for concentrated wealth and for the States Rights big fellows. It means more and better national security legislation, conservation, labor, and corporation

control. Except for the rotten political mess, it would be OK & more. It is a smashing defeat of the few by the many. I can't be very sorry, except for C.B.

11/8 Milford …Dr. vonHagen came…to talk Galapagos. He has put up the Darwin Memorial & secured an ordinance making about half the islands into wildlife refuges (without means of enforcement). Wants to start a research institute. I agreed to trade photos with him but could not contribute. He talked rather wildly.

11/12 Milford All day, nearly, getting the new car C.B. is giving me. A Buick convertible 8.

11/14 Milford …Listened to Yale-Princeton 26-23, about most exciting football game ever.

11/23 New York …Read Readers Digest & found it best magazine I know.

11/27 Milford …I spent some time on a proposed letter to papers urging that all private & public money be cut out of political campaigns…to be replaced by public money, so much per vote at last election.

12/2 Milford Mail etc. Got very little done. C.B. & I walked to village in the rain. Wet snow on the ground made it equal a hard mile walk at least. My left leg felt it somewhat afterward. I get absolutely nothing done these days. C.B. paid for my new Buick today. It is a superb present. It will be delivered in the morning.

12/3 Milford …I am reading Gone with the Wind, & like it. "What better way can an old man die than doing a young man's work?"

12/4 Milford C.B. & I looked over the new Buick she gave me. She likes it & so do I. But the back seat does not fit her. The great question today is the Simpsons. What will the royal Edward do?…Buick most satisfactory, especially because there is so little wind impact in either seat.

12/7 Milford Furious interest everywhere in what Edward VII will do.

12/16 Washington C.B. getting house in order. G.P. reading, marking, & dictating his letters saved by M.E.P. [Mary "Mamee" Pinchot]—first one in 1872, & up to 1912.

12/20 Washington Did not go to church, as I should. Slattery to lunch. He thinks F.D. will go right, and advises me to take up conservation again & help & fight F.D. as necessary

12/21 Washington …Franklin made an excellent talk, roasting papers for the picture of him they made in the campaign.

12/22 Milford …Giff's 21st birthday. Awfully nice to have the children here.

12/24 Milford …Trimming the tree, a white spruce cut from the place, after supper… Stockings pinned to bench in front of living room fire.

12/25 Milford Stockings before breakfast. A very pleasant time indeed…Then after dinner the tree. I never saw so many presents. A grand celebration.

1937

1/1 Washington …C.B. & I alone in Washington; Giff and Sally in New Haven; and Amos and his family in New York

1/3 Washington …Evening, Royal C. Johnson (no longer congressman from South Dakota, but practicing law in Washington) and his wife came to dinner, and we had a most interesting talk. He says nothing to be done for the Republican Party until the Democrats make an opening by their own mistakes. Unlike Slattery, he thinks Roosevelt is going to keep to the left, as I do.

1/6 Oyster Bay Took 9:01 train from New York to Oyster Bay Roosevelt Pilgrimage…Mrs. Roosevelt was able to come, to be with us at Sagamore Hill, and so were Ethel Derby, Kermit, and others of the family.

1/7 New Haven …to Giff's apartment at New Haven for dinner, and spent a quiet evening.

Giff and Sally flourishing, and Sally has made a wonderful job of training the Great Dane Nietsche. Stayed with Giff this night.

1/15 Washington …Bob Marshall came to lunch and we had a talk about forestry in the Indian Office—and conservation generally.

1/16 New York To New York with C.B., just in time for the Explorers Club Dinner—one of the most interesting dinners I ever attended. Wilson of "Free-wheeling Across Africa," Strom, who climbed Mt. McKinley on skis— Dr. Roy W. Miner, with his underseas pictures at Tonga Reva.

1/18 New York …Lunch with Amos, Rosamond [Amos's daughter], and Frank Gannett at Amos's house. A very interesting talk. Agreed that Amos shall call small group together to discuss political situation. Then saw Dr. Ober, who thinks there is no reason why my arthritis should get any worse, if I take care of it.

1/20 Washington Inauguration Day. Raining like the dickens, and cold…Franklin made excellent speech, especially in his recognition that one-third of our people are living below a decent standard. How can the Old Guard expect, with their miserable devotion to money alone, to meet such a policy as that?

1/21 Washington …Arranged books in the library part of the morning, and got that mostly cleaned up. Walked with C.B. in the afternoon. Harry S. to dinner. S. told me of how the regular Civil Service is still subject to "political clearance" in spite of the law, making the whole federal civil service a political machine. The Interior Department, like the rest of the government, is full of politics. Four thousand people have been discharged from the Interior Department, and the P.W.A., in the last two weeks. Evidently a great reduction in the forces is at hand.

1/28 Washington …Commissioner David E. Lilienthal of the TVA came in before I left. This was the first time I had met him. C.B. out to dinner with the Hosiery Workers.

2/1 *Washington* Cleaning up mail and odds and ends. C.B. returned from Detroit where she had a most interesting time with the automobile strikers. At Flint she went into the factory where they were, and reports the utmost good order—the place neat as a pin, and everything peaceful. A most important discovery was that a great majority of the automobile workers get less than one thousand dollars a year—and that the speed-up is driving the older workers out of business. They can't stand it…After supper to a sort of reception at Bob Marshall's house in Georgetown.

2/2 *Washington* …C.B. spent most of the day preparing a statement concerning her trip to Detroit, and what she found there. She hoped to present it in a speech before the Hosiery Workers tomorrow…E.W. Martin (colored), Colonel Frank Elbridge Webb, and another man, came in to talk about the National Allied Republican Council. Martin made ridiculous statements about the strength of his organization. I would have nothing to do with it—but parted on a pleasant basis.

2/4 *Washington* …Dunc came in and was shown upstairs to C.B.'s room. He stayed until after supper, and his general message was that even my enemies thought I was the only man who could win for governor the next time, and that the prospects for my nomination were growing better, if I wanted the job.

2/5 *Washington* Working on G.M. stockholders' letter protesting against Sloan's labor policy for C.B. Walk with C.B. in the afternoon. Feeling pretty rotten. Dinner at 1615 Rhode Island Avenue tonight. Guests: Ambassador of France and Mme. DeLa-boulaye; Mr. and Mrs. William Castle; Senator and Mrs. Warren Austin; the Canadian Minister and Lady Marler; Mr. and Mrs. Dwight Davis; Frederic

Delano; Senator Capper; Mrs. Winthrop Chandler; and Mrs. Hugh C. Wallace.

2/8 *Washington* …Lunch at Cosmos Club with Hoyt of U.S.G.S.; and ex-president Schantz, University of Arizona, who suggested that arrangements should be made with University of Arizona to supply working opportunity for government employees of retirement age, whose knowledge ought to be written down. Pay them, say, two thousand dollars a year. An excellent idea. C.B. to New York. Agitation about Franklin's Supreme Court plan blazing up.

2/14 *Washington* C.B. arranged the people at little tables and in part we waited on ourselves as the custom is at Grey Towers. Everybody seemed to have a really good time, and the last of the guests left at 5:30—which is pretty good proof…Harry Kalish thought things were moving fast in my direction in case I want to run for governor, and agreed with C.B. and me that I had better say nothing.

2/15 *Washington* …Republicans seem to be making the fight on Franklin's court proposal into a party matter, which is the sure way to make Franklin win…Giff's chance to get on the Dean's List looks very good. He thinks he passed the last examination very well.

2/16 *Washington* …My guess is that Franklin is going to win on his rejuvenation of the Supreme Court. The Republican opposition seems to be following precisely the same tactics which led to their blazing defeat in November.

2/19 *Washington* …to dinner with Justice and Mrs. Stone—just we four. The Justice is much better, but not entirely well. Very interesting talk about proposed legislation, in the course of which he expressed himself with amazing frankness. He is emphatically opposed.

2/20 *Washington* …Afternoon to see Men in White at Little Theatre with C.B. and Mrs.

Catherine Drinker Bowen, who is staying at the house.

2/26 Harrisburg …lunch with George Fetzer, who said the Republican organization of Dauphin County was rotten, that he had found committeemen still on the books who had been dead from five to ten years…I am entirely satisfied, as a result of this trip, that, unless the Republicans actually begin organizing within the next two or three months, the nomination would be worth nothing.

3/2 Philadelphia To Philadelphia in the open car to see C.M. Morrison of the Ledger. Lunched with him and had exceedingly satisfactory talk. He is for getting rid of money domination of the Republican Party—limiting individual contributions to $500—abolishing political contributions by public employees.

3/4 Washington …Will and Alberta to lunch. Bill looking fine, but both of them more reactionary than I supposed any human being could be. Their ideal is Hitler…Listened to Franklin's speech to the Victory Dinner on the court. It was an excellent vote-getting speech and makes it still more sure that his plan will go through.

3/7 Washington …to Daisy Harriman's for one of her discussion-dinners, where I said the court question seemed to be, to me, not one of protecting minorities, but of protecting majorities—whether the people of the United States should have the right to go in the direction they wanted to go.

3/10 New York Down to see Amos…Afternoon to the matinée The Eternal Road. It is so different from anything I ever saw that I would like to see it a second time. Rosamond was superb in her part, but it was very short.

3/13 Washington …Giff and Sally arrived with Nietsche and George Rat the first thing in the morning. Fooled around with them a lot during the day and had a fine time. Went to see the Scarlet Pimpernel at the Little Theatre with C.B., and liked it very much.

3/14 Washington The fact that Giff is on the Dean's List gives me the greatest satisfaction. Certainly Sally is in part responsible. Fine talk with her after breakfast. She is clear that Giff is doing right in going into medicine.

3/16 Washington …Short walk in afternoon. Bob Marshall and Mary Heaton Vorse came in to tea.

3/17 Washington …Evening with C.B. to a small party at Bob Marshall's, where I met Ernest Gruening and Gardner Jackson. Excellent talks with both.

3/19 Philadelphia …Doctor Gordon came in and I had a very nice talk with him. His thesis was that in New York and in Philadelphia, both, the people whom he sees (mostly financial, of course) believe it absolutely essential that I should run for governor…C.B. went to musicale at the German Embassy.

3/20 Washington …Went to see Fire Over England in the afternoon, and in the evening C.B. and I to dinner at Canadian Legation—a big and very dull party.

3/21 Washington Meant to go to church but fell down as usual. No one extra to lunch. Walked with C.B. in the afternoon about 3 miles, and evening to most interesting dinner at Daisy Harriman's, where John Lewis discussed the sit-down strikes. Most interesting utterance besides his was statement by James M. Landis that a change in law is on the way by which the right of a man in his job will be recognized.

I pointed out that the sit-down strike is very little in comparison with the boot-legging of coal that is going on with the completely overwhelming approval of the community in Eastern Pennsylvania; and that the stake of labor is vastly more important today than the stake of capital in industrial controversies.

JUST A SONG AT TWILIGHT!

Political cartoon published in the Pittsburgh *Press*, February 1938, portraying Pinchot's attempt for a third term as Pennsylvania governor. Pinchot scrapbooks, Pinchot Collection, Library of Congress.

3/30 Washington …Zerbey [Pottsville Republican] asked me if I were going to run for governor. I told him I would be seventy-two next August, and I thought it was very doubtful…I said to Zerbey with much emphasis that before anybody should be considered a candidate the question to be decided was what kind of campaign the Republican Party was going to make—whether it would make the progressive campaign that had a chance to win, or the stand-pat campaign that had no chance to win.

4/22 Washington …C.B. came back from New York about lunch time. She had been addressing anit-Nazi meeting at which Thomas Mann was present.

6/1 Cincinnati Stopped to see Alice Longworth, who drove me to the airport. Officials tried to tell me they had no space for me, although my ticket was in proper shape. Reached Cleveland about 12:30. Big fuss because they had no seat for me to Newark on plane my ticket called for. Finally they got me place by offering one passenger free transportation if he would stay over.

6/3 Milford This was the day of the Garden Club convention. Cloudy in the morning—looked like clearing—all tables set to the last knife and fork—and then, half an hour before they were due, it began to rain. So we had lunch in the house. 130 or 140, I suppose. They waited on themselves and had a real good time.

6/13 Milford …we had twenty-five for lunch around the Finger Bowl… After dinner we all went over to Amos's house and had a lot of fun trying to find a name for the dog C.B.P. gave Tony.

6/21 New Haven With Charley Gill, Ted Donnelley, and Dol, to High Street. Then to lunch with members of the Class at the Graduates Club, and afterward to the ball game with Harvard. Fifteen-inning game! Said to be the longest ever played between college teams. Yale 7, Harvard 6. Everybody worn out at the end.

6/27 Milford …Ferrara keen for G.P. Says about 60% of the Democrats in Susquehanna County who had supported me before would do so again. Both said that the county would go overwhelmingly Republican next time.

7/6 Milford …My tame catbirds come demanding to be fed, and the grey squirrel spends part of every morning in C.B.'s bedroom often coming to take peanuts off the floor or off the bed.

7/27 Milford …Jack [Owens] is of opinion not only that I could get the nomination easily, but that I could also easily win the election—which I doubt. He mentioned a number of old-timers who had told him I was the only man who could save the party. There seems to be a good deal of that sort of talk.

8/10 Portland, Oregon …12 to Kiwanis lunch with Harry Graves. Nobody seemed to know us. He was introduced as the Chairman Forestry of State of Washington.

8/11 Cascade Head …Left Portland 7:30 with Buck, McDaniel, & ranger. Down the Valley & turned left at St. Helens. Into Clark & Wilson logging. Absolute devastation. Practically no reproduction over most of it. Some willows, etc. Burned & burned. Mostly a clean sweep, taking everything. Cut less than 10 years ago. The men who did this are nothing less than public enemies…Serious danger too much of this marvellous forest country will be classified as agricultural…Logging along road. Slash awful.

8/12 Cascade Head …Sea Lion Caves. G.L.O. let it go when could have saved it for public. Now 2 bits a head to go & see it…Crown Zellerbach nearer on sustained yield basis than anybody in N.W.…Most important thing we have seen so far as far as forestry goes.

8/13 Traveling …In evening Buck showed us his map of sustained yield working circles he has worked out with private lands included for Washington & Oregon. A great piece of work. None in operation yet. I suggested that danger of attack for selling U.S. timber exclusively to big operators without bidding a necessity in working circle plan could be met by buying their land with U.S. timber. Buck thought well of it, & so did Harry.

8/16 Thompson's Lodge …In P.M. Harry & I went fishing again. Poor…Evening discussion of selective logging…I would cut for 2 reasons only—needs of a county. Buy land in exchange if Congress did not demand revenue & if counties would be persuaded…Forest Service keeps forest wild for its visitors. Park Service citifies or better vulgarizes it. Forest Service should absolutely declare against clearcutting in Washington & Oregon as a defensive measure.

If I were "Forester" I would keep a merchantable growing stock on all this N.W. national forest land, preferably by timber sales at +/− 20% cut. And I would make no sales except 1. For counties' need 2. Paid in land. I would keep a growing forest on the land always—which doesn't shut out holes or narrow strips…Lunch at Westfir camp. We had ham, beef, cheese, potatoes, peas, string beans, baked fish, canned corn, cold slaw & sausages, shrimp & celery salad, white & brown bread, cookies, jello with bananas, cantaloups, pickles, fresh & canned milk.

8/18 Crescent City to Willits …Graves Grove given by G. Fred Schwartz. Fine bronze plaque to H.S.G. Fine, fine. Superbly placed on steep slope high above Pacific, which fog hid. "Forester, Educator, Administrator."

[Humboldt Redwood Park] …Wisdom & tolerance, Continuance & peace, Patience & understanding, Knowledge & silence. They made me weak. They were personalities. The whole place was full of personality…S. Franklin Lane Grove, etc.—Much too good for the man it was named for.

8/19 Willits to San Francisco …The national forests belong to the people, but the national parks belong to the concessionaires…Timberline Inn beginning of concessions. Most dangerous thing I've seen on national forests. It should be run by a hired manager on a non profit basis…Even in wild places you can't get away from people.

8/23 Yosemite Great songfest, Harry & I as we got up. With Dol, we had the house to ourselves…You can't get to a national park without knowing it. Same should be true of national forests…to El Capitan. Beyond words. We all stood, Harry, Dol, & I, with our hats off in silence. It must be the most majestic rock on earth…Then to club Mather built for the park rangers. (Entrance to park $2. We didn't pay) …At one place magic lantern was through "Clementine" at seven for singing by the crowd, & one woman came & played the piano. Then we left. Comic songs in Yosemite!

8/24 Yosemite …Washburn Point—incredible. Glacier Point left me all in. Went & stood on the overhanging rock where I threw my bed 41 years ago & looked down. At both points went off by myself. I had to. It was too great. And I thanked the Lord for what I saw.

Yosemite Park & Curry Co. has all the concessions (one little independent restaurant. Old hotel not open). Buck says wrong. So do I. Ranger becomes servant of concessionaire. Buck's horse for a day in Yosemite Park on a pack trip $15. Monopoly. In national forest adjacent where 3 packers compete it is $2. Competition…Dancing, motion pictures, etc. golf in park at Wawona. I saw it.

8/26 Travelling …This was one of the great days of my life. I think the greatest sight I ever saw. If it cost me a year of my life, except for Leila, it would be worth it…Sequoia National Park. Huge sign. Good…On your walk through into national forests. No sign.

11/15 New York …Talked with Amos, who is pretty depressed over the general situation, and after lunch with C.B. at the Colony Club. To see the film The Hurricane, which is a perfect dandy. It made me yearn for the South Seas again.

11/22 Washington …Eric Biddle came to dinner, and afterwards we went to Bob Marshall's for a sort of evening party.

11/27 Philadelphia Took the 10:00 o'clock train from Washington to Philadelphia. Lunched with Morrison of the Ledger and had an excellent talk. Found he agreed exactly about the impossibility of winning without a united party in 1938—the effect of that election on 1940—and the necessity for going after the people we haven't got.

He asked me whether I was physically capable of making a campaign, to which I replied that I thought so, and so had every doctor I had consulted. He said that there was nobody in sight that could make a better fight than I could, and he undertook to find out, if he could, what the position of the Old Organization would be in case I ran.

11/29 New York …Lunch with Amos at an Italian restaurant where we found Ed Rumley. He suggested that employers should be required to make public the terms, rates of pay, and average annual pay of their workers. It struck me as an excellent idea.

12/14 Washington …The following at dinner tonight at 1615: Justice and Mrs. Stone; Mr. and Mrs. John L. Lewis; Lady Ribblesdale; Mrs. Truxton Beale; Mrs. Frank West; Mrs. Robert W. Bliss; Mrs. Robbings; Mrs. Eleanor Patterson; Mr. Frank Kent: Mr. Charles G. Dunwoody; The British Ambassador; Mr. Jules Henry; Senator Frederick Hale; Senator Theodore Green; Mr. Harold J.T. Horan; Mr. John F. Carter; and Dr. William MacCallum.

After dinner Frank Kent opened the discussion on the question, How Far Is Labor Responsible for the Depression?

John Lewis made a masterly statement, pointing out that business in the United States was dependent on government subsidies, giving many illustrations, pointing out also that the great need of the country was leadership (with very strong implications of criticism of Franklin), and suggesting that business, labor, the farmer, etc., ought to be called together by the president to thrash out the present situation and suggest a remedy.

1939

1/1 Washington C.B. & I in 1615, still very much in reconstruction. Eyes & stomach bad …The New Year opens like a set trap. The world will not escape its bite, even if we do not fall into another Great War. In all my life I have never known a more threatening future.

1/2 Washington …House at last nearing completion. Very satisfactory, but cost very heavy.

1/27 Washington At 6:30 A.M. anginal attack.

2/6 Washington Sat up for 20 minutes in a chair.

2/12 Washington Second attack.

2/17 Washington 3rd attack started at 4:55 A.M.

3/1 Washington 3rd consecutive day received fine letter from Giff.

3/10 Washington Whole aspect of universe changed by two table-spoons of Fleets Sodium Phosphate and one hot soda & salt enema. Tremendous unloading. Tired but triumphant afterwards.

3/12 Washington T.O. Andrews of Erie called up to inquire. So did Bob Marshall.

3/20 Washington Started feeding myself today. (Helped self to two crackers.) Proud as a peacock. Began to read a few words.

3/21 Washington I have begun to eat with keen enjoyment. Today for lunch had lamb chop, baked potato, spinach, peas (purée), baked custard.

3/28 Washington Out of bed for first time.

3/29 Washington Fed self for first time sitting up in bed.

4/2 Washington Stood on my feet.

4/5 Washington Harry Graves & Dol Smith in to see me.

4/7 Washington …I had lunch with family in dining room for the first time, sitting in my wheel chair.

4/10 Washington Eight weeks today.

4/11 Washington A beautiful bunch of flowers came this morning with a card: "With the love and very best wishes of the Forest Service."

4/16 Washington Walked from bed to scales for first time today. There & back. Legs pretty darn good.

4/19 Washington Had my clothes on, shoes & all for the first time.

4/28 Washington Bailey Willis, Silcox, & Harold Ickes, all here to see me at one time.

5/28 Washington …Stepped to chair & spent 2 half hours in front of house.

6/2 Washington Harlan Stone came in to see me in the morning and Felix Frankfurter in the late afternoon. Pleasant talks with each.

6/9 Washington to New York Drove to station in Wash., but litter & ambulance to 40 E 61. Sat up nearly all the way on the train & was not tired.

6/15 New York to Milford …It was wonderful. Amos came over. He is much better. C.B. wheeled me to the moat, where I sat with her & Amos for half an hour.

7/2 Milford …To my great astonishment, Reed told me in the course of a talk on the lawn about a civil service revision he is engaged in, that "no man now living has done as much for America as you have through your work in conservation."

7/18 Milford [fishing]…Mr. Geodecke, Levin, Larrabee came to start WPA inventory of my files, which are to go to the Library of Congress.

10/15 Milford C.B. called up & told about

invitation from W.O.L. for nationwide hook up on embargo repeal.

10/18 Washington All day on talk. Got it finished in afternoon. Spoke over W.O.L. at 10:15 P.M.

10/27 Washington Eichelberger over phone told me 1100 requests for copies of my broadcast—more than for any other speaker... [Spelling of my name] in requests for copies. Penshaw, Pincus, Pindral, Pinchhell, etc.

11/23 Washington F.D.R.'s Thanksgiving Day. C.B. & I alone. C.B. read to me. I worked a little turkey for dinner. Slept an hour. Sat in Park for another. Mrs. Stanley Reed spoke to me & came in to see C.B. We talked about Pringle's [biography of] Taft. Then with C.B. to see Beau Geste. It got so unpleasant to her she had to leave. I saw it through. It was good.

11/25 Washington Dol brought Paul Frothingham to see me, & we talked most of the morning. Then at Tommy Shearman's suggestion I went to Cosmos Club to hear Yale-Harvard game. Left at end of first half, & heard rest at home. Yale 20—Harvard 7. Rah!

12/20 Washington Silcox died today of coronary occlusion. A very great loss...Eugene Myer agreed to publish a letter from me about Silcox, which I wrote & sent by messenger. Also a letter to F.D.R. asking him to see me before he decided on S's successor.

12/22 Washington Silcox's funeral. Giff drove C.B. & me to Alexandria. They did not come in to Wheatley's Chapel. Henry Wallace & Ickes etc. there. Place could not hold 100 people. Too bad.

12/25 Washington We had our presents in

Amos and Gifford Pinchot at Grey Towers, August 11, 1939 (Gifford's seventy-fourth birthday). Pinchot Collection, Library of Congress.

my room before breakfast. C.B. gave me Pringle's Taft…I gave C.B. a skin rug…I wrote F.D.R. recommending Clapp to succeed Silcox.

12/26 Washington …I saw Geo. Norris & asked him to speak to F.D.R. about Clapp to succeed Silcox. But he hadn't seen F.D. for nearly a year & didn't think he could.

12/28 Washington …saw George Norris & suggested he speak to Henry Wallace in favor of Clapp to succeed Silcox. He did, & later told me Wallace said he would tell F.D.R. that Norris was backing Clapp.

1940

1/2 Washington …To a White House reception (Eleanor only) with music. A bum crowd. Eleanor was evidently surprised to see us among them!

1/3 Washington Benton MacKaye came in P.M. Harry Slattery to dinner. Said he had suggested to Henry Wallace he should put me in as Forester. Wallace spoke to F.D.R. about it, he told Henry I had no knowledge whatever that this was to be suggested.

1/12 Washington …C.B. had Leon Henderson & some others in evening to discuss help for Spanish refugees in France.

1/28 Washington I have felt better this week than at any time since the occlusion. Thank the Lord.

3/19 Philadelphia Met C.B. in Philadelphia & went to talk with Harry Kalish & McGee. Long conference. They recommended finding out just where we stand on M.E.P. estate—what it is worth. Also that we divide it, since otherwise inheritance taxes & other troubles may be worse than necessary. Decided to deed Grey Towers to C.B. on undivided interest plan. Also 1615.

4/1 Washington Mail. Jim Casey to lunch. He proposed of his own motion to back C.B. for member of National Labor Board if increased to five.

4/24 Washington …Arranging with Dol for Old Timers meeting Society American Foresters at 1615, May 2. He wanted Kauffman of National Parks to speak. I objected.

5/2 Washington Keeping quiet for the Society American Foresters meeting at 1615 tonight. A grand time. Old Timers did all the talking. I read T.R.'s talk to SAF in March, 1903. Lee Kneipp, Arthur Ringland, Dol Smith, John Halton, & Chris Rachford were the speakers. Baked apples, gingerbread & milk, and 2 camp stools broke down. It was a grand time, & seems to have made a grand impression on the younger men.

5/6 Washington To see Dr. McCarthy. He said my eczema was due to nervousness & also in part of stomach trouble. Must stop hearing news over radio before breakfast.

5/16 New York By air through thunder storms. Came out of clouds in middle of cliff of a great thunder squall. It was superb. Landed at LaGuardia field.

6/5 Milford …this day the decisive action in France began. The Germans attacked on the Somme. May God help the Allies to win.

6/14 Milford Paris surrendered today.

6/15 New York …Spoke over NBC on Farm & Home Hour on Arms but Not Men.

6/17 Milford to New Haven France stopped fighting today. Left after lunch for reunion at New Haven. Supper with Dol at Graduate Club.

6/19 New Haven To see Harry Graves get his long & well deserved LLD. But Billy Phillip should not have talked about me in presenting Harry.

6/26 Milford Republican platform adopted. Dol read me Wilkie's article in Saturday Evening Post. Just another plutocrat, accepting what progress has been made, but no more of it. "Free enterprise."

7/12 Milford …To Red Cross concert in

Forest Hall. Mary Pinchot made her first concert appearance. Did awfully well. Mrs. Medlinger handled it all finely.

7/18 Milford …Franklin renominated for 3rd term.

7/19 Milford …At four concert in living room given by quartet from Tuskegee. Just out of friendliness. Then C.B. gave them supper around the Finger Bowl. We all sat in with them.

8/11 Milford Seventy five years old today. And so much, so very much, to be thankful for.

8/17 Milford …Listened to Wilkie's acceptance speech at Amos' house. I thought it bold, otherwise mediocre, & in spots self contradictory.

9/28 Milford C.B., Dol, & I heard Wilkie at Yonkers. A poor cheap speech. I can't be for him with any satisfaction.

9/30 Milford Have finally decided for Franklin. Writing statement. Heard Wilkie's Detroit speech to the Republican women. Still nothing to show he realizes the world situation.

10/6 New York Giff's baby born at 8:15 A.M. Both doing fine. A girl.

10/7 New York to Washington Took 3 P.M. plane. C.B. came later. Saw Dr. Chase. Said I was about well of my eczema, which is hooey.

11/5 Milford Election Day. Voted for F.D.R. …Then to N.Y. to see Dr. Draper. He said eczema is purely emotional, & laid it to my trouble with Ickes, etc.

1941

1/6 New York Day at Oyster Bay for Roosevelt Pilgrimage.

3/25 Washington Meeting of Morale Committee.

4/4 Washington Catching up & finished morale plan…Leila working like a tiger for R.A.F. (Piccadilly Arcade). She is chairman of antiques.

4/7 Washington Went over my plan for a morale service (National Defense. Unity Service) with Pope. It evidently did not strike him. I've wasted a solid week & gotten wore out over it besides.

4/10 Washington Dictated proposed statement for C.B. about Paul Robeson concert. Washington Committee for Aid to China.

4/13 Washington All day on statement about the Washington Committee for Aid to China. National Negro Congress muddle. Statement for press signed by C.B.P. and Eleanor Roosevelt.

4/14 Washington Press conference for C.B.P. on Robeson muddle at eleven.

4/18 Washington All this week in Washington, occupied almost exclusively with getting this Robeson concert matter straightened out.

5/25 Washington Lunch at the Raymond Clappers' outside of Washington, and a buffet dinner at home before C.B. went to the discussion meeting of the Washington Committee of the Emergency Rescue Committee at the Shoreham Hotel.

6/1 Washington To lunch with the Whitehouses. Very pleasant time. Felix Frankfurter advised me strongly to go on and finish my book. I take it that means no government job.

6/28 Milford …The Amoses came to lunch with Mr. Webster, who is reported to have been the founder of America First. He looked like a poor stick.

7/7 Milford C.B. went to Wash'n, leaving at 6:40, to see about real estate matters. Alex Shaw and I were shooting revolvers at the burned garage when Harry and Elsie Reed drove up. We had quite a quarrel about their trespassing on the place before Shaw caught on, to our great amusement.

7/25 Milford …Over the phone from Washington C.B. told me she had not yet discovered just what her job was to be in Volunteer Participation for Defense.

8/6 Washington Various consultations about building an apartment house on our land…an apartment house for women government employees only.

8/9 Washington …Working for C.B. on Volunteer Participation committee and loafing. Not much good.

8/12 Milford …Doctor Martin of the Library of Congress came to arrange for the transfer of my second administration records to the Library of Congress. All my other records will go later on. Worked on the Volunteer Participation Committee for C.B.P.

8/14 Milford …Records left in a huge van which carried 206 file drawers, 121 bundles of newspaper clippings, 140 bundles of personal filing, one package of folio books on budget and highway, and two cartons of printed pamphlets and mimeographed material. These came from the Letter Box, Bait Box, and Barn. Got practically nothing done.

9/5 Milford …Got to Milford at 4:30. Ernesta and Shaw came. The two boys killing flies at five for a cent.

9/11 Milford …Evening Roosevelt's radio closing our defense areas at sea to Nazi ships. We none of us thought it would be as well received as apparently it has been. This action means Germany can't win.

10/1 Milford Elsie finished her remarkable portrait drawing of C.B. Decided the best picture of her I have ever seen.

11/13 Washington Working on plan for C.B. to submit to Eleanor. Five items— Training speeches, sampling pub. opinion, keeping in touch, Awakening the People (White House meeting of heads of organizations), & organizing forum. House voted 121 to 194 to send our ships to Allied ports. Great victory.

11/15 Washington …To lunch, C.B. & I at the W. House. A Mrs. Edith Grey, a woman w. grown children, fr. Long Island. She had never heard that States & Nation had been feeding people, & she was all for letting them die if they couldn't or wouldn't work. Perfect example of her horrible type.

11/26 Washington Apptment w. Rice about priorities for aptment house. C.B. & I waited in his office an hour & a half to see him. Looks favorable, but only if we employ architect he favors. C.B. left for Ohio to look up morale situation.

11/29 Washington C.B. got back from Ohio on her trip for O.C.D. & V.C.P.C. (Vol. Civ. Participating Com.).

12/6 Washington …Eve. dinner for Norris… I never heard so many stories—laughed till I was lame.

12/7 Washington Japan attacks Hawaii & Manila. The very ultimate in treachery, & her peace envoys still negotiating in Wash. And the very ultimate in brass-hat dumbness, to be caught utterly napping at Pearl Harbor.

12/8 Washington War declared on German & Italy. Unanimous in both Houses, except for Miss Rankin. Time for passage & signature 33 minutes, as I read it.

12/25 New York Christmas Day. I have very much to be thankful for, personally, but it looks bad for the Philippines. Churchill's coming will be of immense help…To see Arsenic & Old Lace w. C.B. Very good.

1942

1/1 Washington The most critical year in the whole history of nations begins today. Very tired. Got nothing done.

1/2 Washington Working on plan for a Public Relations Service for Office of Civil Defense & a radio program.

2/11 Washington …A great series of victories

for Japs probably just ahead. C.B.P. appointed head of Emergency Housing & Feeding for D.C.

2/13 Washington At home working on statement for C.B. (and possibly for F.D.R.) for new plan of dedicating warships…Quiet evening. C.B. has a real job.

2/15 Washington Singapore falls. Now we are in the war for fair.

2/16 Washington The War: we are in a tough spot. We need attention to national morale as never before. Paper says we have not yet been told the truth about Pearl Harbor…Morgan of Housing to lunch. Good talk. C.B. to meeting in eve. All I do is listen to radio. 4 tankers torpedoed in Dutch West Indies.

2/25 Washington The Red Cross attempt to take over Leila's work, feeding & billeting in emergency, has fallen down. D.C. Red Cross chapter is no good.

4/14 Washington Saw Dr. Martin at Library & he showed me room my records are to occupy…Blackout tonight.

4/25 Washington …Can't stop thinking about survivors. Can you squeeze water out of fresh fish? Jelly fish? Can you eat plankton? Catch gulls, etc. etc. Eat seaweed?

4/27 Washington To Library with Dol & Alberta, & arranged for her to have access to C.B. & G.P. records in case (Key 15). Martin said it was largest single mss. collection in Library of Congress. Had another long talk with Kaiser about fishing talk & what I recommend is going on all Navy planes collapsible boats—probably 25,000. That's progress.

4/28 Washington …This evening F.D.R. made his best talk to the people so for. Took them into the family better than ever.

5/25 Milford …Heard from C.B. in Washington. No news about whether Emergency Feeding and Housing goes to the Red Cross or not.

5/28 Milford C.B.P. got home from Washington at 2:35 with the good news that the Red Cross will not get E.F.H. Winant telephoned that he got 1 qt. of fish juice from 15½ lbs. of miscellaneous fish, is delivering the juice today on ice to Dr. Smith. Wheeler of the N.A. Newpaper Alliance called me to know if I would give him the story of the lifeboats and the fish juice.

5/29 Milford Started on speech for graduating class of Milford High School.

5/31 Milford …Giff left to begin his internship.

6/2 Milford Working on speech for Milford High School, and article for Readers Digest, if they will take it.

6/5 Milford Commencement address.

6/7 Milford …Mr. and Mrs. J.P. McEvoy, of the Readers Digest, came to lunch. Long talk afterwards about article for the Digest on fish juice, and life-saving equipment. In view of preference of Navy Department that fish juices should not be made public, McEvoy turned article down. He was right.

6/11 Milford …Letter came from Dr. Chasis saying that fish juice had been fed to two men for four days with no bad result. That is really good news!

6/16 Milford …We made 248 miles down and back on six gallons of gasoline.

6/24 Milford …In the evening talked with C.B. She is giving a big dinner before the Russian Aid meeting, over which she presides, on June 30.

7/25 Milford …Letter from Captain Rhea to say that 33,000 fishing kits are to be put on the Navy lifeboats and life rafts, including the lampwick bait. Fine!

8/31 Milford …[C.B.] is doing a grand job and is now deeply interested in doing what she can to bring about a settlement, through Franklin, of the trouble in India.

9/7 Milford Rewrote C.B.'s rewrite of Pearl Buck's proposed letter to Winston Churchill.

10/20 Philadelphia to Washington... Spoke on radio at 6:15...Endorsed Democratic candidates for Congress.

10/21 Washington Dave Lawrence phoned and is pleased with speech and impression it made; says that McInty would like a copy to show the president. With C.B. walked to White House in afternoon to leave copy of speech.

10/22 Washington ...C.B. left to give campaign speech in Bristol, Pa. She is endorsing entire Democratic ticket.

10/25 Washington C.B.P. entertained about 100 for tea, for the Cooperative League.

11/5 Washington ...listened to the radio for the great news of the Allied victory in North Africa.

11/10 Washington ...Goodwin Gibson came to see Leila about renting house for the Canadian government.

11/18 Washington Leila's letter to Franklin finished and sent in, together with mine; both on the subject of a job for her. At it all day.

12/3 Washington ...Admiral and Mrs. Stephenson to dine. Talked with the Admiral about taking Giff with him on his Eastern expedition but he was against it on the ground that to break in on Giff's year as an intern would be bad.

12/14 Washington Working on article. I hope Readers Digest will take fish juice & fishing tackle.

12/16 Washington Finished fish juice article for Readers Digest. Had it checked at Navy Department...and passed by Navy Censor. I only hope Wallace accepts it.

12/17 Washington ...C.B. had one meeting at 10, another at 12, in the Library, latter with Eleanor Roosevelt answering questions to about 40 air wardens.

12/25 Washington Entertained about one hundred members of the Armed Forces for afternoon and supper. Showed movies of South Seas trip.

12/28 Washington ...Giff and Sally had baby boy tonight.

1943

1/1 Washington New Year's Day. Made changes suggested by Coast Guard in fishing instructions and took copies to Admiral Waesche and Captain Shepard.

1/3 New York Saw grandson and Sally. United Nations Committee at Biltmore Hotel during afternoon, with C.B.

1/5 Washington Worked all morning with C.B. on Civilian Defense movie sequence.

1/12 New York ...I saw the new grandson again. He is to be called Gifford.

1/19 Washington ...In the afternoon Kotok, Marsh, and Grainger came in to talk about Earle Clapp, who has been replaced by Lyle Watts—one of the worst pieces of injustice that has happened in this town for a long time, although if Earle had to go, Watts was probably the best man to replace him. Thank heaven it was not an outsider.

1/22 Washington ...Long talk with Clapp in the afternoon about his proposal to leave the Service and work under the Bob Marshall Foundation, which under the circumstances is the best thing he can do, I believe.

2/14 Washington Eyes still very bad, but to a reception for Lyle Watts at the Department of Agriculture. Pleasant time. Nearly froze in cold wind getting there.

3/4 Washington Dinner at Y.W.C.A.—Society of American Foresters. Harry Graves guest of honor.

4/2 Washington Working on letter to newspapers for Ball Resolution. Evening big dinner...also Senators Austin, Pepper, and Brewster. About 335 people. Excellent discussion of Ball resolution and necessary action…C.B. suggested letters to presidents of high school and college classes. Admirable. My plan for letters to newspapers approved.

4/5 Washington Working on the letters to newspapers in support of Ball's Resolution, S.114, and talking with Harry Graves. Am enjoying his visit immensely.

4/6 Washington Marking of newspapers from Ayer's Directory finished. Draft of letter practically finished.

4/8 Washington …practically completed for letter to daily newspapers on Ball's resolution. Feeling rather groggy. Skipped dinner and meeting C.B. held to promote Youth Hostels around Washington.

4/13 Washington …Signed more letters to editors on Ball Resolution.

4/15 Washington Finished signing the 1781 letters today newspapers in the morning and dictated some letters in the afternoon. C.B. got volunteer help in folding. In the evening, meeting of the Washington section Society of American Foresters. At least 100 came. Many had to sit on the floor. Colonel Fisher of the Philippines and Commander Griffiths of the English Navy spoke, one on his experience on Bataan, the other about Burma.

5/9 Milford Had Giff's single trout for breakfast and hung around all day. Walked in to the Falls, etc., etc. It was impossible to keep still. I had to see it all.

5/10 New York Took the 10:25 and attended young Gifford's christening. All the grandparents were there. Also Aunt Sally. I was so glad I could be there too.

5/15 Washington Lunch with Gabrielson at the Cosmos Club. He agreed to have the Fish and Wildlife Service take up the collection of fishing tackle for Army men and will write me after he has seen some of his people in Chicago.

6/7 New Haven Breakfast with Sam & Ned

at Lawn Club. They also believe capitalism is on the way out. I agreed to make and send them a statement to that effect.

6/15 Milford Mail. Tried chewing moisture out of small raw fish. Got it.

6/16 Milford Feeling rotten, I don't know why.

9/10 Milford …Haircut & talk with George Gravy about old times while Cal Tronton operated.

11/11 Washington …Conf. in library w. Rabbi Miller & others on org. of big committee to help get Jews out of Europe, feed those which remain, etc., etc.

12/23 New York …With C.B. to see Paul Robeson in Othello. A wonderful performance.

12/24 New York …sang carols after dinner.

1945

1/8 Washington Accepted invitation from Secretary Grew to become member of a committee for National Tribute Grove.

1/10 Washington C.B.P. to White House to lunch, and conference on the situation regarding nurses for the Armed Forces.

2/1 Washington Little work in the morning. Afternoon with C.B. to 40th birthday celebration of Forest Service. Eleanor Roosevelt, Secretary Wickard, G.P., and Watts principal speakers. Program arranged by Committee of Warren. Admirably done. I enjoyed it immensely.

2/3 Washington [Forest] Service in the morning. Giff came after supper so that I missed the Forest Service dance which followed the 40th Anniversary celebration.

2/21 Washington In the morning to see Phil Murray at the CIO, about the NCPAC situation.

3/7 Washington Helped C.B. with statement for House Committee on India Naturalization bill.

3/27 Washington …C.B. in Harrisburg

testifying for Brown bill against job discrimination.

4/11 Washington Will Clayton and Charlie Taft spoke to group at 1615 after luncheon for United Negro College Fund Campaign. Mr. Glover of Riggs Bank here, also President Colston of Bethune-Cookman College, and President Patterson of Tuskegee.

4/19 Washington …C.B. and I were invited to tea at 5 to see Mrs. Roosevelt and bid her goodbye. She leaves Washington tomorrow.

4/21 Washington C.B.P. to Milford to see Mr. & Mrs. Danniel Roberts of Bristol, Pa., about possibly working at Grey Towers as manager of the farm.

4/22 Washington C.B. returned from Milford. Satisfied with Roberts, and plans to take him on in Vinnies' stead.

4/23 Washington Mail in the morning and to office. Lunched at Mayflower with Mr. & Mrs. McLean of Negro College Fund Campaign.

5/4 Washington …It is hopeless to try in a diary like this to describe what is going on in the world. Now that the German Fascists are on their last legs, and the San Francisco Conference in full swing—so I am not going to try.

7/24 Milford …Tony Smith came up from Washington and N.Y. to discuss plan for Roosevelt Redwood Memorial to include all standing redwoods north of San Francisco.

8/11 Milford My 80th birthday. C.B.P. gave luncheon party—Forest Service sent delegation—C.M. Granger, Kneipp, and Mattoon—to present scroll, made by W. Ellis Grohen, and bound volume of letters from men and women of the Service.

8/14 Milford Radio flash at 7 P.M. from White House—Japan Surrenders. C.B.P. and I went to village to join in celebration, and with many others, rode the fire truck.

8/17 Milford Received invitation from Roosevelt National Memorial Committee to attend meeting at White House on Sept. 5.—President Truman to preside.

8/23 Milford …C.B. and I to Beaver Run to fish for pickerel. A calm water, and beautiful evening—every leaf reflected.

10/28 Washington Board of Directors of Union for Democratic Action meet at 1615 for morning and afternoon sessions.

11/27 Washington …Tony Smith came at 4:30 for a long conference about the proposed Redwood Memorial Forest for F.D.R.

12/17 Washington Telephone rang at 6:45. C.B.P. speaking from London, after long wait call went through. She has invitation from Gen. McNary to go to Germany as his guest, which would take 2 or 3 weeks. I advised her strongly to accept. She wanted to be accredited correspondent of some big periodical. I called up DeWitt Wallace, but he turned proposition down. Then spoke to a lot of other people.

1946

3/1 Washington …Lunch with Julius Barnes and Danielson at the Statler. They wanted me to appear before a Senate committee in favor of the St. Lawrence development. I do not know enough details to risk being questioned. So I am going to write a letter.

3/2 Washington …a tea Leila gave to discuss another proposed International Women's Conference in the U.S.

3/3 Washington [last diary entry] Stayed in bed half the day. Lunch of 14 which was not over until half past 4, after which Giff and his family went back to Frederick. Pretty well worn. GP

THE FOREST SERVICE TRANSFER

"Glory! Once more the Service is saved—for a time"

In 1876 Congress attached a rider to a seed distribution bill, appropriating $2,000 in support of a "forestry agent." This small program would evolve and grow, and in 1886 the Division of Forestry was made a permanent agency in the Department of Agriculture. In 1898 Gifford Pinchot succeeded Bernhard Fernow as chief forester of this agricultural agency. Initially, forestry advocates had sought to place the program in the Department of the Interior. However, the House Public Lands Committee refused to report out the bill, which languished for three years. In desperation, supporters managed the agricultural rider, and for that simple reason, federal forestry began in Agriculture instead of Interior. As the national forest system came into being following the 1891 Forest Reserve Act, the forests were under Interior. Thus the forests were in one department and the foresters in another.

Between 1898 and 1905, Pinchot labored mightily to have jurisdiction over the national forests transferred from the General Land Office in the Department of the Interior to the Bureau of Forestry in the Department of Agriculture. The political situation was such that a much easier route would have been to move himself and his then-small agency to Interior, merging in some way with the General Land Office. But the easy route was not his choice, no doubt partly because of his view that the GLO traditionally harbored corruption. In Agriculture he would have a much cleaner slate. Thus the tradition was carved in stone: forestry belonged in Agriculture, and over the years the Forest Service and its supporters have successfully deflected presidential efforts—including substantial reorganization initiatives during the 1920s, 1930s and 1940s, and two during the 1970s—to move it to Interior to be with other federal land management agencies.

Presidents routinely reorganize the executive branch—that is one of the things that presidents do—largely to reduce administrative inefficiencies. For example, in 1946 President Harry Truman used his authority to merge the General Land Office with the

Grazing Service into the Bureau of Land Management, and the sun still rose the next day—it was no big deal. Of course, both agencies were in Interior, so no one "lost," including the pertinent congressional committees that are as turf-driven as any agency. In fact, Pinchot's (and others') actions notwithstanding, lack of congressional support for efforts by Presidents Harding, Franklin Roosevelt, Nixon, and Carter to move the Forest Service explain why the agency is still in Agriculture. Too, each challenge has caused the Forest Service to chisel ever more deeply into its cultural stone that it must remain as it has been since 1905.

The following diary entries show Pinchot's energetic response to President Franklin D. Roosevelt's several proposals to transfer the Forest Service to Interior, as part of larger reorganization plans. His first transfer entries appear in 1937, with thirty-two notations. The 1938 diary is fragmentary, dealing only with Pinchot's failed bid for the Pennsylvania governorship; he resumes in 1939 with twelve references, and peaks in 1940 with sixty-five, dropping to three notations in 1941. There is nothing again until late 1945 and then two highly speculative notes in 1946, but just a few days later he stopped all entries, so we are left hanging.

Pinchot quickly identifies the players. Secretary of the Interior Harold Ickes, his long-time political friend and ally, becomes the devil, and at times the reader will wonder if the ruckus is more a battle of wills than concern about the management of natural resources. President Roosevelt, also enough of a friend that Pinchot could write "Dear Franklin" letters, receives mixed reviews; his support is essential but he could be infuriating. When Pinchot finally was able to make an appointment with the president to argue his case, FDR was "cordial" but elected to talk about the war, even Socrates, and the topic of transfer did not come up. "I was pretty angry," Pinchot noted in his diary that evening.

Decades earlier, when Pinchot was chief and then president of the National Conservation Association, he routinely used mass mailings to influence events, and he used that strategy again to bring pressure on the president. FDR indeed felt the pressure, and he wrote to Pinchot that his "general reaction [to the letters to forestry faculties] is unfavorable" because special interests are in fact special interests looking out only for their own situation. The president's language was strong, as he saw Pinchot's efforts no more justified than those of cattlemen's associations and even "horrid things like the K.K.K. itself." More moderately, FDR thought a "logical" organization would be having Interior tend to federal lands, and Agriculture to farmers' needs on private lands. Although FDR "was sore," Pinchot repeated his rationale that forestry was better off in Agriculture.

Even so, Pinchot felt hampered by Secretary of Agriculture Henry Wallace, who in the diaries appears indecisive, if not weak. Since FDR would select Wallace to be his vice-presidential running mate for the 1940 election, during the height of the transfer controversy, it would seem that Wallace would have had some sort of unique presidential access. If he did, he was reluctant to oppose the reorganization plan. It probably did not help matters that Pinchot, a life-long Republican, had campaigned against FDR for his first two terms, although by 1940 he had declared his support for a third term. A suspicious reader may see bits of evidence that Pinchot believed he would gain presidential favor on the transfer issue by this shift.

Generally, written history is not about things that did not happen, but the series of failed efforts to combine land management agencies into a single department is instructive when looking at today's condition. Forest Service advocates continue to see the Department of the Interior as much more politicized than the Department of Agriculture, at least the corner that includes the agency. If the Forest Service can only remain in Agriculture, their argument goes, it will also remain a professionally managed, as opposed to a politically managed, organization. As the century-long debate continues, no doubt the contrasting of agency cultures will remain prominent.

1937

1/12 Washington F.D.R.'s message to Congress seems to make it certain that the Forest Service will go to the Interior Department. Tough luck, after stopping it so many times.

1/13 Washington Franklin's proposal to reorganize the government is meeting with great opposition. It is ridiculous that it proposes economies amounting to only from one-half to one and one-half per cent over the present emergency setup. Unquestionably the attempt will be made to transfer the national forests to the Department of Conservation.

1/27 Washington Worked on the Brownlow Government Re-organization Report in the morning. It is not a bad document, but written from the point of view of men with little experience in actual administration. This is curious, because Brownlow as commissioner for the District ought to know something about government work.

1/28 Washington Munns, of the Forest Service, and his wife to lunch. Very interesting discussion about floods and the transfer of the Forest Service. Went to see Norris in the afternoon and discussed the transfer question with him. He agrees that the Service ought to remain in the Department of Agriculture, but I don't know whether he will fight for it.

2/10 Washington Called up Holman to see if I could get a body of farm leaders now in Washington to protest against the transfer of the Forest Service. Later learned that they had actually passed a resolution while here.

2/26 Washington Attended meeting of Allegheny Section Society of American Foresters in the afternoon and spoke against transfer of the national forests, ripping Ickes up the back, in the evening.

2/28 Washington Talked with Henry Wallace about transfer. Perfectly evident he will make no fight.

3/27 Washington In the afternoon Dol Smith came to talk about the transfer…

4/26 Washington …to see George Norris at 11:30, who heartily agreed in opposing the transfer of the Forest Service, and said he expected to make a speech about it when it came up. He hoped it would not come up this year, the danger being that the hot weather in the late season might drive Congress to hasty action. I left him with a draft of a speech.

5/3 New York Attended dinner of Camp Fire Club of America, Williams Club, 24 East 39th Str., New York. Spoke on Transfer of U.S. Forest Service from Department of Agriculture to the Department of the Interior.

5/15 Washington To see George Norris in the morning, who said he did not believe the reorganization bill would come up at the session of Congress, but in any event he would be unwilling to speak about it until he knows what bill is reported.

5/31 Cincinnati Arrived at banquet of American Forestry Association at Cincinnati while Henry Wallace was making what seemed to me an excellent talk. Then Reddy of Red Cross spoke—and then I made my talk. Afterward, conference with Harry Graves and Jim McClure, urging action by American Forestry Association; and again at breakfast with the same and Butler and Collingwood. Final decision to put Collingwood in charge of stirring up action by agricultural representatives on members of House and Senate—at my suggestion.

6/29 Washington …to meeting of agricultural and other leaders at the American Forestry Association, to discuss government re-organization. Fred Brenckman, Chester Gray, Hunt, Major Brookings of the U.S. Chamber of Commerce, Butler, Collingwood, and another man whose name I don't know. Suggested to them a joint letter should be written to each member of the House and Senate, and another to all the newspapers of the United States. Plan adopted by groups, which I think is wiser than a single letter signed by all interests. Was obliged to leave before the meeting ended.

7/20 New York Met Dunwoody at the Century at 10:30, and with him a former Forest Service man by the name of Neeper, who is raising money for the fight against the transfer. Dunwoody, contrary to my advisers from Washington, still thinks there is serious danger that they will attempt to pass the transfer at the session. In any case he is building up public opinion against it.

8/10 Portland …At 2 conference with Wentworth, West, etc. on transfer…At 3:30 to see Jackson about transfer. He seemed interested. Then Kelty of Oregonian who promised editorial **& delivered**. Then talked with Greeley…dinner with Greeley, Dol & Harry…Decided with Greeley, Dol, & Harry on telegrams to Byrnes & McNary on hearings about transfer, following Dunwoody telegram to me.

8/17 Roseburg, Oregon …Called Senator McNary at Salem. He gave me his assurance that when S2700 is reported Forest Service will be exempt from transfer. Grand!…Spoke over radio (local station) at 7:30 this A.M. about Forest Service transfer etc.

8/17 Crescent City, California …Show showed me message from Wash—Ickes appeared before Byrnes committee & said chief blame for opposition to transfer to me.

8/19 [San Francisco] With Show & Kotok. Harry & I to meeting [of] directors [of]

California Chamber of Commerce [illeg] & others. About 40. Spoke about transfer.

9/16 Washington Lunched with Dol Smith and Harry Graves at the Cosmos Club, and afterwards had a long talk with Rachford at the house. He agreed thoroughly with my statement of what the Forest Service needs to do in publicity and otherwise.

9/17 Washington Talked with Glavis in the morning at the house. Then long talk with Silcox at his house in Alexandria. He is much better. He also agreed thoroughly with my point of view; the Service must use the powers it has to prevent the Park Service and the Interior Department generally running away with it.

11/17 Washington Prospect for beating Harold Ickes seems excellent, thanks to Dunwoody who has been here for ten days or two weeks.

11/18 Washington Buck McGovern and Ralph Flinn came in about 9:00 and left at 5:00. We talked solidly all day except for short trip to see Henry Wallace concerning Harold Ickes' raid. It was a very satisfactory talk…Bob Marshall came in and turned over a thousand dollars to be contributed anonymously to the Transfer War.

11/20 Washington To see Vice-President Garner in his office at 10:00 o'clock about the proposed transfer. Most satisfactory talk. He

President Franklin D. Roosevelt with Cornelia and Gifford Pinchot, 1934. Pinchot Collection, Library of Congress.

said, "The transfer will not be made if Congress has anything to say about it." And went on to talk very freely about the president and the Cabinet—said that there were three members of the Cabinet who would talk back to Franklin—and that, when they did, Franklin was apt to weaken. Referred several times to his own differences of opinion with Franklin, and said definitely that he himself was against the transfer of the Forest Service. It was a highly satisfactory interview…[at dinner] I talked about the transfer—William Draper Lewis about the Constitution—and a man named Sims from Alabama about nothing much.

11/22 Washington Saw Senator Byrd in his office at 11:00, to discuss the transfer. Found him, of course, very vigorously on our side. He asked me for a short statement to include in his minority report on the Reorganization Bill …Then called on Capper, who is also very much with us…Talked with Dunwoody and Clapp at 4:30.

11/23 Washington Tried to see Senator Smith, but failed. Had long talk with McAdoo who seemed to be fairly friendly, and said he would consider the transfer matter. Like so many other government officials, he talked a tremendous lot before getting down to business.

11/24 Washington Long talk with Senator Smith of South Carolina, who made me speech after speech, and actually with tears in his eyes declaimed how he had been marked for slaughter politically because he would not follow the New Deal. He is red hot with us against the transfer to Ickes.

11/25 Washington Talked with Dunwoody in the morning, who reported sixty-six senators opposed to the Department of Conservation— and a lot more doubtful.

11/26 Washington Talk with Senator Green in his office on the transfer. He rejects emphatically all arguments based on Ickes and the Department of the Interior—and wants to know only what is good administration. So I told him the best I could…[in afternoon] Dunwoody came in…

11/29 New York …to see Roy Howard about the transfer. He referred me to Deacon Park in Washington, and said he would let him know I was coming…

12/3 Washington Dunwoody and I went over to see Max Stern with the story of Harold Ickes' defeat in his attempt to use the meeting of Advisory Board Taylor Act stockmen to accomplish the transfer. A Legislative Committee was selected. Chapman urged them to recommend to the full meeting that they undertake to sabotage the Department of Conservation if the committee reported to the meeting against it, and their report was unanimously adopted.

12/15 Washington …to see Vandenberg, who said three things: 1) That he had heard no one speak favorably of the transfer on the whole; 2) that all his people in Michigan were against it; and 3) That he thought there was no doubt where he would land when the question came up.

12/25 New York …Telegraphed Alberta to bring down the Ickes Presidential circular letter…

1939

1/15 Washington …Charley Dunwoody came in about 11. Good talk…

3/3 Washington …Dunwoody told C.B. strong possibility [of] relieving Forest Service from transfer in new re-organization bill.

3/28 Washington …Mr. Dunwoody in for 5 mins.

4/19 Washington …Dol, Tom Healey, & Dunwoody came in. Dunwoody said Ickes has opened new drive to get grazing & recreation away from Forest Service in spite of fact that

F.D.R. promised Pittman & 14 other senators no functions of FS would be transferred.

6/2 Washington Dol Smith showed me a copy of F.D.R.'s correspondence with Key Pittman which should settle question of transfer for good & all.

11/13 Washington …[Henry Wallace] suggested I see Pittman first about transfer & then Byrnes & Garner.

11/17 Washington …Tried all this week to get to see Pittman. Put off & put off. Sick, his secretary said, but I doubt.

11/30 Washington …At 12:30 saw Pittman about transfer. He is uneasy. He suggested stirring up the friends of forestry. I suggested a letter signed by faculties of all schools of forestry. After lunch, Ellen (Thoron) Leonard lunched with us, went to see Dol & Clapp about it. They approved.

12/5 Washington …letters about transfer.

12/6 Washington Finished letters on transfer with Dol.

12/18 Washington …Signed about 250 letters to faculty members of forest schools on transfer.

12/23 Washington To see George Harris. He could do nothing about the transfer. To see Fred Brenckman. He is to write F.D.R. Learned this morning that F.D.R. asked Henry Wallace to name Silcox's successor. That looks to no transfer…

1940

1/1 Washington …I wrote F.D.R. on the transfer…

1/13 Washington …Took 139 replies of forestry school faculty members to White House. Col. Watson promised F.D. would get them. To see Pittman. He said no hope to stop transfer of F.S.

1/14 Washington …Chapman assured me he believes transfer is out—no chance of it. Ickes asked for CCC & got a firm refusal.

1/15 Washington …Continual rumors back & forth that the transfer will be made, that it won't & da capo. Saw McNary, who says flat there is no danger, that not five senators are for the transfer, that Congress would smash it, & that F.D.R. won't do it "unless he is a damned liar, because he told me definitely within the last two weeks that he wouldn't."

1/16 Washington Very sore letter from Franklin on the transfer. He is bothered. Took it to Felix, who thinks as I do that he is sore, but does not intend to act. Then showed it to McNary, who thought it didn't mean anything, but wouldn't head any protest. Also wouldn't introduce bill to cut down political contacts or forfeit election for violations. Must have walked a mile. Pretty used up. P.M. tried to write letter to F.D. on Felix advice.

1/17 Washington Spent morning on answer to F.D.'s letter. Dol helped.

1/18 Washington I believe it was this day I went to see McNary again, & got him to arrange for me to see Joe Martin. He was very cordial & agreed I should send him a statement on the transfer.

1/22 Washington At 10:45 to meeting at American Forestry Association. Mostly farm leaders (Brenckman, Ogg, etc.) to prepare protest against transfer. I see joint statement for F.D.R. & all members of Congress. P.M. called Henry Wallace. Urged him to fight. He said (confidentially) he had asked for appointment with F.D. to protest against transfer. I had urged him strongly to fight. Some progress, anyhow. On 24th (I think) joint letter was sent.

1/23 Washington …Afterward phone[d] a man & heard that Harold was low in his mind, F.D.R. having told him he had just about made up his mind not to transfer the Forest Service.

1/24 Washington That was great news last

night. Dol came in as usual…Telegrams sent to Dunwoody's 21 names beginning to get action.

1/25 Washington Working on transfer.

1/26 Washington Mail. Working at last on material for Martin. Saw Professor Creel at 11 at Willard. He is strong against transfer & will tell Henry Wallace to get busy at lunch today. Saw Congressman Doxey. Strong for us. Said it was Joint Committee on Forestry that asked for conference with F.D. before his decision on transfer. Even Fulton Lewis radioed F.D. will make decision probably next week, gave impression Ickes would win.

1/27 Washington Heard last night things were not going well. So went to see McNary. He said no danger at all. Said F.D. would get licking of his life if he tried transfer.

Senator Bankhead had "Talked rough" to F.D. Everything OK. Then saw Norris. He said F.D. had promised Ickes in writing. Norris wrote F.D. suggesting Ickes for War Department. Norris told Tom Cochran he would fight transfer to the last ditch. Talk with Creel & President Lory of Association Agriculture Colleges & Experiment Stations. They are red hot to help. Working P.M. on statement for Martin.

1/29 Washington To see Senator Bankhead. He has sent word to F.D. that Joint Committee on Forestry is unanimously against transfer by Watson & asked for interview Wednesday or Thursday. Is very encouraging. Saw Doxey. No news. He is for G.P. sending letter to all members. Saw Martin. Is with us strong. Says vote on reorganization order will not be rushed. Fine. Also said absolute confidence Ickes will have very hard time getting approval [of] transfer through House. Saw Bert Wheeler. With us strong.

1/30 Washington …Telgraphed Dunwoody I thought [he] had better not come…

1/31 Washington …Dinner at Bob Taft's. Met Senator Holman of Oregon. He's agin transfer.

2/2 Washington …Either this day or yesterday saw Cotton Ed Smith & asked him to call his committee to protest against transfer. Asked Norris & Capper to urge him. Capper introduced me to Carl Sandb[u]rg.

2/3 Washington Finally got out letters to senators & congressmen. 2 pages mimeographed. Hope it may help prevent transfer. Bankhead still sick. Henry Wallace & a lot of people to dinner. Henry said as he went down stairs: Transfer still uncertain. There has been some kind of commitment (to Ickes). It may be that the situation will invalidate the commitment, cause it to be overlooked or words to that effect.

2/4 Washington Joe Martin—a lot more to lunch. Martin very positive F.D. can't put the transfer through the House. He approved my sending the letter.

2/5 Washington Got out letters to all state foresters on transfer. Asked George Norris to speak to Senator Smith about calling Senate Agriculture Committee to protest against transfer to F.D. Also asked Capper. Both had agreed to do so.

2/6 Washington Replies to Congress letter. 13 for us. 11 non committal. 1 for transfer (Cochran).

2/7 Washington Replies 9+ 15+/− 0− Talk with Governor Pierce of Oregon now congressman. He's with us strong. Will see Ben Cohen today & tell him transfer would be beaten. Also will see Marvin Jones…Harris Reynolds came in this evening. He will stir up Massachusetts & all N.E. against transfer. Great luck.

2/8 Washington 4+ 5+/− replies

2/10 Washington All these blank days busy with transfer. Sent letter to all state foresters etc.

Seeing people etc. Gradual feeling things are going our way. Contradictory reports, more than I ever knew about anything else. Eleanor told newspaper man F.D. would not make the transfer. Other reports that order is signed etc., etc.

2/12 Washington Talk with Worth Clark of Idaho. He will confer with Bankhead as to possible hearings to spread news of opposition, & with McNary. Doxey with us but not in fighting mood. Tried to talk with Fulmer, but he was ruder than any congressman has ever been to me, & I couldn't say a word for fear of his opposition. He says he's for us.

2/13 Washington Word that Byrnes of South Carolina is against transfer. Conference with Butler, Collingwood, Korstian, Clepper, Gillette. All agreed order will go in in next two days or not at all. They will get wires sent. Later news from Earle Clapp & others that no action on transfer at present & none on any reorganization order till March 10 or 15. Newspaper men say transfer is dead. If so, thank God. I am profoundly pleased & relieved.

2/14 Washington Reports from newspaper men no reorganization order till March 10 or 15 & that transfer is dead. Worth Clark told me Bankhead sent 2 messages to F.D. yesterday protesting. Also that half a dozen senators saw F.D. yesterday & told him probability of defeat if order was sent. Order was actually signed. One of them read him Pope's (Idaho) speech— would vote for reorganization order 2 because of promise not to transfer. Fulton Lewis on the air said F.D. said that was enough for him & tore up the signed order. Said Forest Service safe, at least for the time. I <u>am</u> thankful. Work all day on radio speech for Farm & Home Hour.

2/17 Washington Finishing radio talk. Spoke over WMAL on Grange hour on why USFS belongs in Department of Agriculture…Dinner with Bill Hard—Brenckman confirmed story I

got Tuesday. He was doubtful about transfer, but when Emsley of Colorado made about the finest endorsement of F.S. I ever heard, I think he was converted.

2/18 Washington Earle Clapp at 10:30. He will send my talk to Forest Service officers. Said he liked it. Thinks I can go away on 12 day cruise safely…Glenn Frank, who agreed to C.B.'s suggestion that Republican Platform should speak out against transfer…

2/19 Washington Some approval of my Sat radio…Talk with Fred Brenckman. Suggested Grange ask all governors to protest to President against transfer. He agreed, & will ask other farm organizations to do same. Great! Will also send my talk to all local Grange officers.

2/20 Washington Went to see Worth Clark. He thought the decision against transfer was not final.

3/11 Washington …At 5 young Collier (son of Indiana congressman) to see me about Morris Cooke's new organization to save the land. Told him I couldn't come in unless it stood against transfer. Gave him a lot of free advice. He told me Ickes had told his father about three weeks ago that the transfer was dead. May be. I hope so.

3/14 Washington Dinner with the Justice Reeds. Senator Barkley there. Talk about Big Trees led to my asking about transfer. He said it was dead. Also confirmed strong protest made to F.D. by New Dealers in Congress. Told him about harm done to Forest Service by uncertainty & he said he would speak to F.D.R. about it. A very good talk. He told F.D. he was & would vote against it.

3/18 Washington Talk with William H. Finlay, V.P. Nature Association, at wildlife conference. Suggested question of taking national forest lands for national parks be referred to Joint Committee on Forestry. He agreed.

3/27 Washington The fat in the fire again. Not the transfer but the dismemberment of the national forests is now the plan. Recreation, wilderness areas, areas suited to recreation, & areas more valuable for grazing to be transferred to Ickes. Also Rural Electrification. Also Food & Drug. Ickes has been denouncing Forest Service to F.D.R. & others—demanding transfer to him.

3/28 Washington To see Henry Wallace at 9:40. Appleby said plan not executive, but reorganization order. Got nowhere with Henry as usual. Saw Norris. Urged him to write protest to F.D. Said he couldn't. Then got him to call Bankhead. Bankhead didn't want to see me. Same with Byrnes. Then saw Pittman in his office. He was mad. Said he intended writing F.D. fierce letter. I urged to see Bankhead & Byrnes. He agreed, & took with him copy reorganization order, which he had already.

3/29 Washington Writing telegram to Finley to be read to Izaak Walton League in Chicago after Harold Ickes makes speech denouncing G.P. Telegram shows how bad proposed partial transfer is. About 4 this P.M. got news from Clapp that F.D.R. had announced in Cabinet meeting there would be no reoganization order! Glory! Once more the Service is saved—for a time. Harry told me Norris had written fierce letter to F.D. against reoganization order. He then got word Thursday evening from White House that he need not worry.

3/30 Washington Wire from Finlay. My message not read. George Norris, Slattery, Dol, Clapp etc. to dinner. Very pleasant eve.

4/2 Washington …Saw Boylin in P.M. Thinks we are out of woods. Asked me to prepare plank on transfer. Bankhead will back it…Clapp called on phone after supper to say Forest Service reorganization still threatened.

4/3 Washington Phone talk with Slattery. Says Barkley gave public notice another reorganization order was coming, which would have no trouble in Congress. So I guess that's OK.

4/8 Washington …Fulton Lewis on radio said F.D. considering putting dismemberment of Forest Service in 4th reorganization order due this week. I notified Slattery & Earle Clapp. If true it's no credit to F.D. Talked with Slattery & Earle. Probably not serious.

4/9 Washington Got in touch w. Trent (to see Pittman), Brenckman (to see Bankhead & McNary), Criel (to see Pittman), Worth Clark (to see Byrnes) & Ogg.

4/10 Washington …Apparently no trouble coming on transfer.

4/11 Washington …About 11 Marquis Childs called me on phone to say that the 4th reorganization order had been signed with no mention of the Forest Service. Thank Heaven again. That saves the Service for this session. Saw Fred Brenckman about putting Ickes' Izaak Walton speech & the Izaak Walton anti transfer resolution in Record.

4/16 Washington Brenckman came in. Good talk. He's strong for a western association to prevent transfer. Also for Republican plank against it.

4/18 Washington Got Brenckman & Trent to look up report F.D. will transfer grazing parts of national forest into public domain. Brenckman reported nothing in it…Phoned the good news.

4/22 Washington F.D. gave notice of a tour West in June in which he will talk on conservation. Will dedicate Kings Canyon steal & Olympic steal. Looks dangerous…

4/23 Washington …Suggested to Brenckman that he see Worth Clark about pressure on him from Interior Department to get grazing in national forests transferred to Interior by changing boundaries, & make it public on Senate floor.

4/29 Washington Brenckman came. He has same idea as I to make Inter Mountain Association take on defense of Forest Service. Report today that Ickes is after executive order to abolish certain national forests & turn land over to him for grazing.

5/8 Washington Working on letter to delegates to Republican Convention concerning transfer.

5/15 Washington Mail & letter to Republican Delegates on transfer…

5/21 Washington [Ickes's] article full of misstatements—omissions. Provoked of course, by Ickes' defeat (transfer).

5/23 Washington …Alf Landon came in after [lunch]. C.B. suggested speech against [illeg.] & his wire tapping, & Ickes'…Asked we send him Republican planks on labor & conservation.

6/5 Milford …Finished transfer plank for Boykin…

7/9 Milford …Henry Wallace's nomination as V.P. raises many questions for Forest Service.

8/13 Washington Harry Slattery came in early. At 1 P.M. lunched with Henry Wallace. At his invitation sent by Slattery last week. Told him there were three things I was interested in. Public statement by F.D.—no transfer of FS or any of its functions. Appointment of Clapp as head of Forest Service. Recognition of Pinchots through C.B. Henry had no proposition, but said F.D. had sent word by Henry that F.D. wanted to see me. He was not going to speak for F.D., but wanted me to do it all. I told him I didn't see why he should be afraid. Henry agreed with my three points. Afterward told Slattery & Clapp about talk.

8/15 Milford Wrote Franklin that I would come any time he set…

8/20 Milford …Letter from Franklin saying he'd be "delighted" to see me. Called up Watson & made date for 27th at 11.

8/24 Milford …Chapman & Arnold both of strong opinion that Franklin has got to have me & that he will publicly guarantee Forest Service where it is.

8/27 Washington …Saw Franklin at 11… Franklin cordial. Talked about the war. Socrates. But so far as his bringing up anything, might just as well not have come. I was pretty angry. Saw Norris. He knew nothing of proposed article with Brandeis answer to Ickes. Told Henry Wallace, Slattery, & Chapman about interview.

9/9 Washington … At [C.B.'s] suggestion to see Pittman & others about transfer, & if possible get my position on presidency determined.

9/10 Washington Saw Key Pittman at 11:30 & told him I wanted a public statement from F.D.R. He said he could not speak to F.D. about it lest F.D. retract his written promise but he would speak to others, meaning, I took it, Chairman Flynn. Good talk. Harry Slattery came in late P.M. Said Franklin had told him he (F.D.) was going to see me soon. Also of his talk with Rodden, Flynn's assistant. Then he called up Byrnes & made appointment for me tomorrow. Harry told of his talk with the new secretary of agriculture who decided at Harry's suggestion to tell F.D. he would stand no more interference from Harold, & would appoint Clapp.

9/11 Washington Talk with Senator Byrnes of South Carolina. Told him I wanted public statement by F.D.R. there would be no transfer of Forest Service or any of its functions. He said he would see F.D.R. "within the next two or three days." He had told Harry Slattery yesterday that I would be "worth ten thousand men." Harry came in at five. He had talked with Rodden over phone, apparently with good results. Byrnes said F.D. had promised him definitely there would be no transfer, & said F.D. had never signed the order transferring the national forests—which I doubt.

1941

3/3 Washington …Reported that F.D. will soon have introduced new reorganization bill …Tried again to see McKellar. Sick. Saw Harry Stimson. Told him about Ickes…& the Forest Service. Said he was with me on account of me.

4/20 Washington C.B. talked with Henry Wallace. He told her critical time for transfer would be week beginning April 28. Suggested I see McNary.

8/6 Washington …In the late afternoon saw Earle Clapp and Jud King. All quiet along the transfer front at present.

1945

12/13 Washington …Afternoon saw Anderson who told me Ickes had written a letter to the president 10 days ago recommending transfer of the Forest Service to the Interior Department. Anderson hot under the collar and determined to fight, which is fine.

1946

2/26 Washington …Harold Smith of the Budget was for transferring the national forests to the Interior Department on the ground that all public lands ought to be there.

2/27 Washington Talked with Henry Wallace in the morning about Krug's appointment and the threat of transfer. Later he told Anderson about our talk and Anderson gave me an appointment for tomorrow. G͜P

FEDERAL REGULATION OF INDUSTRIAL LOGGING
"The two control questions of foresty, public control and public ownership"

During the latter third of the nineteenth century, as Congress debated the proper means to protect western watersheds, no thought was given to federal regulation of privately owned forest lands. Instead, Congress in 1891 authorized the president to create federal forest reserves by proclamation. In this way, essential watersheds would be protected by keeping them in federal ownership. However, the 1891 statute was defective, in that it failed to provide means to manage the forest reserves, and Congress immediately began consideration of a remedy. This effort resulted in the 1897 Forest Service Organic Act, as it is now called.

During the six-year debate leading to the 1897 statute, many in Congress voiced their strong opposition to logging of any kind on the proposed reserves, giving priority to full protection of water supplies. However, Bernhard E. Fernow, Pinchot's predecessor as chief of the Division of Forestry, was able to convince key committee members that regulated logging would not impair water quality or quantity. Thus, the Organic Act authorized sale of federal timber, but it also prescribed in detail just how the cutting would be done. Congress would not be involved again in debating logging prescriptions until the 1920s.

Pinchot succeeded Fernow in 1898 and immediately began to develop a cooperative program that was to bring management to privately held forest lands. Under this plan, the owner would pay the costs, and the agency would provide the expertise. Eventually, more than seven million acres of private forests would have a Pinchot-approved management plan. In addition, Pinchot's law officer, Philip Wells, developed a strategy by which the Forest Service would enable cooperating companies avoid antitrust constraints on price fixing if they would adopt "conservative" logging practices. Too, Pinchot testified in Congress in support of protective tariffs on lumber imports. Finally, he announced publicly that the Forest Service would withhold national forest timber from local markets that were adequately served by private supply.

Those several actions resulted from his belief that a financially healthy industry was more likely to voluntarily adopt suitable logging practices. The industry did not respond as Pinchot had hoped, and he began to turn his attention toward obtaining statutory authority over the private sector. But this happened after he left the Forest Service in 1910; from his platform at the National Conservation Association, he urged an unspecified "forcing" of lumbermen to practice forestry. Ultimately he wrote in 1919 a *Journal of Forestry* article titled, "The Lines Are Drawn"—the line being the one between federal regulation and voluntary action. The conflict, often bitter, continued for five years before it was officially resolved by passage of the 1924 Clarke McNary Act, with its cooperative programs. Congress was not of a mind to pass regulatory statutes. The Forest Service, led by William Greeley, had lobbied hard and effectively for the Clarke McNary Act, much to Pinchot's chagrin.

During the 1930s the Forest Service with Chief Ferdinand Silcox resumed the debate by once again insisting that federal regulation of private logging practices was essential to American well-being. And again, those who were opposed did so with vigor, some going so far as to compare Silcox to Hitler. But Congress still would not support regulation, and beginning in 1941 the states stepped in with so-called forest practice acts that placed private forest lands under their control, mainly to assure reforestation following logging and prudent fire protection measures. Strangely, Pinchot's diary is mute on the regulation issue until 1941, except for a single entry in 1937, even though his 1930s correspondence contains files on the topic.

From the entries, we can see that Pinchot and Acting Chief Earle Clapp saw eye-to-eye on the need for federal regulation, but Clapp's successor, Lyle Watts, preferred control of logging by the states. While Clapp was still in office, Pinchot mounted his tried-and-true bulk mailing approach to influence Congress via newspaper articles and editorials. He made the issue a wartime issue: "To win this war we must have wood." He also stated, "No forests in all the world are safe against destruction unless they are under governmental control." The forest industry through its primary trade association labeled Pinchot's statement "ambiguous and misleading." Too, the lumbermen saw that the war was "being used as the excuse again to urge federal forestry legislation."

Lyle Watts became chief in 1943, and Pinchot thought him a good choice. They could speak to each other with candor, and they could disagree on issues without discomfort. Pinchot consulted the chief about his pending approach to the American Forestry Association, whose president, W.S. Rosecrans, was a lumberman from California. The exchange obviously did not go well from Pinchot's view, and he resigned from the association in 1943. The diary entries peter out about this time, but we know that nothing came of the regulation effort other than imbedding ever deeper in corporate culture that the federal government needed close watching.

Ironically, during the late 1940s after Pinchot's death, Chief Watts began a major effort to obtain statutory authority over logging on private lands, a campaign that ended in January 1953 when Ezra Taft Benson, President-elect Eisenhower's choice for secretary of Agriculture, directed recently appointed Chief Richard McArdle to drop the regulation effort. The chief complied, and regulation was not seen again until the 1970s, when a series of federal statutes asserted authority over logging and other activities. But it would not be the Forest Service that acquired that authority. Rather, it fell to the Environmental Protection Agency, the Corps of Engineers, and the Fish and Wildlife Service to carry out congressional mandates.

1941

3/18 Washington Talk with Clark of Idaho about government control. He says Joint Committee is practically unanimous against federal control.

1942

6/17 Milford …C.B. called about the form letter on government control of forests. It is to go out next week and is being prepared in Washington.

6/22 Milford …Began signing letters to newspapers in support of government control of lumber during the war.

6/23 New York Signed more letters…

6/25 Milford Finally finished signing all second sheets of that letter about government control.

8/27 New York Lunched with Clapp at the Century. Most satisfactory talk about control.

11/9 Washington …Afternoon, talk…with Earle Clapp, who brought me a long statement on the two control questions of forestry, public control and public ownership, which I have got to rewrite.

11/14 Washington …Long talk with Clapp in the afternoon about proposed letter urging control of cutting on private forests by Executive Order.

1943

4/7 Washington Work on proposed letter to president American Forestry Association.

4/15 Washington …In the evening, meeting of the Washington section Society of American Foresters…I praised Clapp and denounced state control as against federal, and read a chapter on origin of conservation policy.

5/5 Washington To see…Watts, with whom I had a good talk about the American Forestry Association, and a less satisfactory talk about federal control.

5/6 Washington Spent nearly all day on drafting of letter to Rosecrans. Probably time wasted but I have a desire to answer him.

5/15 Washington …Talked with Watts who went over my proposed letter to Rosecrans, which Dol thoroughly and rightly so, [found] defective in some respects.

5/17 Washington Working on Rosecrans letter.

5/18 Washington …letter to Rosecrans.

11/24 Washington…Long talk with Lyle Watts…Most satisfactory. While he sticks to state control of cutting under federal regulation, he is perfectly willing to have the rest of us stand for federal control straight. G͟P

Conservation as the Foundation of Permanent Peace

"Fair access to natural resources for all nations"

In his autobiography, Gifford Pinchot allocated twenty-two pages to the description of four conferences: the Conference of Governors (1908), the National Conservation Commission (1909), the North American Conservation Conference (1909), and the World Conservation Conference (1909). The first three were convened and produced proceedings, but the fourth was "killed" by President Taft as part of his larger attempt to rein in his chief forester.

Pinchot continued to press for a world conference and petitioned Presidents Wilson and Hoover, but to no avail. In late 1939, as World War II drew ever closer to American shores, he began again to push for a conference, this time with special emphasis on "permanent" peace. Even though direct American involvement in the war was still in the future, Pinchot wanted to get his plan to the president so that it could be worked "into the peace terms at the end of this war."

He accepted an invitation to speak at the Eighth American Scientific Congress in May 1940, and his paper was published that August in *Nature*. The paper would go through several subsequent revisions, but the main points were firmly in place. He traced the history of his belief, beginning with the conservation philosophy of Theodore Roosevelt. With the war already upon Europe and Asia, Pinchot stated, "War is still an instrument of national policy for the safeguarding of natural resources or for securing them from other nations. Hence international co-operation in conserving, utilizing, and distributing natural resources to the mutual advantage of all nations might well remove one of the most dangerous of all obstacles to a just and permanent world peace."

For another year, Pinchot continued to tinker with his proposal, then the diaries are fairly silent on the topic until 1945, when he worked through Franklin Roosevelt's daughter, Anna Boettinger, and others to gain presidential attention. In August 1944 Pinchot wrote to the president, "I enclose for your consideration a suggested draft of a letter to Allied Governments proposing a Conference on the conservation of natural resources as a necessary requirement for permanent peace." The State Department added its cautious support, concerned that it might conflict with the proposed creation of the Food and Agricultural Organization of the United Nations. On March 28, 1945, Pinchot again wrote to Roosevelt that he would continue to refine his proposal for the president to review, following his return from Yalta.

FDR died on April 12, and during the funeral four days later, Pinchot discussed his peace plan with Henry Wallace, the former vice-president and former secretary of Agriculture. On May 8 President Harry Truman wrote to him, "My lamented predecessor placed great faith in your judgment and I shall like to think that I, too, can seek the counsel which you can give out of so rich and so long an experience." On May 23 Pinchot noted in his diary, "Highly satisfactory talk with President Truman on World Conference at White House."

When he met the president again during an FDR Memorial Committee meeting in August, which Truman chaired, Pinchot asked for two minutes to explain his views on atomic energy; could he write a proposal for the president's consideration? Truman said that he could, that "he was thinking about that subject all the time." To Pinchot, nuclear energy was another natural resource to be included in his broader plan for peace, and so the pertinent diary entries are included in this section.

Pinchot died in 1946 without knowing whether his long-held idea would ever bear fruit. The editor of *Breaking New Ground* noted that Truman sent Pinchot's plan to the UN Economic and Social Council, and it was accepted and placed on the 1948 agenda. M. Nelson McGeary, Pinchot's chief biographer, states that the 1949 United Nations Scientific Conference on the Conservation and Utilization of Resources was the official result.

It is fascinating to read Pinchot's diaries and watch him as he writes *Breaking New Ground* at the same time he is developing support for the world conference. In the autobiography he goes so far as to speak directly to his readers and explain that for the conference he is suspending the book's 1910 cutoff and will bring the reader up-to-date, that is, to the 1940s, when he is writing. He even quotes in full two letters by President Franklin Roosevelt. This blatant present-mindedness may be a bit of a jolt to the historical purist, but along the way Pinchot bent many conventions, some major and some minor, and the reasonable among us will agree that the world is better off for his pragmatism.

1939

11/12 Washington …Dol, Earle Clapp, & Dick Basset, & their wives to lunch. Told Clapp about plan for world agreement in natural resources as part of peace…Will take peace plan to F.D.R..

11/13 Washington I think this was the day I saw Henry Wallace, told him in confidence about plan for conservation & peace. He said Franklin most anxious to be known as peace maker in this war. He thought well of my taking it to Franklin.

11/16 Washington Long talk with Dol about Conservation & Peace.

11/18 Washington …Talk with Graves about Conservation & Peace plan. He is strong for it. Also with Dol in P.M.

11/19 Washington …Harry Slattery to lunch. Talked with him about conservation inventory & peace. Am to show him plan when ready.

11/20 Washington Graves, Dol & I spent the morning working over plan for F.D.R. to work conservation & fair access to natural resources for all nations into the peace terms at end of this war. Harry read us a superb memo that set the whole thing in train. C.B.P. & Dol had urged us to get at it..

11/21 Washington We three spent the morning again at the plan. Made real progress.

11/22 Washington Working over statement on peace plan…

11/24 Washington Working on peace plan. Excellent letter from Harry Graves as to what we ought to find out for that purpose.

11/29 Washington Peace plan & book.

11/30 Washington Working on peace plan & book.

1940

4/27 Washington …Invited to speak at Pan American Science Congress.

5/4 Washington …Working on speech for Science Congress.

5/6 Washington …Finished speech on conservation as foundation for permanent peace for American Science Congress.

5/11 Washington Spoke before 8th American Science Congress section of Agriculture & Conservation—about 140 present—on Conservation as the Foundation of Permanent Peace. Good talk, I think, but not especially well received. With Dr. Shantz will try for resolution. at Friday session of section.

5/13 Washington …Arranging to have Science Congress paper mimeographed. 500.

5/14 Washington Wrote resolution for Inter American Congress on conservation to advance permanent peace. Saw Schantz of Forest Service & Kellogg [illeg.] soils about resolution. They approved. Saw Bennett & Holt. They approved. Saw Dr. Rowe. He said it was of "major importance." Also saw Wetmore. He approved.

5/15 Washington …P.M. called Holt. He said resolution approved by Resolution Committee & now before Section. Called Shantz & he went at once to meeting. Reported in a few minutes resolution passed with addition referring to Pan American Union. No opposition. Dinner at Henry Wallaces. Showed him resolution. Also Grady, assistant secretary of state, who seemed favorable.

5/25 Washington Talk with Dr. Rowe. Am to send him outline plan for making resolution on conservation & peace work. Very good talk.

5/28 Milford Finished & sent off to Holt & Rowe outline for action under my conservation & peace plan.

1941

2/25 Washington …at Department. Harry Graves came in & we talked Pan American Conservation Committee. He

The library at 1615 Rhode Island Avenue, Washington, D.C. Grey Towers Collection.

advised conservation inventory of what each nation needs, not only of what it has. Good sense.

2/26 Washington Saw Hull A.M. & outlined Inter-American conservation plan. He approved vigorously. Left resolution & description with him. He seemed old. Met Berle. He seemed to approve.

1945

1/17 Washington ...Memo from Franklin enclosing Stettinus suggestion for area conferences instead of International Conference on Conservation.

1/19 Washington Buffet luncheon at the White House. Roosevelt to take up proposed International Conservation Conference with Churchill and Stalin.

1/20 Washington To F.D.R.'s Inauguration with C.B.P. We stood in the snow on the South Lawn to hear him speak from South Porch of White House. Afterwards finished draft of letter for F.D.R. for 40th birthday of Forest Service. On C.B.P.'s suggestion, will enclose copy of letter to Franklin to Mrs. Boettinger.

1/21 Washington On C.B.P.'s suggestion, enclosed copy of letter to Franklin and draft for Forest Service to Mrs. Boettinger, and Mrs. Mather delivered letters to Franklin and Mrs. Boettinger at White House Sunday afternoon. About 6:30 Mrs. Boettinger called up to say that she had read parts of my letter to the president and he suggested that I prepare an outline for the international conference, to reach him not later than 4 o'clock Monday afternoon. *1/22 Washington* Worked on short statement for F.D.R. on International Conservation Conference. Talks with Lorwin, Wetmore, Zon & C.B.P. Statement delivered to White House by Mrs. Mather at 10 minutes to 4. Immediately afterwards Miss Tully telephoned to say that Franklin would send letter to Forest Service and authorized me to see government experts in preparing longer statement during his absence. That was fine! Quite fine!

1/24 Washington Henry Field came at 10:30 to talk of plans for conference. To Soil Conservation Service in afternoon—to see Bennett on getting data together for conference.

1/26 Washington To the office. Talk with Watts about International Conference. Saw Wheeler of R.E.A. who agreed to prepare material promptly.

1/27 Washington To the office. Talk with Watts and Wheeler about conference… Afternoon Henry Field brought in Dr. Thompson and Field's assistant with a Russian name. Thompson will help with preparation for conference.

2/2 Washington …Working on agenda for Conservation Conference.

2/5 Washington …Henry Field brought Oscar Cox in to talk about the conservation conference. He will prepare an outline for the meeting. Very satisfactory talk.

2/8 Washington Amos Taylor for lunch. Good talk about the proposed conference. He will send some material.

2/10 Washington To see Finch at the Carnegie Endowment for material for the conservation conference. Didn't get much.

2/12 Washington Conference work in the morning. Book and conference in the afternoon. Talk with Zimmerman of the Soil Conservation

Service who brought material for conference prepared there. As I pointed out they had left all consideration of permanent peace out of the picture.

2/13 Washington …Henry Field and Harry Slattery to lunch. Long discussion with them about conference…Talk with Dr. Wrather about conference afterward.

2/14 Washington Busy day. Work on conference. Nearly two-hour talk with O.C. Merrill in the morning about place of power in the plan. Then with Mrs. Burns, formerly of the Natural Resources Planning Board. Good talk with Morris Cooke at 3. Monroe Smith at 4, and I went to see Miss Janet Richards afterward. Good & tired.

2/17 Washington To the office…Dr. Gerayd Johnson, of Columbia University, whose name was suggested by Bruce Bliven, came in to talk about Conservation as a Basis of Permanent Peace, and very kindly agreed to dig up some examples of war caused by the lack of natural resources.

2/18 Washington C.B.P. and I to see Felix Frankfurter and tell him about proposed international conference, over which he showed great enthusiasm.

2/22 Washington Work on the conference all day. In the morning talk with Amos E. Taylor, who submitted a statement, and in the afternoon with Dr. Langer who agreed to supply historical data on natural resources as causes of war. So far I have not struck anybody who was not enthusiastic over the conference plan.

2/23 Washington Working on conference in the morning. Lunch with Lorwin at the Cosmos Club and long talk about the conference. I left him a big envelope full of papers to go over. He sees clearly the very great danger of stepping on the toes of other existing organizations.

2/28 Washington Long talk with Harry Graves about the conference at the office. Zon was there, having recovered from his cold. Talk was a real help.

*3/6 **Washington*** Lewis Lorwin came in at 5 to look over manuscript for conservation conference. Made some excellent suggestions.

*3/16 **Washington*** Met Wickard at 10 o'clock in his office, with Watts, Tolley, and Wheeler. Wickard had understood from F.D.R. that the proposed World Conference would deal only with forestry and was obviously afraid it would interfere with the plans of the Food and Agriculture Administration. After I explained the situation Wickard agreed and repeated several times that there was no conflict. After lunch, Hassett, secretary to the president, called me up and said the president wanted to see me and that he would arrange for a time early in the coming week and let me know.

*3/27 **Washington*** Hassett phoned from White House that the president wants to see a copy of the plan.

*3/28 **Washington*** Completed the plan, with a few very small changes and Leila & I, with little Jimmy took it down to the White House. It was addressed to the president and in the corner "Attention of Mr. Hassett."

*4/10 **Washington*** Henry Field came to talk about World Conference. Sent letters to F.D.R. and Miss Tully to White House, about Conservation as a Basis of Permanent Peace.

*4/12 **Washington*** …Late this afternoon, C.B. called me. At first I couldn't understand what she said. Then came the dreadful news of the president's death. At first I didn't believe it. But it was true.

*4/14 **Washington*** The president's casket on a caisson drawn by 6 white horses was accompanied from the station at 10 A.M. by battalions of blue jackets, field artillery, air forces, women's auxiliary forces, and the streets lined with a saddened people. The funeral service was at 4 in the East Room of the White

House. Talked with Henry Wallace about plan.

*4/16 **Washington*** Truman made admirable address to Congress. Wrote to Mrs. Boettinger and saw Charlie Taft who disagreed about natural resources being the principal cause of war but he was strong for a World Conference just the same.

*4/17 **Washington*** …Wrote letter to Hassett at his suggestion summarizing correspondence with F.D.R. for plan. He was to put it in Connelly's hands with the hope it might reach Truman.

*4/19 **Washington*** …Stettinius called about 4:30 to talk about proposed World Conference. He is for it on basis of conservation and said repeatedly he was heartily for it as a step toward permanent peace. That is a great surprise, and a great satisfaction. There is nothing to be done at San Francisco [formation of United Nations], but whole question will come up when first meeting of new world organization takes place. He said the American delegation would back it. Stettinius has whole correspondence with F.D.R. and copy of my completed plan.

*4/27 **Washington*** To office in morning. William Hassett, formerly Franklin Roosevelt's secretary, came in at 3, to talk about plan.

*5/6 **Washington*** …Lunched with the Fergusons. Told him about the plan for conservation & peace. Very pleasant time.

*5/23 **Washington*** Highly satisfactory talk with President Truman on World Conference at White House.

*5/24 **Washington*** …Henry Field came in to hear about talk with President Truman.

*7/26 **Milford*** Working on chapter on World Conservation Conference [for *Breaking New Ground*].

*8/6 **Milford*** …Atom bomb dropped on Hiroshima today.

*8/20 **Milford*** …Wrote scratch of possible

newspaper release on atomic bomb, and its future control.

9/5 Washington Meeting F.D.R. Memorial Committee in White House, Truman presiding. I asked for 2 minutes talk after meeting. Truman said I could see him whenever I wanted to. Authorized me to see Wallace & Anderson at his request on international conservation conference. Said I could get help from government officials as F.D. had authorized. I said I would give him outline of proposed conference by December 15. Truman said OK. He might want to mention it in his message to Congress. I said I would write him a letter about atomic power. Would he be sure to see it? Truman said he would. Truman said he was thinking about that subject all the time. Very satisfactory talk.

9/12 Washington With C.B. saw Henry Wallace about World Conservation Conference. For it, of course, but at first didn't see where Department of Commerce came in. I said atomic power must be considered. He agreed. Suggested I see Amos Taylor.

At 3 P.M. saw Secretary Anderson. Enthusiastic for conference.

9/13 Washington Talk with Amos Taylor about atom.

9/14 Washington Talk with Marquis Childs. Showed him letter to president. He strongly approved.

9/15 Washington Good talk with Senator McMahon on atom. Showed him draft letter to Truman & letter to newspapers. He strongly approved. Suggested change in his bill as in letter to Truman. He approved. Work on letters all day. Finished Truman letter & signed it.

9/16 Washington–Milford …Finished draft of letters to editors before leaving, and left letter for Truman at White House en route to airport.

9/17 Milford Material for letter to newspaper editors on atomic power taken to duplicating

company today. Stationery will be printed this week, and letter gotten out next week. To be put in mail in four groups, October 2 for Rocky Mountain states, October 4 for southern and prairie states west of Mississippi, October 5, states west of Alleghenies, October 6, New England states. To be printed [by newspapers] not before morning of October 8.

9/20 Milford Received letter from Truman that there will be no monopoly control of atomic energy, and that when his program is finally outlined, I will be "entirely satisfied with it," and that he is "more than happy" to have my views on it.

9/24 Milford …Proof of letter to editors approved today, and work is under way.

10/12 Milford Talk with C.B. about atomic bomb. She wants to do more about it. We heard Gram Swing on radio on that subject.

10/20 Washington C.B.P. suddenly invited to New York to meet with atomic scientists— afternoon, dinner, and evening. To return by plane tonight—but to meet again every other Saturday. An interesting opportunity.

10/23 Washington Several atomic scientists here for lunch—Dr. Farmer of Tennessee and others.

10/31 Washington …Evening with C.B. to Cooperative Forum. Heard Dr. Urey on the atomic bomb. Most interesting.

11/1 Washington …C.B.P. talked with Dr. Present and arranged for a dinner of scientists and senators for Saturday night.

11/2 Washington Dr. Present came to talk about how the atomic scientists could best get their story before the president and the public, and to remain for the dinner C.B.P. is giving for them tomorrow night.

11/3 Washington …a dinner to atomic scientists with Drs. Present, Bruce, English, Szilard, Coudan, Kaplan, et al., at which were present Senators Hill & Morse, Will Clayton, and a number of ladies. Most interesting talks by the scientists. I urged Coudan & Kaplan to send a telegram to the president telling who they are and why they want to see him. And do it before Attlee lands in America. Got to bed at 1 A.M.

11/11 Washington Took things easy while C.B.P. telephoned all day invitations to various people for the atomic dinner tonight. About 30 people came, including Senators Downey and McMahon with Congressman Kefauver, Patterson, and Clare Booth Luce. 8 or 10 atomists came: Borst, Coudan, Present, Szilard, Rush and a number of others. The meeting began at 5 o'clock. It was intensely interesting that in the end C.B.P. had to give the crowd scrambled eggs and ham, because they refused to go home.

11/12 Washington Long conference with Borst and Curtis, atomists, over the May-Johnson bill. They came at 11, stayed until nearly half past one. Henry Field came at 5 to discuss including people in the world conservation conference. Good talk. Pretty tired.

11/16 Washington …Meeting of atomists and heads of civilian organizations at the Mayflower with C.B.P. in the afternoon.

11/18 Washington …Good talk with the atomists and especially with Henry Field about World Conference.

11/26 Washington Mail and work on World Conference. Saw Henry Wallace in the morning, who thought there was no hurry in turning material in to Truman on account of Ickes…Talked with atomists. They will take up letter for C.B. from Urey and statement of what they want her to do in Paris.

11/27 Washington Harry Slattery to lunch. He made some good suggestions about the world conference.

12/2 Washington …Henry Field came in to say he would send me material on conservation and people…

12/4 Washington Good progress on the material for the World Conference…

12/8 Washington …In the afternoon Dr. and Mrs. Compton dropped in for a talk which I greatly enjoyed. The doctor was not easy in his mind about the atomic bomb.

12/13 Washington …Saw Truman at 10:45 and submitted plan for World Conference on Conservation. He spoke highly of the plan but made no final decision saying he would submit my papers to "some of my intimates." I am very hopeful.

1946

1/9 Washington …Zimmerman of Soil Conservation Service came to talk over the prospects for a World Conservation Conference, with which he had been concerned while Franklin was alive.

2/9 Washington Oscar Chapman dropped in Saturday morning to talk about World Conservation Conference. I suggested he should see Henry Field and he was for it strongly.

2/10 Washington …Afternoon: tea party for atomic scientists, and others. The atomists came about 5 and stayed believe it or not until 9:30 talking to C.B.P. I went in only for half an hour.

2/25 Washington Oscar Chapman & Beany Baldwin to lunch. Long talk with Oscar about the World Conservation Conference in which he is deeply interested and which is now in his hands. I do hope he gets promoted to full secretary.

2/26 Washington …In the afternoon to see Clayton who is represented by Willard Thorp and Clair Wilcox on the committee on the conference. Satisfactory talk but nothing definite. Ꮹ

THE WRITING OF *BREAKING NEW GROUND*

"Only 2½ more chapters to go, and one week to finish them in"

Gifford Pinchot's final entry related to his autobiography, *Breaking New Ground*, was that for March 1, 1946: "Book in morning." He died on October 4, and Harcourt Brace published the book the following year.

Harcourt Brace was only one of several publishers that courted Pinchot, even coming to Grey Towers to emphasize their interest. But Harcourt Brace's offer of 15 percent royalties and freedom to publish excerpts elsewhere, along with supportive advice from close associates, tipped the balance. The lengthy manuscript (the book is 522 pages, including index) had been rigorously trimmed and polished before Pinchot's death, according to diary entries, so the posthumous version fairly represents what he wanted to say. The title itself, *Breaking New Ground*, no doubt stems from the chapter on natural resources in Theodore Roosevelt's 1913 autobiography, drafted by Pinchot at the former president's request, describing the forester's work as "breaking new ground."

On April 13, 1945, Pinchot wrote to Harcourt Brace that he was sending "a number of chapters" that were "not all consecutive" but were "practically in final form." The publisher responded a week later reporting that "Breaking New Ground" had arrived. This exchange settles a minor historical point, whether Pinchot himself had selected the title or whether it was added after his death.

"The Book," as Pinchot referred to it, was a major part of the last decade of his life, accounting for 378 diary entries beginning in 1936 (the 1938 diary is fragmentary and 1944 is missing). He sought, and received, a great deal of help. Herbert "Dol" Smith, Yale classmate, life-long friend, and Forest Service associate, with his wife Lillian (sometimes spelled Lilian), actually lived at Grey Towers for months at a time and worked daily with Pinchot. We can even see Pinchot's note that he went fishing while Dol stayed back at the house and produced drafts. After Smith died in 1944, Raphael Zon, eminent Forest Service scientist and Pinchot contemporary, provided nearly daily assistance, even moving in next door to Pinchot's Washington, D.C., home.

Others helped, too. In his introduction Pinchot thanks John Lydenberg, Harvard professor, and R.P. Holdsworth, professor of forestry at Massachusetts State College, whom we often see in the diaries. Three other consultants who left their own historical trail are Professor Edmond S. Meany, Jr., who wrote his doctoral dissertation on the history of the lumber industry in Washington State; Alpheus Thomas Mason, author in 1941 of *Bureaucracy Convicts Itself: The Ballinger-Pinchot Controversy of 1910*; and Supreme Court Justice Louis Brandeis, who was Pinchot's legal adviser in 1910 during the congressional hearings following the forester's dismissal from federal service. Forest Service old-timers jotted down their experiences and sent them in, at Pinchot's invitation, and of course active Forest Service personnel assisted along the way. In fact, the Forest Service provided him office space in its Washington, D.C., headquarters, as did the Library of Congress.

The first diary evidence we see for *Breaking New Ground* is early in 1936, when Pinchot records a conversation with Zon. "He holds we were exactly right in our position toward forestry in the early days. We were." With that thought firmly in mind, Pinchot began his decade-long effort, or in his own words, "A personal story of how forestry [led] to conservation."

In February 1937 Pinchot listened carefully as historian Charles Beard explained just how he had become such a prolific writer. Beard said that he made "a very elaborate lay-out of a book before he begins to write it. Sub-division after sub-division of each subject until, he said, 'All you have to do is to put in the verbs and the book is done.'" Two days later, reflecting on this advice, Pinchot jotted, "If I had had it when I started this wretched book, the darned thing would have been done and out by now." Throughout the year he continued to apply the "Beard method," but we know that completion lay a nearly decade in the future.

Also in 1937 he returned to Biltmore and then traveled west to bring his thinking up to date, and generally to refresh his memories of times past. He spent four days at Biltmore but more than a month in the West. With his long-time chauffeur Bill Hinkel at the wheel, Pinchot, Harry Graves, and Dol Smith drove more than five thousand miles as they met with Forest Service old-timers and others. Only fragments of both trips follow here, and the August 1937 entries come from a supplemental diary Pinchot kept for his travels.

There is much in the diaries not related to the autobiography, so the apparent gaps in diary entries are due to other activities, such as his long contest with Secretary of the Interior Harold Ickes to keep the Forest Service in the Department of Agriculture, and much about World War II. Also his health; Pinchot suffered three heart attacks early in 1939, which greatly reduced all activities for a time. He always seemed relieved to get back to "the book" after each distracting episode, but shortly thereafter he would take up yet another challenge. The many entries that reported only "book," or "worked on book" have not been included in the following excerpts.

A scan of the table of contents in *Breaking New Ground* pretty much tips us off as to what topics are noted in the diaries. Noteworthy is his battle with Secretary of the Interior Richard Ballinger, which accounts for 10 percent of the book-related diary entries (and nearly a third of the published book itself). His autobiography would have us believe its author was vindicated, even won a moral victory over Ballinger, and went happily along with the rest of his life. Yet the diaries reveal his near-obsession with the affair even decades later, and the need to prove that he had indeed been on the side of right. Looking back at how things turned out, it is difficult to share Pinchot's view of the importance of the specific controversy—what happened afterward as a result is very important—but then an autobiography is supposed to be a personal statement. And *Breaking New Ground* is that, as well as an extremely valuable historical document.

1936

1/21 Washington Long talk w. Zon. He holds we were exactly right in our position toward forestry in the early days. We were.

6/17 New Haven [Yale] Commencement…Arranged w. Harry Graves & Dol Smith to get Holdsworth to help on my book if possible.

6/22 Milford Woke up early. Worked out beginning of chapter on origin of conservation policy. Dictated it. At the Book again!

6/25 Milford Catching up. Reading TR's autobiography on conservation.

7/8 Milford–Philadelphia–Milford With C.B. to get my records of conservation fight out of safe deposit. Couldn't find Prices's letter when I told him of conservation fight. Got TR's two letters from Africa when he heard I was fired in 1910.

7/15 Milford …Holdsworth here to help with book.

7/16 Milford …John Lydenberg reading over papers on Ballinger case while I sit [for portrait].

7/17 Milford …Amos came from New York & gave me a lot of his most valuable material about the Ballinger case.

7/18 Milford …Fishing Burch place in late P.M. with Holdsworth, who is taking hold finally. John continues reading the Ballinger documents while I sit.

8/6 Milford Book all day. Describe Taft & why he went wrong.

8/8 Milford Book. Spring of 1909…Tennis. One hard set. C.B. & Holdsworth against John Lydenberg & me. We won.

8/10 Milford …a little on book. Got idea of publishing all my original documents on forestry & conservation. Wrote plan to Dol…Tennis. John & I beat C.B. & Holdsworth, 7-5.

8/15 Milford–Ocean City Stopped Philadelphia in one more effort to find Price's letter on origin of conservation. No good. Holdsworth & John L. took train to Washington.

11/6 Milford Book again, thank goodness [after Landon campaign]. Rereading & correcting early chapters.

11/13 Milford Working all day on 1889 diaries, life at Nancy.

11/14 Milford 1889 diaries again.

11/16 Milford ...Finished abstracting 1890 diary.

11/17 Milford Mail & 1889 & 1890 diaries. Dictating to Gregg.

11/28 Milford ...Getting old diary records dictated etc.

12/12 Washington Working over old letters for Book.

12/14 Washington Saw Silcox, Zon, Lydenberg & etc. at Forest Service. Lydenberg arranged I can have installments of old Forest Service records at home for study.

12/20 Washington...Some work on diaries. Harry is to help me get dates.

12/27 Milford John Lydenberg came, & Ralph Hetzel...Ralph will come & give half time to my book.

12/30 Milford–Washington ...Arrive Wash just before nine. Big load of documents etc.

12/31 Washington Getting straightened out on book material. There is a vast amount of it. John Lydenberg has done a real job.

1937

1/1 Washington For the first time in many months really got a chance at my book, and reviewed and re-wrote nearly the whole of the first chapter. All necessary material is here, and there is no excuse for me if I don't make progress.

1/4 Washington All morning and part of the

Gifford Pinchot at work writing *Breaking New Ground*, August 11, 1945, his eightieth birthday. Forest Service.

afternoon on old diaries and note-books of 1889 and 1890. Getting material for chapters one and two.

1/12 Washington Got Ralph [Hetzel] started on reading up the material already prepared for my book.

1/14 Washington Finished Chapter 1, and did some work on correspondence.

1/20 Washington Inauguration Day…Spent the day on my letters home from Nancy, and listened to Inauguration over radio. Franklin made an excellent speech.

1/21 Washington Going over my own and Fernow's letters of 1889, '90, and '91, bearing on the story of forestry.

1/25 Washington Got in a little work on the book in the morning…To lunch at the Cosmos Club with Ralph Hetzel, and then to the Atlantic Building [Forest Service headquarters] so that he could get acquainted with the material on file there, using John Lydenberg's analysis—which Ralph said afterward was excellent.

1/30 Washington …called on Mrs. F.H. Newell, who has much material, including complete diaries of F.H., and is most willing I should use them.

2/2 Washington Working on Chapter II. John Lydenberg came from Harvard to help Ralph get better acquainted with the material for the book, and we had a very pleasant time with him.

2/7 Washington Book in morning. Luncheon party at 1615. Guests: Congressman and Mrs. Coffee; Mr. and Mrs. Leon Henderson; F.E. Silcox; Dr. and Mrs. Beard. Talked with Beard after lunch. He told me how he works with his beaverboard and makes a very elaborate lay-out of a book before he begins to write it. Sub-division after sub-division of each subject until, he said, "All you have to do is to put in the verbs and the book is done." He said this was the secret of his enormous production of books—

that very few people ever used it, and that he got it from Alexander Hamilton's notes of speeches and reports in the Congressional Library.

2/8 Washington Trying to apply Beard's method and making some progress, but it goes slow at first. On book all day.

2/9 Washington Working on Beard's method. If I had had it when I started this wretched book, the darned thing would have been done and out by now.

2/10 Washington Working on the book nearly all day. To Forest Service in afternoon to look up facts about F.V. Coville, for a notice on his work on grazing.

2/11 Washington Book in the morning. Working on the Brandis excursion by the Beard method. Finished article about Coville's part in grazing regulation.

2/27 Washington Decided with Ralph to drop the chapters of book before 1900 and get at later chapters immediately.

3/3 Washington Getting straightened out on available material for the book all day.

3/4 Washington Book in the morning. Getting ready to get at story of the Bureau of Forestry.

3/5 Washington Getting a reasonable start on the history of the Bureau of Forestry for the book. Read over a lot I had already written. It isn't so bad.

3/15 Washington Really made some progress on the Beard method of dealing with the book, and got most of the year 1898 fairly worked out.

3/16 Washington Made some progress on story of Division and Bureau of Forestry.

3/17 Washington Long talk with Raphael Zon in the morning. Found him in practically entire sympathy with my point of view about how to treat the Division of Forestry, Bureau of Forestry, and Forest Service parts of the book.

3/22 Washington [Harry Graves] thinks the best time for our western trip this summer would be to start in August. We discussed trailers.

3/23 Washington Spent too much time looking up the question of a trailer for the trip Harry Graves, Dol Smith, and I are planning to take in the West. Arranged with W.S. Domer, Covered-Wagon Trailer distributor, to make plans for fitting up a trailer with four single beds. Gertrude Smith, Harry and Marion Graves, and Dol Smith to lunch. A very pleasant time indeed. Made plans for Western trip.

3/24 Washington Still working on trailers.

3/30 Washington Getting ready for Southern trip starting tomorrow.

3/31 En route With Bill Hinkel in Buick. Left for Asheville en route through Shenandoah National Park…Spent night at Colonial Inn, Wytheville. About 340 miles.

4/1 En route Left Wytheville at 7:15. Arrived Asheville…at 12:05. Town completely changed…Met H.C. Ochsner at Arcade Building…to meet C.R. Beadle at Biltmore Village…left for Pisgah Forest, taking new Forest Service road to Pink Beds…George Vanderbilt tried to sell the Pisgah tract to the Weeks Committee at $15 per acre. The committee turned it down, then George died, and Edith sold the standing timber to Carr for $10 per acre, and Pisgah Forest to the government, subject to the contract, for $5 per acre…This is the finest forest property I ever knew an individual to have…In spite of the bad logging the reproduction of the tulip poplar is everywhere superb.

4/2 Biltmore …The view down Big Creek from the veranda [of Buck Springs Lodge] is breath-taking…down to the old splash dam at the Big Creek cutting. The spillway and the rock piles of the cribs were still there. On the way down in the coves the Poplar reproduction was superb.

4/3 Asheville …In my time we floated cord wood and logs to Asheville for the Asheville Wood Working Company. We had a boom on the French Broad River. Beadle says this work paid back. It covered several million feet of lumber.

4/5 Roanoke Left for Roanoke. Still feeling the effect of that long walk down Big Creek.

4/22 Washington Book all the morning. Working over Forest Service reports for 1908 and '09.

4/23 Washington Working over the old annual reports of the Service from 1906 to 1909, written by Dol Smith. They are admirable documents, showing between the lines just what our difficulties in administration were during each year.

6/6 Milford Bob [Marshall] and Bennett Cerf reading my book, what there is of it…Steve [Stahlnecker] and I told Bob Marshall the story of the Ballinger case after dinner.

6/25 Milford Spent morning with Dol going over the principal points in the history of forestry in America. He regards Carl Schurtz's recommendations in his annual report as of the first importance. I do not, for I think they had little influence on the progress of affairs.

8/13 Eugene–travel …McDaniel said: Binger Hermann burned G.L.O. books, was indicted. Jury 11 to 1 for conviction, & yet he was received with a brass band when he came home to Roseburg. John Meldrum surveyor general of Oregon was convicted & went to the Pen.

8/19 San Francisco …To Forest Service with Harry & Dol. Mrs. Shinn there. Greatly delighted to see her. Met a lot of FS people. Long talk with Lou Barrett, who will write. So will Mrs. Shinn. Am to write all supervisors for names [of] old timers, & ask them. Barrett recommends consulting records of creation of national forests.

8/22 Pine Crest …Dol & Harry & I spent the morning going over old times for the book. Most useful morning. Notes in binder.

8/24 Yosemite–travel …John T. Noddin, old ranger on the Sierra, knows all about running the sheep out of Sierras. Get Lou Barrett or Ayers to get story from him. Noddin also knows of the delays in the proclamations so others could get the timber…Worst of the June 11, 1906 [Forest Homestead Act] trouble came under Graves. Classification under Graves practically knocked it out. Lonny Stewart suggested it, then assistant secretary of Senate. Stories about G.P. current in the Forest Service should be collected. Kotok is to write me about Congressman Curry & the bear traps. John E. Raker & the Raker law.

8/26 Travel …Potter came in at dinner (Dol, Hutchinson & I) & we had a fine talk over old times.

8/25 San Juan Experimental Range … Benedict will write. Down in to foothills O'Neal's P.O., where McGee, Newell & I must have stopped for lunch in 1908.

9/24 Milford With Dol Smith all the morning talking over plans for the book. He and his wife left after lunch.

11/11 Washington Dol Smith came in about 9:00 to go over history of forestry in my files.

11/13 Washington Getting my room and the material for the book in order.

1939

2/16 "The Biggest Question of All"—title for book. A personal history of how forestry lead [sic] to conservation and how conservation began or how conservation was launched.

4/24 Washington Sat outdoors half an hour on balcony. First time. Also worked 15 min on book. First time. Formulated title: [blank]

5/30 Washington Can sit up two hours today. Working on book. Note: Use E Pluribus Unum in describing the conservation policy. Many problems make a policy, just as many states made a nation.

6/24 Milford …Giff killed a big rat, and I got Chs. I to VII practically all done.

7/13 Milford …Got in a good morning's work on the book (Big Creek).

9/1 Milford War began today. Harry Graves, who came Tuesday, went back w. Dol. Most useful visit to book.

10/14 Litchfield To see Sam Fisher. Went over, he & Dol, a lot of the book. Mighty fine time.

11/11 Washington Working on Ch. X. Dol came to lunch & thought well of Ch. I to VI.

11/18 Washington …Worked on Ch. X, but got little done…

11/22 Washington …Dol came in late P.M. Is doing great work getting USFS behind collection of forester biographies.

12/10 Washington …Signed letters to old timers asking for personal narratives.

12/18 Washington …Matthew Josephson came to lunch. 2½ hours talk about Ballinger case & Taft & TR etc.

12/30 Washington …to see Louis Brandeis with C.B. Told me in detail how he caught on to Wickersham & Taft & the misdated report.

1940

1/1 Washington Happy New Year. Finish the Book this year. Sure…Chapter on National Forest Commission & Special Forestry Agent about done. Hope to finish it promptly & go about finishing Ballinger case. Brandeis wants to go over it as I get it done.

1/12 Washington Got in a fair day's work— the first since the flu [illeg.] in. Started in on Taft-Ballinger, so that I can go over it w. Louis Brandeis, as he suggested.

1/16 Washington …Felix [Frankfurter] agreed with me that Pepper, not Brandeis, took Stimpson's place in the Ballinger case.

2/7 Washington …Read Louis Brandeis what I have about Taft & Ballinger. He approved.

2/13 Washington …Long talk with young Pomeroy about Ballinger case.

2/22 Washington Very busy this morning cleaning up. Sent a lot of stuff to Forest Service through Dol for safe keeping. Mss. of book etc. etc.

3/8 Washington Dol came in. Came again later to say that Ickes had written Wallace for permission to go through Forest Service files in his attempt to vindicate Ballinger. So we went over some of the old papers.

3/12 Washington Mail & Book. Going over briefs in Ballinger case.

3/25 New York Saw Cheney. Told him of Ickes' intent to rehabilitate Ballinger & about Colliers' great part in that fight. He agreed at once to have Walter Davenport see me about replying.

4/4 Washington…Ernest Gruening to breakfast. Asked him about effect of Ballinger-Pinchot scrap on Alaska.

4/9 Washington …Jim [Garfield] told me reason for Ballinger resignation from G.L.O.

4/24 Washington Got at last an hour or two on the Ballinger case. Book. Should have said before that old timer narratives have been coming in all winter, & very good stuff indeed.

4/25 Washington …Got first work in rewrite on book. About Ballinger & why he resigned as commissioner G.L.O.

5/6 Washington…work on Ickes article on Ballinger going right ahead.

5/7 Washington …With C.B. to see Louis Brandeis. Told him [about] Ickes' effort to clear Ballinger's memory. He said: Only possible reason for clearing Ballinger (logical reason) would be to clear Taft's memory in order to help Bob Taft. Said Taft had been guilty [of] what no other president in all our history had done—deliberately deceived

Congress in a message when he sent Wickersham's misdated report. Said it was the worst thing ever done by a president. He wanted Ickes' Ballinger attempt stopped. I said I'd see Norris, but I doubt anything can or should be done.

5/21 Washington Ernest Gruening & Oscar Chapman to dinner. Read aloud Ickes' blast & made notes. They are both sore. Article full of misstatements—omissions. Provoked, of course, by Ickes defeat (transfer).

5/22 Washington …Working on possible statement in reply to Ickes article Not Guilty in Saturday Evening Post. C.B. strong against any answer at all. Saw Brandeis. Very indignant but strongly opposed to my making any answer. 28 page letter from Harold full of abuse. Almost if not quite a crazy letter. Harry Slattery read letter aloud after dinner. Agrees with Brandeis about making no answer.

7/12 Milford …Dol fell against table & cut his head very badly…But Dol was not to be stopped. He ate his lunch, slept well & today (Saturday) is on the job again.

7/15 Milford Began again on the Book. Whoops! The week of loafing is over.

7/17 Milford Got something done on book. Ballinger case. Fishing with Dol in late P.M.

7/19 Milford Book, & got something done.

7/26 Milford Book. Some progress on Ballinger case.

9/12 Milford Book & mail. Found I had been duplicating some work I did last year.

10/1 Milford …I am immensely better than last spring, but what with mail, bad eyes, and what not I have almost nothing done on the book. Dol has made real progress or so I judge.

11/15 Washington …Harry Graves after lunch. Harry Slattery at dinner…Help to finish book…Call with C.B. on the Brandeises. He is for letting Ickes answer go & finish book.

1941

2/24 Washington To Room 2519 (Rm 2767) which Clapp has turned over to Dol & me. Awfully glad to be working in an office again. Book. Ballinger chapter & made some progress.

3/5 Washington …Arranging with Dol to finish book. (This was on 5th.) Rereading some of John Lydenberg's work on Forest Service. Excellent.

3/6 Washington Read more of John's work, & more impressed.

3/10 Washington Book. Good walk. Read Ballinger text late.

3/18 Washington …Started having Book copied for last time.

5/20 Washington Book. I am actually making some progress.

6/15 Milford Laid around and did nothing except try to find Chapter 11-a, which has been mislaid. Anna May kindly came up to help me look for it. No luck.

6/23 Milford Working on Ballinger chapter. Went fishing…

7/2 Milford Book and separating material for Yale Forest School Library. Wrote to [Sam] Record yesterday suggesting that material collected by Phil Wells on water power, coal, etc., should be kept separate as a memorial to him.

7/16 Milford …Really made some progress on the Ballinger chapter of the book. Dol and Lilian came in the evening.

7/17 Milford I am really making some progress on the book, getting fairly close to the end of the Ballinger chapter.

7/18 Milford Book and making real progress. Dol and Lilian still here.

7/23 Milford Book. Working on Kerby's part of the Ballinger case.

7/29 Milford Really got some work done on the book. Worked on it five hours in the morning. Fishing in the afternoon.

8/1 Milford Made real progress on the book.

Anna May found my letter of December 31, 1909, to T.R., in Africa—a great help.

8/8 Milford Reviewing old correspondence, 1909 and '10 for the book.

8/25 Milford Made some progress on the book…the Ballinger case story is almost complete.

8/26 Milford Still on the Ballinger case.

8/27 Milford …working on book, autumn of 1909.

8/28 Milford Book, mail, and fishing in the afternoon…Dol went with us.

9/1 Milford Nearly all day Dol read me his work on the book. I was greatly pleased. He has done a fine job.

9/6 Milford …Professor Alpheus Thomas Mason and his wife came for lunch, and we spent the rest of the day going over chapters on Ballinger, most helpfully for me.

9/7 Milford The Masons both fine. We finished the Ballinger chapters and went over some other questions. His visit most helpful.

9/8 Milford Morning and much of the afternoon going over the book with Dol.

9/9 Milford Spent most of the day with Dol going over his suggestions Volumes I and II Ballinger story.

9/10 Milford Ballinger story almost complete.

9/19 Milford Got a little done on the Division of Forestry.

10/28 Washington With Dol called on Siousat and then Martin showed us our 2 rooms in the Library [of Congress] Annex & all the stuff sent down from Milford—an incredible amount. Got a little settled in A.M.

10/29 Washington Library working on Black Hills story.

11/7 Washington Library. All morning wasted looking for Holdsworth's chapter I, which Dol finally found.

12/4 Washington Working on Philippine Islands chapter along here.

12/24 New York Some work on Trans-Siberian trip.

1942

1/5 Washington …Some work on book. Stupidly did some work twice.

2/17 Washington Library. Near end of Philippine trip.

2/19 Washington Library. Getting near end of Philippine chapter…Went to see George Ahern. A little better.

2/26 Washington Library. Dol read me many notes about 1901 & 2. Got a little done on book.

3/7 Washington …Got practically nothing done on the book.

3/19 Washington …Dol Smith and Dr. Meany to lunch. Meany considering work on book.

6/18 Milford Working on the book and making progress.

6/19 Milford Working on T.R.'s first Message to Congress and the Lacey Bill.

6/22 Milford …Professor Edmond Meany, professor of history at the Hill School, Pottstown, Pa., came to talk over the book. He has been reading the copy Mrs. Crocker made.

6/24 Milford Long talk with Dol and Meany about book. Got many excellent suggestions. It was well worth while, his going over it.

6/25 Milford …Mail and another talk with Dol and Meany.

7/11 Milford … Mail and some work on the book. Fishing with Dol in the afternoon. Poor luck.

7/15 Milford Mail, book, and fishing with Meany in the afternoon.

7/17 Milford Talked about the book with Meany.

7/27 Milford …Dol and Lillian returned from weekend at Wacabuc, and Professor Meany arrived in the afternoon, to work again on the book.

8/1 Milford Fishing with Dol and Lillian at Beaver Run.

8/17 Milford Book all morning. Minnesota national forest. Meany arrived. Read Dol and me his recent material on legislation.

9/16 Milford …Professor Meany arrived.

9/18 Milford All day Friday on the book. Mrs. Meany and her little girl, Margie, arrived to spend the weekend. Interesting child.

9/30 Milford Dol and Lillian left for the summer. Iva still here. Good talk with her. Collecting books out of the library for working collection in Letter Box. Mail and some work on the book.

10/1 Milford Long talk with Iva. Mail and book. Starting to collect materials to take to Washington and close Grey Towers for season.

10/28 Washington Almost all day on book. Some progress. Dol was in first thing this morning.

11/6 Washington Working on mail and chapter on Inland Waterways Commission. Dol Smith came in.

11/7 Washington Book. Charlie Squires and Dol Smith to lunch. Long talk about Land Office and Forest Service methods of handling national forests. Squires agreed to write up his reminiscences.

11/9 Washington Book in morning. Afternoon, talk with Tom Shearman who will help on legal matters in the book, if desired.

11/11 Washington Mrs. Mather came in spite of the holiday, which was very nice of her.

11/14 Washington …Talk with Dol Smith in the morning about power control in national forests.

11/16 Washington Long talk with Dol Smith in the morning about the book.

11/17 Washington Spent the morning at the Library with Dol checking over second copy of the book and making plans.

11/20 Washington Book—Inland Waterways Commission and Governor's Conference.

11/24 Washington A photostat of my letter

to Secretary Wilson about conditions of permits to power companies on national forests arrived from Archives. Dol Smith came in for a long talk about our work.

11/25 Washington Book. With Mrs. Mather to the Library to check up on how much of the master copy has been copied. Parts of the copy seem to be missing. After much difficulty, opened the drawer and got out a copy of the preliminary report of the Committee on Organization of Government Scientific Works.

11/28 Washington …Went over the book with Dol at the Library to see that there is a complete duplicate copy. Could not locate copy of the Philippine chapter.

11/30 Washington …Book at the Library. Getting master copy straightened out.

12/1 Washington Book. Talk with Dol in the morning.

1943

4/7 Washington …Got carbon copies of chapters from my book to show to McEvoy when he comes.

4/14 Washington Dol Smith called—talked about book.

4/20 Washington Started in again on the book. Governors Conference.

4/21 Washington Book in the morning…Dol came in the morning to talk over summer work.

4/22 Washington Book. Chapter on Conference of Governors and North American Conservation Conference.

5/3 Washington Book in the morning. Good progress on National Conservation Commission.

5/20 Washington Book—North American Conservation Conference.

5/26 Washington Got the story of the Public Lands Commission pretty nearly finished.

5/27 Washington Some progress on the book. Talked with Dol in the morning about the chapter on the Public Lands Commission. And that is about all.

5/28 Washington Book and mail. Getting near the end of the Roosevelt Commissions.

6/1 Washington …Dol went over the finished chapters on the Roosevelt Commissions (all but the Keep Commission) and approved the job. That's fine.

6/2 Washington Hot! Mail and book. Long talk with Dol about chapters on Forest Service. I am going ahead with that.

11/10 Washington Office in A.M. Working on last chapter—which doesn't mean the book is done.

11/11 Washington …Some work on last chapter.

11/12 Washington Work on last chapter at home.

12/16 Washington To the office. Working on last chapter with Dol. Harry Graves and Tommy Shearman came to lunch.

12/17 Washington All day on the chapter on "American Forest Congress." Making real progress.

12/20 Washington Working on "American Forest Congress" chapter, in the morning.

1945

2/2 Washington …To Forest Service in the afternoon. They have moved Zon and me to a smaller room and were quite justified in doing so.

2/5 Washington Working on chapters 1–10 of the book. Got all but two into final form.

2/9 Washington Working on book…Took Vol. I to the Dept. for final copying.

2/10 Washington …Worked on book in afternoon. Zon came in.

2/17 Washington To the office. Took down a couple more chapters in so-called final form.

3/29 Washington To office in the morning and back to some uninterrupted work on the book.

3/31 Washington Book all day. Getting ready to send some sample chapters to Harcourt Brace and working on completing others. Zon came in on his way home.

4/9 Washington …to Forest Service with volume of mss.

4/10 Washington …To office at 11, and to Library with Zon in the afternoon.

4/12 Washington To office all morning. Getting chapters ready to send to Lambert Davis of Harcourt Brace.

4/13 Washington …Worked on book all day and sent several chapters to Lambert Davis for review, and possible publication.

4/26 Washington …Letter from Lambert Davis of Harcourt Brace. He likes book & they want to publish it. Very flattering comments from him.

5/3 Washington Spent most of the day getting ready for the talk to the Society of American Foresters. There were not far from 100 present and they seemed to be satisfied with my talk (the last chapter in the book). Although I know the majority seemed to be satisfied, some were very much against it. I asked for questions but nobody would ask any.

5/4 Washington To the Forest Service with material to be copied. Otherwise got very little done.

5/6 Washington …Long talk with Wang of Thos. Y. Crowell Co., who spent an hour or two going over my book. He wants to make suggestions and to consider publishing it.

5/7 Washington VE Day! Getting ready to leave. Saw Dr. Leonard and with Mrs. Mather to the Library of Congress. Brought down material for Lillian Smith.

6/14 Milford Book. Then Burnshaw & Ambler of the Dryden Press came to look it over—11:30 to 4:30. They will submit an offer.

6/28 Milford Chapters 42, 45, and 96 to Lilian. And did some work besides on other chapters.

7/2 Milford Sent off chapter 46 to Lilian, and got some work done on Lieu-Land Law.

7/6 Milford Went over with Harry [Slattery] all the Ballinger chapters. He had a few suggestions to make, but on the whole, approved decidedly of what I had written. That is a big help.

7/11 Milford C.B. to N.Y. with Harry Slattery. He had finished reading my manuscript. Made some excellent suggestions, and thought it was a good book. Marking on book all day.

7/12 Milford …completed and mailed 2 chapters to Lilian.

7/17 Milford Completed revision of Zon's Ch. 38—Forest Products. Will mail it tomorrow.

7/19 Milford Finished Chapter 52 and found that 57, 58, and 61 of Lilian's list have been completed, although marked the other way. That leaves eight more to do, together with a revision of the last chapter. And the shortening of the whole book. And I have got 21 days to do it. A mighty cheerful situation.

7/20 Milford Practically finished Chap. 64. Will mail it tomorrow, after dictating it to Mrs. Mather, so that, if lost in the mail there will still be a record. Suggestions came from C.B.P.

7/21 Milford Finished and mailed Chapter 64…After finishing 64 I tackled 63 and practically finished that.

7/25 Milford Sent Chap. 73, National Conservation Commission, to Lilian for final copying. C.B. just suggested a final chapter to bring story of conservation briefly up to date. I think it is a fine idea. If adopted, as I think it will be, that will make six still to do.

7/26 Milford Working on chapter on World Conservation Conference. Received from Lilian final copies of chaps 36–40, 44, 50 and 52.

7/31 Milford Letter from Bruce Bliven endorsing Harcourt Brace as publisher for the book.

8/1 Milford Chapter 67—New Forest Science

completed today and sent to Lilian and Zon. Three chapters to go.

8/4 Milford "Country Life Commission" finished today, and only 2½ more chapters to go, and one week to finish them in.

8/6 Milford Working on book all day. Finished "Holding the Line." Only 1½ left to do. The back of the main job is broken. Chapts 66 and 68 sent to Lilian for copying—she is on vacation this week, so copies made here also.

8/10 Milford …FINISHED BOOK! Final chapter typed today.

8/13 Milford Counted pages, lines, and spaces of mss.—and compared to T.R.'s "Autobiography," Wells' "Outline of History," and Beveridges "Lincoln." Will need to cut manuscript almost a quarter.

8/23 Milford Letter from Lambert Davis of Harcourt Brace unable to come for weekend with Mr. Brace, but will come on Monday next to review manuscript of book. Not sure, but it looks more and more like Harcourt Brace.

8/24 Milford …Working on final review of book—finished second volume…Letter from Didier—wanting to publish book.

8/27 Milford Lambert Davis came at noon and Ray Kane in the evening. Working on the book and talking it over with Davis.

8/28 Milford The Kanes left after lunch. Got a little done in the morning. After they had gone, long and very satisfactory talk with Lambert Davis. Harcourt Brace & Co. offer 15% of the retail price and freedom to sell any part of the book to magazines or newspapers before publication. Returns to go to me. Dog tired tonight.

9/26 Milford …Mark on mss. Cutting all morning.

9/27 Milford Worked on mss. in morning, and went fishing.

9/28 Milford Working on cutting mss. 1100 lines out to date.

10/12 Milford …Cut 42 lines out of chapter 24.

10/15 Milford Finished cutting out in 2 more chapters—25 and 26.

10/26 Washington …Sent material to Library study room for use for manuscript—had been in Letter Box.

10/27 Washington Working on reducing chapters in book…

10/31 Washington Book in the morning. Zon came in the afternoon. He will be here for the winter.

11/1 Washington …Afternoon: a little work on the book. Finished another chapter.

11/2 Washington …A little work on the book in the afternoon. Called on Zon and his wife next door.

11/7 Washington Working on the book. Chapters 47–51. Reduction of first two completed.

11/14 Washington Book…Zon finished chapters shortened, 1, 2, 3, 5, 47 and 48, 49 and 50, and was much pleased.

11/29 Washington Zon came at 8:30 for another chapter.

12/3 Washington To the Library to lunch with Luther Evans. Good talk about additional manuscript material which he would like to have from the Forest Service men.

12/10 Washington Going over Zon's suggestions in earlier chapters. Up to the Library to get material.

12/14 Washington Book in the morning. Mrs. Mather took me up to my study room in the afternoon to get material to work on.

12/15 Washington Book all day. Went as usual to see Zon next door who has been under the weather.

1946

1/1 Washington Celebrated the New Year by working on the book. Zon and his wife came to lunch.

1/3 Washington …Real progress with the book.

1/4 Washington To the Forest Service to take a lot of Dol Smith's papers to my study room. Mrs. Mather drove.

1/7 Washington Book and mail. Getting chapters cut down fast.

1/8 Washington Made real progress on the book…

1/10 Washington …Afternoon with Mrs. Mather and Lilian Smith to the Library to get more chapters to work on.

1/11 Washington Mrs. Mather finished copying 7 chapters. I finished reducing 3. Good progress…Lilian started copying chapters of the book.

2/23 Washington Work on the book and not much else.

2/26 Washington Book. Zon came in with suggestions for reducing some of the earlier chapters.

3/1 Washington Book in the morning. GP

Gifford Pinchot. Grey Towers Collection.

Index of Names

The following names appear in Pinchot's diaries, where not all are well identified. He had the habit of including everyone who attended a meeting, but many did not leave their own historical trail. Those who have not been identified or are incidental have not been included here. Rarely, Pinchot incorrectly identified a person, for example, reporting that a particular congressman represented such and such a state when the official record lists another state. What follows comes from formal records and on occasion varies from the diary notation. The identifications stem from examining traditional sources, such as the various sorts of *Who's Who*, directories of persons elected to Congress or appointed to the Cabinet, plus *Breaking New Ground*, M. Nelson McGeary's biography of Pinchot, and related works. People are identified here mainly as they related to Pinchot at the time he wrote their names in his diary.